S. A. Southworth

Hester Strong's Life Work; or, the Mystery Solved

S. A. Southworth

Hester Strong's Life Work; or, the Mystery Solved

ISBN/EAN: 9783337055226

Printed in Europe, USA, Canada, Australia, Japan

Cover: Foto ©ninafisch / pixelio.de

More available books at **www.hansebooks.com**

HESTER STRONG'S LIFE WORK;

OR,

THE MYSTERY SOLVED.

BY

MRS. S. A. SOUTHWORTH,

AUTHOR OF "LAWRENCE MONROE," ETC.

"Life is only bright when it proceedeth
Toward a truer, deeper light above;
Human love is sweetest when it leadeth
To a more divine and perfect love."

BOSTON:
LEE AND SHEPARD.
1870.

Entered according to Act of Congress, in the year 1869, by
LEE AND SHEPARD,
In the Clerk's Office of the District Court of the District of Massachusetts.

STEREOTYPED AT THE
Boston Stereotype Foundry,
No. 19 Spring Lane.

CONTENTS.

CHAPTER		PAGE
I.	The Loverings and their Friends.	9
II.	Life and its Changes.	18
III.	Sad Scenes at the Small House.	31
IV.	The Pain and its Cure. — The Confession and Revulsion.	42
V.	Alone with the Dying and the Dead. — The Sad Return.	51
VI.	What became of the Children. — The Midnight Call.	64
VII.	The Children's Prattle. — The Wife's Burden, or a Synopsis of Mr. Giles.	73
VIII.	A Tragic Scene in Village Life.	83
IX.	Mr. Trueman's Family. — Pleasant Memories.	93
X.	Mr. and Mrs. Stillman. — A Domestic Scene.	99
XI.	Christmas Morning. — Reminiscences of the Past.	106
XII.	The Christmas Party. — Miss Patty Stearns.	112
XIII.	What Santa Claus left. — Judith Lovering's Advice.	122
XIV.	Winnie's Visit, and the Party.	128
XV.	Making Calls here and there.	136
XVI.	The Separation. — The Aged Christian's Death-bed.	143
XVII.	The New Home and its Trials. — Mr. Wiley's Family.	151
XVIII.	The Good Shepherd's Watchfulness. — The Disclosure. — The Burial.	162

CONTENTS.

XIX.	Morgan Lentell, or the Broken Web. — The Accident.	172
XX.	Mrs. Giles' Sickness. — Miss Ann Thropee, or Sympathy wasted.	179
XXI.	Winnie's Thoughtfulness. — Sunshine and her Freak.	189
XXII.	Hester's Visit to Mrs. Giles. — Little Johnnie's Death. — Removal of Mrs. Giles to her Father's House.	195
XXIII.	The Struggle and the Triumph. — The Council. — Mr. Giles' Visit.	213
XXIV.	About the Baby. — Trouble upon Trouble. — The Proposal.	227
XXV.	Hester rescues the Baby from its unnatural Father. — Dr. Edward's timely Arrival.	233
XXVI.	Midnight Musings. — The Discovery. — Conscience disturbed.	243
XXVII.	Passing Events. — Scenes and Incidents.	251
XXVIII.	About Hester's Call. — Winnie's Talk, and Grandpa's Wedding.	258
XXIX.	Self-Communings. — The Still Small Voice. — Light in Darkness.	264
XXX.	Bitter Memories. — Welcome News. — Love rewarded. — Elevia saved.	279
XXXI.	The Day of Miracles, or Mr. Giles and Mr. Lovering made Friends.	289
XXXII.	Fostina's Mission.	304
XXXIII.	Sunshine and Shadows. — Deception unveiled.	318
XXXIV.	Scene in a Factory Boarding-House. — The Tempter foiled.	333

CONTENTS.

XXXV.	Hester's Faith rewarded. — A Leap in the Dark. — Deceived and deserted.	352
XXXVI.	Fort Sumter is fallen. — The Call to Arms. — Weeping at the Village Depot. . . .	368
XXXVII.	Fostina's Life Work begins. — Hester's Story of her own Childhood.	375
XXXVIII.	Love's Golden Key, or a New Era in the Lentell Family.	385
XXXIX.	Uncle Levi. — Sad Scene at the Supper Table. — The Noble Wreck.	396
XL.	Elida's Visit. — The Soldier's Funeral, or the Laurel Wreath.	411
XLI.	Our last Call on the different Families in our World. — Harmony's dying Wish accomplished, her Faith rewarded, or the Conclusion of the whole Matter.	429

HESTER STRONG'S LIFE WORK.

CHAPTER I.

The Loverings and their Friends.

Just on the outskirts of one of New England's most enterprising cities, the Lovering farm-house has stood for at least a century. The old house was kept in excellent order, and in process of time the shed roof on the back side was raised, and a porch added, to make room for the third and fourth generations. Three tall, trim poplars stood sentinel in front of the house; a maple at one end; a Balm of Gilead spread its leaves and shed its healing buds at the other end, shading the porch door. Just over the way, on a gentle eminence, stood the corn-barn, ample in dimensions, and under it the cider mill and storehouse for farming utensils, with bench and tools for repairing. On this bench the children and grandchildren (little ones, I mean) used to sit, and watch the apples fall into the hopper; while Old Tom, the family horse, went round and round, with his sleepy eyes half shut, a miracle of patience and docility.

It was an important epoch in the life of each succeeding child when he or she was taken down from the carpenter's bench, and assigned some post of honor about the cider mill. Just back of the house, at the left, stood a capacious barn, with all the conveniences necessary on a large farm, even to the "little yard," as it was called, especially for milking. But the pleasantest, the most delightful spot on all the premises, was the "river road," or cart path, which led from the barn through well-cultivated fields, under fruit and other trees, down even to the smooth, sweet waters of the Merrimac. Dear old river! How the young people loved it! What moonlight, morning and midday walks they used to take, back and forth! If there is magic in music, so there was magic in the moonbeams as they fell upon the bosom of the sparkling water, and came dancing and flickering to you through the silver leaves of a cluster of willows which stood just at the right hand of the terminus of the river road. Beneath these willows were rustic seats, placed there many years agone, by young, brave hands, which are now folded over the silent bosom of a weary sleeper, who is resting in the village burial-ground. Of these willows we shall speak again. About half a mile down the river, and farther from its sloping banks, Nathan Sharp built a small, inconvenient house; married, and made it the business of his life to get rich; ignoring all refinement of manners, all adornment of his person or premises, and despising "book larnin'," as he called it; counting no labor too hard that would pay well. His worldly goods increased, as well as his family, until he could count more acres than Mr. Lovering; had more cattle crowded into his little shabby barn, more children in his inconvenient, uninviting house, and more money. He was satisfied, — as much so as a selfish, narrow nature can be. Money was his idol; work, his pride and boast. Mehitable, the eldest daughter, was her father's exact counterpart, except in one item — *she* was neat and orderly, even to a fault.

Mr. Manlie, an educated gentleman, lived at the village about two miles from the Loverings. His wife was a pleasant, cultivated lady, so that their children enjoyed excellent advantages, and were every way worthy of their parents. Horace Manlie, while a medical student, became engaged to Miss Hester Strong, an adopted daughter of the Loverings. Between these two families there had always existed a firm friendship, which ripened into a warm and permanent attachment. So when the eldest son of Mr. Lovering asked timidly for the hand of Mary Manlie, it was cheerfully bestowed. This connection was pleasant to all who had a right to be concerned, if the different members of Mr. Sharp's family did prophesy evil, and that continually. Mary and Hester had long been as sisters, and now they felt that they were sisters indeed, as they were in affection.

Both were looking eagerly forward to the time when Horace should complete his studies, and cement the bond of union between them. They spent many happy hours in talking over their future plans, their hopes and bright anticipations, little dreaming that a net was even then being spread by envious, artful hands, which would change their plans, and bring sorrow, ay, anguish, to many hearts. Mehitable Sharp had some claims to beauty of face and figure. She was of medium height, fair complexion, blue eyes, rosy lips, and very sprightly. With other training, and different influences, she might have been a noble woman. But as it was, all the good aspirations of her ardent nature were crushed out, all the envy and avarice of her heart were cultivated.

Her girlish fancy first fastened upon Charles Lovering; and she lost no opportunity to cultivate his acquaintance, and went into many extravagances in dress in order to captivate him. But in vain. His true, noble heart found its mate in Mary Manlie, and he bore her to his home joyfully in spite of hints and unpleasant innuendoes thrown out by Miss Sharp. About the time of his marriage, she was accidentally thrown from her horse very near Mr. Manlie's. She was conveyed to the house, treated with the politeness and attention her situation demanded, and then carried to her home by Horace, who was spending his vacation at his father's. The young lady was charmed with the fine person and agreeable manners of the student, and wished, in her inmost heart, she could win him for herself. Instinctively, she saw how hopeless the task while in her present circumstances; the difference between them, intellectually and morally, was too great; but she used all the arts she was mistress of to interest him. She was brilliant, pleasant, and witty. He looked upon her as one who had been neglected, and sought to lead her into new channels of thought, to stimulate her to cultivate her mind and heart. And after this he often called at her home when passing, on his way to visit Hester. His prejudice against the family was not so great as that of his parents and sisters, because he had seldom come in contact with them since quite young.

His mother warned him that he would see trouble if he made so much of the girl.

"O, I think not," was the reply. "I am trying to

bring her out, to make something of her. She feels her deficiencies sadly. Hester approves of my course. She pities her sincerely."

"She must have changed," said his sister Martha. "She used to despise learning, and make sport of you, and all educated people."

"Well, that was when she was young and thoughtless," was the reply. "She told me she did. I am going to lend her some books; and, Martha, I wish you would join me in the good work of bringing this young girl up out of the slough of ignorance in spite of her parents." The student returned to his studies with buoyant, hopeful spirits. His affections had never wavered from his first and only love, no, not for a moment. But into Hester's heart had finally entered a vague doubt, a nameless fear, a secret and scarcely recognized pain. Soon his letters became less frequent: she made no complaint, but her step became less elastic, her voice more silent; she was changed. When he chided her gently for her remissness in writing to him, she smiled almost bitterly, and strove to still the throbbing of her wounded heart, little dreaming that the perfidy of another had robbed her of those tokens of remembrance which she so much craved. Had either of them been less patient and uncomplaining, the artful web which was being woven about them might easily have been broken, and all would have been well. As Mary sat writing to Horace one day, Hester said, —

"Are you writing to Horace?" "Yes, dear," was the reply. "May I put in a note to him? I do not feel able to write much." She wrote and sealed these fatal words : —

"Horace, our engagement is at an end, and forever. Seek not to see me until we can both talk calmly of the past and its broken vows. Farewell.

"Ever your friend, - HESTER STRONG."

As she handed the sealed note to Mary, she sank back in her chair pale and exhausted, crushed and broken-hearted.

"Hester," said Mary, "what is it? Why will you not tell me? Surely you do not attach any importance to that rumor about his engagement to Mehitable Sharp? You should know Horace better than that. I have not even mentioned it to him. He would be offended. I knew he would be here soon, and then the cloud would pass. Cheer up, darling, or I shall laugh at you." Hester tried to speak, but her lips were mute. She wanted to tell her, now that the letter had gone, of all that she had seen and heard; of the letter she had been allowed to partially read; of the strong professions of love he had lavished on one so unworthy of him; of his great joy that the time of his release from an irksome duty was so near at hand, and the full fruition of enjoyment so soon to come. But she could not pain the fond heart of her more than sister by the recital of her brother's faithlessness.

No, she could not call it that; it was a strange fatality that had separated them, hard to bear, harder to understand. Days passed: all the friends looked for Horace with the greatest anxiety, feeling sure that he could explain all, and bring the old smile back to Hester's face, joy to her heart, and light to her eyes, which were now dull with weeping. But instead came kind, affectionate letters to all but her he loved most and best. Hers read, —

"Hester, I accept the freedom you have so freely given me, and its conditions. We will not meet until you wish it. I should have been better prepared for the cruel blow you have given me, but I was slow to believe what our mutual friend, Mehitable Sharp, so hesitatingly told me. And when you neglected to answer my earnest letters of devoted attachment, I should have believed, but I could not, O, I *could not!* But when my last, eager, hopeful letter was returned unopened, and my sister's letter came to hand, containing your cold, cruel renunciation of me, my heart grew sick, and my very soul faint, with the bitter disappointment of its most cherished hopes. Farewell. To-morrow I shall be far away from all I have counted dear; a restless wanderer to — I know not where.

"Ever your friend, HORACE MANLIE."

Weeks and months passed away before Horace Manlie was again heard from. His unexpected departure, Hester's tears, all, all was a painful mystery to the family and friends. All that they could do to cheer and sustain Hester they cheerfully did, although their own hearts were sore and sad. At length letters came containing his address. If Hester had been hasty in dismissing her lover, she now hastened to confess her fault. She wrote to him of all her doubts and fears, her painful suspense, of all she had seen and heard, closing with the words, "Horace, my dearest and best beloved, come home. I shall never be happy till I hear from your own lips that I am forgiven."

Letters came and went, the light came again to Hester's eyes, the smiles to her lips, and yet something of the old buoyancy had gone. Hester was wiser now. It was sweet to be reconciled and at peace with her heart's chosen one, but the time seemed long, very long to wait. Horace had engaged himself as tutor for three years. He had the privilege of attending medical lectures in one of the best of schools. He must fulfil his engagements, he wrote, though the heavens fall. Very soon after the mysterious departure of Horace Manlie, Mehitable Sharp married Morgan Lentell, a distant connection of the family. There was quite a disparity in their ages, as well as dispositions. He was fine-looking and amiable, but not very energetic. He made a home for his wife on a farm (rented, at first) about seven miles from her father's. Her outfit, although not elegant or extensive, was perfectly satisfactory; as Mrs. Lentell had, like her father, a supreme contempt for the beautiful or the ornamental. But more than all things else she prized her spinning-wheel, reel, and loom. Poverty stood sentinel at their humble door for several years, but he was bravely met and conquered. Mrs. Lentell was, indeed, the more shrewd and capable of the two, and acted well her part as far as the accumulation of property was concerned. The rest we will leave our readers to learn as our story progresses.

The Loverings and the Manlies had never been on terms of intimacy with the Sharp family. But since they had proclaimed to the world that Horace Manlie had broken his engagement with Mehitable, and fled through fear of the Loverings, there had been no communication between them. They met and passed each other without recognition. So that when, two years after, the emaciated form of the gifted young man was borne to his childhood's home to die, and Hester, patient, faithful Hester, watched tenderly over him, there were no prying eyes or curious ears to disturb the mournful pleasure of those few remaining days. None knew how much they suffered, nor how much they enjoyed, except the immediate family and friends. And as the flickering light of that beautiful, manly life went out, and they laid their beloved dead in the churchyard near at hand, the two families drew nearer and nearer together, forming a circle, as it were, around Hester, the stricken, smitten one, as if to shield her from the sorrow which had fallen so heavily upon them, — but with a more crushing weight on her.

"It is all a painful mystery," they said; "who shall fathom it? A deep, deep wound; who but the Infinite One can heal it?" It was there Hester looked; and after months of weary, prostrating sickness, she came forth calmly, and serenely took up the burden of life, consecrating herself to God, and devoting her time and talents — *all* — to the work of ministering to the sick and suffering of earth.

And; verily, she will not lose her reward.

CHAPTER II.

Life and its Changes.

Twenty-five years had not passed over the families, which we have introduced to our readers, without making great and important changes. The dear old father and mother of Charles and Mary Lovering, after years of patient waiting, passed on to the reward of the righteous, blessing God for the gift of such kind and devoted children, such loving and respectful grandchildren.

"It is only the fruit of your own judicious training," Hester, the child of their adoption, used to say. Mary Lovering had found her a source of never-failing comfort and help. "What should we do without Hester?" was a household word; and many other families said and felt the same. All these years she had been like a ministering angel to the sick and afflicted, not only in her own, but often in neighboring towns, whenever home duties would permit.

"Mary and I have six children," she used to say, laughingly. "I don't know which loves them best. But sometimes *they* think they love their auntie a little mite the best, for I never punish them." It would be difficult to imagine a more pleasant and joyous family circle. But Hester began to say the harvest time had arrived. Olive was gathered into a home nest of her own, Frank next. Edward was at college. Charles, junior, said he must wait and look after his lovely sisters — Harmony, the beautiful pet lamb of the flock, and Elivia, the sparkling, brilliant baby of the household. Those were happy days at the farm-house, as the children gathered around the ample fireplace in the large, old-fashioned kitchen, in winter, talking cheerfully, reading, sewing, or singing, while the father led with his deep, bass voice and his violin. Martha Manlie often made one of their number; for, like Hester, she had been down into "the valley," and seen one nearer and dearer than life go over the river and leave her standing *alone*, with life's blasted hopes, and sweetest, fairest flowers lying faded and fragrantless at her weary feet. "O Hester, sweet sister," she used to say in the first months of her grief, "how is it that you are strong enough to bear your own and other people's sorrows?" But we must pass hastily over these events, and remain silent about many things that would be of interest to the reader. Mr. Lovering is "*grandpa*" henceforth, and Hester is "aunt" to everybody. Harmony was her especial darling — from her striking resemblance to her uncle Horace. It was but simple justice to call her beautiful. She had small, regular features, black, glossy, and very luxuriant hair, and eyes full of tenderness, deep and dark. Her complexion was very fair, with rosy cheeks, a bewitching smile, and voice soft as sweetest music.

It was not strange, then, that she who was so much admired at home should be sought after, early in life, to bless and brighten another home. So it was.

"Keep her in the home nest closely, mother," grandpa used to say, "or we shall lose her *too soon*."

Changes have been wrought also in the family of Mohitable S. Lentell. The rented farm has been bought and stocked, and increased in size. She has eight children; three boys and five girls. Some have married and gone from the din of the loom and the buzz of the wheel. Morgan, the eldest son, is his mother's pride.

"I should like to have them Loverings see him," she used to think. He was, indeed, a noble specimen of young athletic manhood; six feet in height, well proportioned, with deep-blue eyes, brown hair, and comely features. As he excelled in all youthful sports, he was a great favorite in his circle. He had also his mother's business talents; so the care and burden of the farm fell naturally upon him. Mrs. Lentell had grown prematurely old in the race for money; deep lines of care were marked on her once comely features. In her family she reigned a sort of queen; her word was their only law. Her house was kept in order, and the family were happy in their way, by due submission to the ruling power. Mr. Lentell was a cipher in his own house. He was often reminded of his great indebtedness to his wife for the property he possessed. Sickness and death had never entered their dwelling. This was owing to her excellent management, she thought. She was never sick; why should others be? Morgan had become a famous rafter of wood and lumber to a seaport town not very distant, and in that way brought much gold to his mother's coffers. On one of these occasions, he was taken suddenly and severely sick. He remembered the cluster of willows, the delightful road, and the neat farm-house but a few rods distant. He had often caught glimpses of young men and maidens seated beneath the willows. Some one might be there now. If not, he might reach the house. This thought nerved his arm till he arrived at the spot. Two young and very lovely girls were seated there. He hesitated to accost them, but they soon discovered his situation, and Harmony Lovering stepped timidly and gracefully forward, as she said, —

"You are sick — are you not, sir? My father's house is near, and my brother is at work in the next field. Shall I call him?"

"If you will do so, I shall be greatly obliged," was the reply. "I have never been so sick before." Charles came at his sister's call. He saw at once that it was a case of cholera morbus, if not of cholera, but he was too generous to leave him in this hour of need. Elivia went forward to inform the home circle, Harmony lingered by the sick man. Simple remedies soon relieved the symptoms, but grandpa prescribed rest and a cup of tea. By that time it was night. "Stop with us till morning," they all said, "and take a fresh start." He was nothing loath, for in such a family it would be pleasant to spend a lifetime. These, then, were the Loverings he had heard his mother speak of with such bitter contempt. Surely she did not know them. Was it possible that Mrs. Lovering was about his mother's age? How young and fair she looked! And Hester, he had thought, was a monster; but no, she was a noble-looking lady, with a calm, sweet face. And Harmony! Never before had he seen or dreamed of such a vision of loveliness. What a contrast to his uncultivated sister! what a contrast in everything!

"You said your name was Lentell," said grandpa, at the supper table. "What was your mother's maiden name?"

"Mehitable Sharp," was the reply.

"Ah! indeed," said grandpa. "Mary, you remember her; she used to be neighbor. They lived on the place where Mr. Stearns lives. Charles, they left when you were a baby." Hester's keen eye rested on the young man's face for a moment, wondering if this noble-looking, agreeable young man could be the son of her youthful enemy. Was he like her? She felt uneasy and anxious. Her quick eye had seen the glances of bashful admiration pass between Morgan and Harmony, and that the two would be fitly mated so far as beauty was concerned. But, like one of old, she queried, "Can any good thing come out of Nazareth?" Reader, this was but the beginning of the end of my story. The visits of the son of Mehitable Sharp became frequent, and agreeable to Harmony, at least. And while sitting under the willows, watching the moonbeams dance and flicker in and out through the leaves, listening to the ardent professions of devotion uttered by the rich, manly voice of Morgan Lentell, little Harmony fell a victim on the altar of sweet, young love. She was wholly his. The young man soon won a place in the affections of the family, so that sooner than they intended, sooner than their judgment dictated, they consented to part with their darling. Hester remonstrated when she found Harmony was to board with her husband's mother. But all in vain.

"It will only be for a short time," was the reply; "just long enough for them to build." This silenced, but did not convince her of the wisdom of the plan. Mrs. Lentell was not pleased with her son's marriage into a book family, and that the Loverings. "What good is their larnin' going to do 'um?" she used to say. "It won't help 'um hold a plough, or swing an axe, or

cook a dinner, or make a shirt, or darn a stockin', to say
nothin' about spinnin' an' weavin'." But these objections
were carefully concealed from Harmony and her friends;
for Morgan had assured them, firmly and decidedly, that
he should leave them, and forever, if obstacles were
thrown in the way of his marriage. The old house had
grown too small for them. A new one must be built
immediately; and who but he could lift the mortgage and
build the house? And so the young, inexperienced
child-wife was actually settled in their midst before she
knew their prejudices or the real character of the family.
But she was soon made to feel herself an intruder; and
the future opened out before her like a dark, dreary wilderness, with just one light to illumine the darkness —
the ardent love of her husband. This, she thought, would
always be left to cheer her. Her affectionate, trustful
nature clung to its first and only love, never dreaming that
what had seemed to her so sacred and pure, so much like
heaven, could ever be covered up or blotted out by the
blight and mildew of sin. She did not see the terrible
monster that was winding his hideous folds around the
noble form of her husband, paralyzing both body and
mind. She was used to seeing the wine-cup passed
around in her father's house, but intoxication she had
never seen; to real intemperance she was a stranger.
She knew not that her husband's feet were even then
ready to slip, and that he was being goaded on by the
perplexing cares and conflicting influences which sur-
rounded him. Poor child, she did not know the power of
the intoxicating cup, or of a strong-minded, managing
mother over a son taught from childhood to obey. At
first, Morgan defended his young wife from the insulting

treatment of his mother and sister and two younger brothers. The elder sisters, being married and well settled in life, received her kindly, and treated her with respect.

He astonished them all one day by informing them that he had entered into an engagement with an aged widow in the neighborhood, to take a deed of her property, giving a bond for her proper care and support. That was a terrible blow to them, as Mr. Lentell had become disabled for active labor by a fall, and was depending on his son to pay up the debts, build the new house, and take care of them in their old age. He, from the first, had treated the young wife with respect and tenderness, and had often been pained by the cold, unkind treatment she received in his house, especially by the bitter taunts of his wife; but he was powerless to improve her condition.

"I don't blame you, Morgan," was his only reply when his son made known his decision; "I *can't* blame you, but God only knows what will become of us." And the tears fell slowly down those patient cheeks.

His mother was silent and sullen, attributing it all to his marriage with a good-for-nothing Lovering.

He would be sorry before long, beg her pardon, and come back on her own terms. She was sure he would never get on with such a slack, shiftless wife. "She didn't know a distaff from a reel when she come here, to say nothin' about spinnin' an' weavin';" and so she let them go, apparently well pleased. She was mistaken. Harmony was young, far *too* young to assume the duties of housekeeping, being only sixteen at her marriage; the consent of her parents being gained only by the assurance of Morgan that she should be a boarder in his father's family, without care, till matured both in strength and judgment. But the kind, motherly instructions of the aged widow enabled her to succeed better than might have been expected. She bade fair to make an excellent housekeeper. She often referred to this period as the two happiest years of her life.

By that time Mrs. Mehitable Sharp Lentell began to fear that her son *would not* return like the Prodigal of old. She saw that she was losing her power over him. The farm, in spite of many days' labor bestowed on it by Morgan, junior, was running down; the debts were not being paid, nor the new house built. She changed her tactics at once, and by a series of skilful manœuvres, by prayers and tears, warnings and entreaties, caused him to break his engagement with the widow (who had been as a mother to him and his wife), and return, like a fool to his folly, a little less than a year previous to her death; which would have left him in possession of competence and happiness.

Morgan Lentell never failed in obedience and respect for his parents. That was an overshadowing influence with him, while his own family took a secondary place in his thoughts. He might have had a deed of all the property when he returned; but regard for their feelings induced him to let writings remain as they were, and transact business in his father's name, lending his own as security. Harmony and her three little children spent the summer at grandpa Lovering's while the new house was in process of erection. It was to be large and convenient for two families; therefore the confiding wife wove many a fanciful web of happiness for herself in the future, interwoven, more or less, with dark forebodings, which were more than realized. Mrs. Mehitable Sharp Lentell was sagacious enough to have the half she was to occupy finished first, and move into it. She then insinuated that her son might move his family into the *old* house, until he should be able to finish the other part, advising him not to hurry about it; for, said she, "Harmony won't have any dairy, and it will be better for you to pay up that note, that will be due next year, first. The old house is enough sight better than it was when your father and I commenced housekeeping. Harmony has got too many notions now." Her parents were opposed to her moving into the old house. Indeed, they would gladly have kept her with them henceforth. "Let her stay where she is," was her father's reply to his son-in-law, "till the house is done; and I will furnish it in good style, if you will only sign the pledge, my son."

But Harmony felt it her duty to go with her husband; so they gave a reluctant consent. From that day her vassalage to her husband's mother was complete. Little by little she artfully estranged the husband's affections, and left her heart an empty, aching void, with nothing to bind her to earth but the love of her childhood's friends; with nothing to bind her to her husband but the children she *could not* leave, and from whom *he* would not part.

The new house was at length completed, and partially furnished, and the family were staying in it, when grandpa Lentell sickened and died suddenly while Morgan was rafting timber to a distant town. His grief and that of his wife were unfeigned, and the little children wept when their mother told them grandpa had gone to heaven.

"Who took him?" said Wallace, sobbing.

"God," said the mother.

"Why didn't he take grandma," said the child, bitterly, "and let my grandpa stay?"

"Her would be too c'oss up there — wouldn't her, mamma? and her can't have her loom — can her? God won't 'low it," said Elida, in a whisper.

"Hush, hush, children!" said the startled mother, looking anxiously at the door.

After the funeral, the inhabitants of the "great house," as it was always called, were thrown into terrible commotion, and the feelings of the community greatly agitated, by the reading of a will, written a day or two before the death of Mr. Lentell, giving his entire property, new house and all, to his two younger sons, and leaving the "Atwood place" to Morgan; a little, uncultivated farm, with a poor, miserable house and tumble-down barn upon it. It was well known that the kind old gentleman would not have done such an unjust deed knowingly, and also that his reason failed in the very first of his sickness. The whole thing was illegal: it would not stand the test of law.

But here, again, the power of the mother was brought to bear upon the yielding son.

"Would he take the law on his own brothers? and at such a time, too? What difference did it make? They should always consider him the same as a father; he would still manage the property just the same."

Alas for his credulity! Six months had not gone by when he was compelled to leave all, and retire to the little house, where we shall soon find them. He was advised to seek redress, and felt disposed to do so; but a few tears and entreaties from his mother changed his purpose. Strange infatuation! "Honor thy father and thy mother," was a lesson he had learned most thoroughly; while, "For this cause shall a man leave father and mother, and shall cleave to his wife: and they twain shall be one flesh," had found no place in his heart; or that other scripture, teaching, "If any provide not for his own, and specially for those of his own house, he hath denied the faith, and is worse than an infidel."

At the time of grandpa Lentell's death, the debts were nearly paid by the industry and hard labor of Morgan; aided considerably by the liberality of father Lovering, and a lift now and then from his wife's brothers. His own family had cost him very little in any way. But the mason work in the new house was not paid for; the workmen had tried to collect it from the new owners, but in vain. They saw plainly that the intoxicating cup, family bickerings, &c., were rapidly breaking down the once strong, noble man. He was, even then, almost a wreck of his former self. So, in the midst of haying, they seized the person of Morgan, and sent him to the county jail; consoling themselves with the idea that the mother, who was still the ruling power on the place, would not permit him to remain there; especially at that time, when he was so much needed at home, as well as on the old place, where he still did much effective labor. They were mistaken: they either could not, or would not, pay the debt. There was something of the old time tenderness in his voice, as he bade his family a sad good by, and rode away with the sheriff.

"I shall be back in a day or two, Harmony," he said. "Good by; keep up good courage. Mother 'll contrive some way to pay it up right off. I'm going to do better when I get back. I'll send somebody to see to you. Don't go home, Harmony, don't: I'll be back in a day or so."

These few kind words were like dew on the thirsty earth: she lived on them many days. On his way to the jail, he called on a friend whom he had often aided, told him his circumstances, asked him to take care of his family until his return. His case excited much sympathy, and several gentlemen volunteered to give bail; which his mother urged him, with tears, to allow.

But as he was resolved not to pay the debt, he refused to return. He had the liberty of the yard, however, and gained the esteem of the jailer's family, besides good wages. And many, very many fondly hoped that this experience would emancipate him from his mother, who went often to see him, and wept bitterly at what she called his obstinacy in not being bailed. But he was firm, saying, —

"I shall remain here till the term expires, unless you pay the debt. You could do it *easily* if you chose."

"Marm," said Abigail, the next day after Morgan left home, "Miller Drake has just gone along. I'll bet a dollar he's gone to see Harmony; and he thinks so much of Morgan, that he'll go and provide for her. It's too bad, the little, proud, puttering thing! I hoped she'd git brought down a peg. Let her go home if she wants to, and cogitate Latin varbs with her larned brothers."

Fortunately Abigail was the only one in the family who inherited her mother's aversion to books and refinement of manners.

"Nabby, you talk like a fool about her goin' home. Morgan would foller her, an' we couldn't git along without him. Hum, I wish to the land we could. I wish he could be prevailed on to send her home: it would mortify them Loverings some, I guess. But don't you fret about

Miller Drake; I'll hail him when he goes back, and you see if I don't manage that now."

And she did manage it. She told him, —

"She was glad he had called on poor Harmony. She *means* well enough, but she don't know how to manage. Everything goes to ruin. I shall see that she don't want for anything, though. We are going to send over their food, and do their washing; so it won't be necessary for you to call again. We can see to them; Morgan ought to have known we would. I will go right over with some things now. Poor Morgan! I pity him, and would contrive to pay the debt, but we have to maintain the whole family most of the time, and he might as well be there as at home. He's an *altered man*, Mr. Drake; yes, an *altered man* since he married. I pity him, and his family shan't want while he's gone, I promise you."

So Mr. Drake wasn't seen at the small house again. Perhaps his gratitude wasn't very deep; perhaps he was glad of a poor excuse for not keeping a solemn promise to one who had befriended him in a similar case. The resolute, determined character of the elder Mrs. Lentell was well known in all that region, as well as her unnatural and unaccountable prejudice against her son's wife and the Loverings generally. At all events, he should have kept his promise, so solemnly given. But the food was not carried over, the washing was not done, and the family *did* suffer.

And Mehitable Sharp Lentell was careful, when she went to see her son, not to inform him of Mr. Drake's unfaithfulness or her own.

So the poor man felt comparatively easy about his family, and made many good resolutions for the future.

CHAPTER III.

SAD SCENES AT THE SMALL HOUSE.

"Hum! You needn't ask me to send for Hester Strong, for I shan't. It's nothin' but 'Hester,' 'Hester.' I hate her. She shan't come here to lord it over me in my old age."

"Why, what did aunt Hester ever do to injure you?" said a faint voice from the bed, which stood in a corner of the low, dark, dingy-looking room. "O, I must have her, or I shall surely die, and baby will die, too."

"Hum! you won't die; no danger of that. That child ain't worth raisin'; she looks like a monkey. I've made gruel 'nuff to last till mornin'; there's bread and meat 'nuff for the young 'uns. You've nothin' to do but lay there, and let 'um wait on ye."

"O, I am too sick and faint to tell them," said Harmony Lentell, the young and beautiful wife of Morgan Lentell. "O, do send for Hester, or mother, or some one. Don't leave me alone with these children another night."

"I shan't send for none of 'em; you've been babied to death; 'tis time you's weaned," said Mrs. Mehitable Sharp Lentell, as she turned to leave the house. "Cruel and unsympathizing," mused the sick one, as she covered her face and wept silently. The three children, Winnie, Wallace, and Elida, drew nearer and nearer together, looking into each other's faces in silent sympathy.

"I think grandma is real c'oss," said Elida. "I don't love her — do you, Wallace?"

"No, I don't," said Wallace; "she isn't a bit like grandma Lovering or aunt Hester."

"Hush!" said Winnie; "mamma is very, very sick. Don't you see how pale she is? She is whiter than the sheets. O, what if God should take her away from us!" she whispered close to Wallace's ear.

"He won't," said Wallace. "We couldn't live here then. We can take care of her."

"So we can," said Winnie; "let's go and tell her about it. Mamma, mamma," she said, going to the bedside, "Wallace and I can nurse you — can't we? Look up, mamma! We love you, *all* of us."

"Darling, precious children! I know you love me, and for *your* sakes I will try to be calm. Perhaps God will send grandpa Lovering to see us; then all will be well."

"Shall I warm you some gruel, mamma, or bathe your head? O, what *can* I do to make you better?"

"You may do both, darling, and then you may put little sister to bed, while you and Wallace sit by me a while to comfort me. You are my little comforter, you know."

Baby was a pale, sick, hungry-looking little thing; the whole expression of the face inexpressibly sad. They named her little Fossie. The children called her funny; the doctor very gravely remarked, —

"Your child is altogether too old of her age, Mrs. Lentell. But have you no one to stay with you but these children? No sister or friend?"

"My sisters are all married," sighed the sick one.

"I am expecting a very dear friend, Miss Hester Strong, every moment. I wrote her a note since I was taken sick."

"Glad to hear it," was the reply. "You will need her. Good day, ma'am. If I am wanted, please let me know, and I am at your service."

"Yes, you needn't come unless you hear from us," said grandma Lentell, who entered the room just in season to hear the remark. When the doctor had left the house, Harmony inquired, timidly, "Isn't it almost time for Hester to come, grandma?" She was answered with a derisive laugh. "I guess not. I burnt that letter. You don't need her. I told you so before." A deathly faintness passed over the sick one for a moment. She felt stunned by the cruel blow, but the thought of her helpless condition roused her.

"How could you?" she murmured, "O, how could you? You will send Levi for her—won't you? Don't say no," she pleaded.

The reader has already been made aware of the cruel obstinacy with which the elder Mrs. Lentell refused to send for Hester, or any one to take care of Harmony. So she had but little nursing except what her children bestowed. She was rapidly sinking, and the wee baby grew more wee daily, until grandpa and grandma Lovering arrived on the fourth day after its birth. "God has sent you," said little Winnie, as she met them at the door. "Mother said he would."

"What's this! what's this!" said grandpa, turning around hurriedly, and clinching his hand firmly in his hair, as usual, when he was surprised or indignant. "Harmy, where is the nurse?" "We's the nurse, said little Winnie. "Wallace and I is nurse." "Ah, indeed!" said grandpa, "you are nice children. But this won't do, Harmony. Father must look after you better than this, dear child. You must come home when you are able to ride." He stooped, took little Elida in his arms, stroked her shining hair, patted Wallace's dark locks, praised Winnie, peeped in at the half-starved babe, stroked the hollow cheek of his faded daughter silently for a moment, and then said in a half whisper, "Take the things out of the chaise-box, mother, and make *her* something nourishing," nodding towards the bed. "You must stay and take care of her till I get back with Hester." Mrs. Lovering found things in a sad condition. She fed the hungry children, and smiled at their joyful demonstrations; but her heart was full, almost to bursting, as she stood over her child, and combed gently the matted locks of hair which were once so beautiful.

"I feel so much better!" said the sick one, languidly. "How good you were to come, when I have been so obstinate about going home! Now I shall sleep a little. You will see to them; and baby, my poor baby, it seemed very hungry till this morning, and now it don't want anything. I haven't any nourishment for it, hardly; it won't starve — will it?"

"No, dear, I think not; go to sleep now. I will see to it," said the mother, softly. But how that word startled her!

Starve! Harmony's baby *starve!* Soon as possible she opened the little, blue, silent lips, and poured a few drops of warm nourishment into its parched mouth. Again and again it was repeated, while the little, cold, wet infant was wrapped in warm, dry clothing. But as she looked around on the destitution of the house, thought of the feebleness of the mother, and the almost hopeless degradation of the father, she had many doubts and misgivings respecting her duty.

"O, how infinitely better off the little one would be in its Father's house above!" she thought. "But I cannot let it starve; no, I must not, if I can prevent it. Poor darling, surely the lines have not fallen to you in pleasant places. But God is good; he knows what is best; I must try to save you, and leave the result with him." After a few hours of careful nursing, the infant opened those strangely beautiful eyes, and raised them to the loving face bending over it, as if to express its gratitude. Mrs. Lovering was astonished at the change produced in the little sallow face by their expression. She combed the tangled locks of soft, bright hair, which curled into graceful little ringlets, and called the children to see how pretty she looked.

"O, she is so *beautifuler* now!" said the children, capering about. "She was real funny before. O, I'm so glad you came, grandma! Now grandma Lentell won't say she looks like a monkey, and make mamma cry — will she?" "I knowed she wasn't a monkey," said Wallace, proudly. "Monkey's has got hair all over, and they hasn't got such nice little mouths and eyes — has they, grandma?" "No, darling, she is a sweet little sister, and when she is strong and well, she will be very pretty, I think."

Mrs. Lovering was surprised to find that Morgan Lentell had been confined nearly a week in the county jail, leaving his family to the tender mercies of his mother and sister. They had succeeded, long ago, in convincing him that Harmony was a poor, slack thing; that she wasted faster than he could earn. And so they undertook to spend his earnings, and carry in provisions as they were needed; and, in their opinion, it took very little to support a shiftless woman and three miserable children, and they dealt out the provisions accordingly. But for the care and thoughtfulness of grandpa Lovering's family they must have suffered ere this.

"My father is a naughty man, sometimes," said little Wallace, confidentially, to his grandma, as he was being undressed for the night. "He is cross, and doesn't love mother, nor me, nor anybody. He talks bad words, and I don't love him much. Mother says I must, though, for he wouldn't act so if he wasn't intoxicated. He tells mother to go home to her rich old father, and I wish she would. Mayn't I go home with you, my dear, good, kind, little grandma? Mayn't I?" persisted the child. "Mother will let me."

"Perhaps so, darling," said the grandmother.

"Aunt Abigail said mother would go, if it wasn't for her *prideness.* She wouldn't — would she, grandma?"

Just then aunt Hester arrived. She was now a maiden lady of sixty, and one of those individuals whose name and nature are perfectly coincident. Except that her black hair was slightly frosted, one would not have supposed her more than forty. She was received with demonstrations of delight by the children, and deep, heartfelt joy by the sick mother, some of the earliest and pleasantest recollections of whose life were connected with Miss Hester, who had been in the family of her grandfather, or father, or among their friends, all her life. So she was considered one of themselves. Her broad chest shook with emotion for a moment, as she bent over the pale face and sunken eyes of her early pet; but the resolute will kept the strong, sinewy body in subjection. Her great soul always obtained the mastery in the sick-room, where she was perfectly at home under all circumstances. So grandfather and grandmother Lovering left with a safe, satisfied feeling, saying, as they went, —

"Well, if anybody can bring her round, Hester will. She will have good care, and Hester won't allow of any interference from any one."

Grandmother Lentell called very soon, and made some sharp criticisms on the baby and baby's mother, as well as upon things generally.

"Folks have changed since we were gals together," said she to Hester. "They didn't lay in bed only a few days then; I'm sure I never laid by more'n a week in my life."

"Yes," said Hester, "they have changed. People are not so healthy as they used to be; and you and I, Mehitable, have been highly favored. We don't know what it is to be sick. Let us thank God, and be kind to those who do."

"Hum," says Mrs. Mehitable; "some folks can feign sickness rather than work. For my part, I'd rather work than be sick."

"Pretty likely," said Hester, dryly. "I'm afraid you are not a good judge of sickness. *I* ought to be, for I've spent my whole life among it. Folks that *feign* sickness don't often pine till there's nothing left but skin and bone. O!" she exclaimed cheerfully, to change the subject, "there is Mrs. Bartlett, the dear, kind soul. She is coming to nurse our little, wee, sick chick. Its poor mother is so low I am going to take good care of her, and hope she will rally in a few days. . She has had a hard time, poor darling."

"Hum," said Mrs. Mehitable, trotting her foot vigorously; "hum, that child ain't worth all that fuss. Why didn't you let it die, Hester? You are just the same as ever: you don't look ahead a bit more'n you did when you refused a good offer, from a sense of gratitude or what not, to them miserable Loverings. You'll git yer pay for it yet," said she, in a sarcastic, insinuating tone.

Hester cast a furtive glance at the bed. Yes, *she* heard it all. A bright red spot glowed on each sunken cheek.

"I've got my pay for all I've ever done for them years ago," she said sternly; "and as to looking ahead, I try to live for eternity, and not altogether for time. And as Harmony is tired out, we won't talk any more here; but if you will stay till I get back, Mrs. Bartlett, I will take a walk with Mrs. Lentell."

"Certainly," said Mrs. Bartlett; "go, by all means."

"Thank you," said Hester, as she bent tenderly over Harmony, and said some low, sweet, brave words to her, arranged the pillows, gave her a drink, and left her. Both walked on in silence a few moments, when Mrs. Lentell remarked, —

"I suppose you know Morgan never can pay you for staying there."

"Yes, I know it," said Hester, looking her steadily in the face. "Is money the only thing worth living for?"

"Why, you're a fool to spend all your days workin' for nothin', that's all;" said Mehitable, somewhat disconcerted by the steady gaze of her companion.

"Perhaps not," was the reply; "perhaps I am not so

foolish as you take me to be. I was not so stupid that I could not look ahead and see that sorrow, disappointment, and suffering would come upon Harmony Lovering if she married your son and went to live with you. Was I mistaken — do you think? Don't we all know what you have done to her? For shame, Mehitable! From beginning to end you have abused and tyrannized over her. She hasn't complained, dear lamb! I told her how it would be; so she is as silent as the grave. I told her folks you would grind her to the earth. She is too good and patient to live with you. Didn't I know you? There came a time, Mehitable, when I could read you through and through, and learned you all by heart, and could reckon you up as well as I could a sum in addition. Ah, Mehitable, I fear *you* don't look ahead any, but you've got to answer for your conduct to that child somewhere. Her folks didn't believe me. O, they didn't know what good reason I had to know you.

"What a shame that my poor, dear lamb should be treated so! My beautiful little Harmony, that might have married into the best family in our town, and been treated like a lady, as she is! For shame, Mehitable, to ruin your own son's prospects for the sake of gratifying a mean, contemptible, jealous disposition. Be sure you can't go to heaven with that spirit." She had been standing right before Mrs. Lentell, with her great, broad palm upon the shrivelled shoulder of the little, wizened, wiry-looking woman ever since she turned to address her.

She had moved her back and forth slowly, and now drew her near enough to whisper, —

"Vile woman, *you* know why I did not marry Horace Manlie. You remember the cruel slander you brought to me, and the letters — you remember them. I had not learned to read you then; I believed you. It was you that sent him across the ocean, and consigned me to a life of honest labor, which is not without its reward. But the pain is over now; I am cheerful, and happier than you are. I would not change places with you. Horace and I understood each other before he died: we shall meet in heaven." Holding her back, and again looking her steadily in the face, she said, —

"How dared you allude to that painful subject now, after all these years, and falsely attribute our separation to Harmony's folks? You did it to pain her; you mean to kill her. Go, now, and do not come into that house again while I stay in it."

She released her, and turned to depart; but Mrs. Lentell, who had been surprised into silence, now found her speech.

"You shall be paid for this," she said, slowly. "I don't bear such insults. Prove what you say about Horace Manlic, or I'll make you."

"I can and will," was the calm, steady reply, "and many other falsehoods, if you wish it. It might help to break that tyrannical power you have over Morgan, and secure the happiness of my darling, who never saw an unhappy hour till she married him. And he would do well enough away from you. Shall I prove what I have said?"

"Prove what you like," was the evasive reply; "and I shall come into my son's house when I like."

"I should think you would call that a house!" said Hester, looking at it significantly; "or perhaps you mean the new house on the hill; that is his, not yours. You can't expect to prosper, Mehitable; you never will. Sooner or later you will have to meet a terrible reckoning. But I must go: I can forgive you all the wrong you have done me and *him*. *He* is at rest, and *I* am happy in making others so. But mind, now, don't come near Harmony while I stay, unless you repent of your wickedness to her, and come to ask her forgiveness. I can't allow it: she is the sickest person I ever saw left alone; and if she dies, her death will lie at your door. And God knows there is guilt enough there now. Good by. I wish you well."

Hester turned, leaving her standing as if riveted to the spot. She never imagined that Hester was aware of her duplicity; ay, treachery and hypocrisy. She never knew that Horace and Hester had become reconciled; that Hester had watched over his dying bed, and wept bitter tears of regret over the manly form, and sealed by a kiss on the noble forehead her vow of consecration to the sick and sorrowing. She did not know with what heroic fortitude Hester had refused to yield to the entreaties of Horace and the pleadings of her own heart to be united to him in the last hours of his life, that he might bestow on her his entire effects.

"Do not ask me, Horace," was always her tearful reply; "I do not deserve it. I will not come between you and your lawful heirs."

She consented to receive five hundred dollars as a dying gift, and had sacredly laid it aside for a time of need, which had not yet come.

"O, hum!" said Mrs. Mehitable; "then they found me out. Well, I suppose it wasn't right, but I liked him in spite of his larnin'. If I'd had more on't, he would liked me better. O, hum! I don't look much now as I did then. He told me once that I was pretty — better lookin' than Hester. He wouldn't say that now, I reckon. Well, it can't be helped. I knew he loved Hester: how red he'd git in the face when I run out ag'in her! O, hum! How he shook that last night that he called, when I told him she was false-hearted! O, well, he knew better, and so did I; but I meant to get him. Well, I didn't play the right card *that* time, sure. I'm glad my folks sold out jest as they did, and moved off. I'm glad I never went there after he got home. I shouldn't 'ave dared to."

CHAPTER IV.

The Pain and its Cure. — The Confession and Revulsion.

"How cruel!" murmured Hester, clasping her hands firmly, and walking with a measured step back to the house; back and forth in the small yard. "How cruel she was to pry open that secret chamber of grief! O, I thought I had buried that great sorrow, with all its bitter memories, so deep that no mortal could drag it forth again.

"That fatal letter! How came she by it? I should have known that it was written to me, for me, every word of it, and not for her. O, I didn't know then that any one could be so false, so treacherous. How real it all seems to-day! And yet, more than forty years have passed since it commenced, and more than thirty-eight since I buried it in the inmost recesses of my soul. To-day is the first time I have spoken of it, only to God. I laid my burden at the feet of Jesus when Horace died. How faithfully He has helped me to bear it all these years! But now it comes over me like a flood. O, Horace, we shall meet in heaven; I believe it.

"O thou pitying Father, help me. Thou suffering Saviour, comfort me; even me, and help me to lay down this vain regret, and take up the burdens and duties of my own chosen work. Help me to think of the blessings left. How kind, tender, and thoughtful the Loverings were to me in that day of darkness! Now I have the opportunity to repay them. Poor, dear Harmony, I fear I shall not be able to save her. And why do I desire it? She is one of Christ's little ones, and if he calls her from this prison-house of bondage, I must be willing, hard as it will be for us who love her so well."

She stopped at the humble door, and resolutely drove the shadows from her usually sunny face, and entered it with a smile. Baby was having a sweet, satisfied nap. Elida was cuddled away in kind Mrs. Bartlett's arms. Winnie and Wallace were at school. All was quiet, and yet the sick one could not rest. A tear glistened on the long, heavy lashes, as Hester, bending over her, inquired, — "How is my pet?"

"O, auntie," she whispered, "I feel so! The bed is all pins, or something. I can't lie still. What shall I do?"

"Why, auntie will fix it for you, darling," was the reply.

"O, it isn't in the bed, I guess; it is in me. *She* thinks I am feigning it; I am not — am I, auntie? and baby *is* worth saving — isn't she? and we didn't prevent your marrying uncle Horace — did we?"

"No, no, darling; don't think of what she said. I know you are a poor sick lamb. I will take you up in my arms, and Mrs. Bartlett will make up your bed all clean and nice before she goes."

Hester forgot her own sorrows as she took the attenuated little form in her strong arms, and walked back and forth gently a few times, asking her to see from the window how beautiful things were looking out of doors.

Then seating herself, and placing Harmony's head tenderly on her broad chest, she commenced singing, softly, the hymn,
"Jesus, Lover of my soul."

Thus she not only soothed the restless invalid, but her own soul was refreshed and comforted by the beautiful hymn. Harmony fell asleep upon that loving bosom, where she had so often rested in childhood.

"Shall I help you lay her down?" said Mrs. Bartlett.

"No, dear; I shall hold her till she is refreshed. She isn't as heavy as she was at ten, I verily believe. Now I think of it, I wonder where that rocking-chair is that I gave her when she moved into the new house. She might be laid in that sometimes, if I could find it."

"I can tell you where it is," said Mrs. Bartlett. "Abigail was having a delightful rock in it when I called there the other day."

Hester's black eyes flashed as she inquired, "Is that so? How came it there? do you know?"

"It is there for safe keeping, I expect. Why, Harmony isn't supposed to know how to take care of things, because she can't spin and weave. But I must go now, and will come in to-morrow and give baby a good dinner."

"You are very kind, and God will reward you," said Hester, "and your husband will accommodate me greatly if he will let one of the boys come and carry me to ride a little way, after the children get home. It won't take more than half an hour, and I will pay him for his trouble."

"O, he'll like to accommodate you," was the reply.

The old white horse drove up to the door in good season. Miss Hester threw on a sun-bonnet, and took a seat in the wagon.

"Drive up to the great house on the hill as fast as you can," she said to the boy. "Mrs. Lentell seems worse. Drive as near the front door as possible. I shall go in for a moment. But mind, as soon as I get into the wagon, turn round and drive off without delay."

It was scarcely a moment when Hester returned with a large rocking-chair in her arms, and placed it in the wagon as easily as if it had been a cricket.

"Wait for me," she said to the boy. "There is one thing more that I want for present use."

She came back again with a small stand, just as Mrs. Lentell, her daughter Abigail, and the two boys, had left their supper to see what the disturbance was.

"Marm," said Abigail, "see there now! Are you goin' to bear that? *I* shan't, if *you* do."

"You may both have to bear worse things than that," said Hester, quietly seating herself in the wagon. "I thought my chair and table would be convenient to use just now. There are some other things in there that belong to Mr. Lovering. I should have spoken to you about them, but Harmony has been worse since you called, and I am in great haste. Good by."

By this time the carriage was out in the street on its way to the small house near the swamp, leaving the group at the large house standing there in utter amazement.

Harmony was restless all night. Several times Hester took her up in her strong arms, as if she had been an infant, and laid her for a little while in the soft easy-chair. Harmony looked pleased when she saw it, and inquired, —

"Did *you* get it for me?"

"Yes, dear," was the reply. "Why didn't you tell me they had it?"

"I was so sick I couldn't think," she said; "besides, you know how angry I was when you told me how it would be; and I didn't like to. O, auntie, I ought to have heeded your warning; but I loved him, and was so young! And father did want me to come back, but I wanted to please Morgan. I feared he would be entirely weaned from me, and I thought I couldn't live then. But I have," she said with a ghastly smile; "yes, I have lived to lose that for which I left the best and dearest of friends — a happy, peaceful home. We can't die always when we wish to — can we, auntie? — or live either. I have longed to die, again and again; but the tone and manner of Morgan when he left home, make me think his heart is still mine — that his love for me, which was ardent, has been stifled, not extinguished; and now I want to live, O, so much! I wonder why he has not written; he said he would, and I believe he has," she said, in a whisper. "She wouldn't allow me that little drop of comfort, if she could help it."

"Child," said Hester, "I don't doubt that he has, for your father has written him a kind letter; and I am sure he still loves you; so now try to sleep while I write him a note. I will send it to the office by the children. You will hear from him; he shall direct it to me."

Thus the night wore away at last. It was the most restless one Harmony had experienced. Just what Hester wrote we know not; but the answer came soon. It was full of sorrow and contrition for the past, full of hope for the future. He entreated his injured wife to forgive him; told her she was dearer to him than ever before; said he had written twice, but had received no answer. He did not say his letters were sent by his mother; but so it was. He closed by saying, —

"My dear wife, I am ashamed to say that my mother is the means of all your sufferings. It shall not be so any longer; do not leave me; stay in the small house till I return. These last acts of theirs have opened my eyes. Who would have thought she would let me stay here at such a time to pay their debts? or act as she has, in many respects?

"They hate you for your superiority; they rejoice at anything that will annoy you. They have sacrificed me to their malice against you and your folks. How monstrous! and what a wretch I have been to allow it! O, Harmy, I have been thinking, and my own conduct appears most hateful and cowardly; yours, beautiful and forgiving as an angel's. The tables shall be turned soon. I have already taken measures to regain the property they stole from me. I shall sign the pledge, and, as far as possible, redeem the past: so keep up good courage, darling; we will be happy yet. Kiss little Fostina for papa. I hope she will never be ashamed of me. Tell the little ones that I love them all, and want to see them. I shall bring them each a present when I come. How good Hester was to write me. She shall not lose anything by her kindness. Try to persuade her to make her home with us. I mean to have the new house all to ourselves. Mother (I can hardly bear to speak of her), and Abigail, and the boys can go to the small house near the swamp. My lawyer says their fraud and deception will give me entire power over them. And they deserve it. I don't mean to forget my duty to them; but I have learned that my own family have the highest possible claim upon me. O, why did I not learn it before! But the past is gone, the future only is left us. God grant I may make a wise use of it.

"Yours, with much love,
"MORGAN LENTELL."

Harmony remained very calm and quiet while her kind friend read this letter, looking up now and then to ascertain its effect. She closed, and both remained silent a few moments, when Hester, observing the extreme paleness of the invalid, stepped to the bed and inquired, —

"Isn't my darling very, very happy? Isn't it all bright and beautiful in the future?"

She reached out the little thin hand, which Hester clasped in hers, and said softly, —

"Yes, auntie, all bright and beautiful; but not here; no, not here; it is too late. I am going, auntie; don't you see it?"

"I see that you are feeble," was the reply; "and I hoped this letter contained a cure. Is it not so, darling? Surely you do not wish to leave poor Morgan now, and these little ones."

"No, auntie, I did not wish it; but God has helped me to be willing," she said, with a sweet smile. "How I have hungered and thirsted for just such a letter as that was! How I have prayed for it! A few days ago I think it would have made me unwilling to die ; but now, thank God, I can leave them all. O, auntie,

> 'There is a land where beauty does not fade,
>   Nor sorrow dim the eye;
> Where true hearts will not shrink, nor be dismayed,
>   And love will never die.'

It is there I am going, auntie. How glad I am that he knows how I have been wronged! that he will love my memory! Tell him how dear he was to me; tell him I forgave him day by day, and pitied him so much!"

"But think,". said Hester, "how sad it will be for Morgan to lose you under these circumstances. Perhaps God will yet raise you up to care for your family and assist your husband to do right. It will be hard for him to break away from old habits alone."

"I know it," said Harmony, almost sadly. "I have thought of it. It has distressed me very much; but now my peace is like a river.

> 'When we hear sweet music ringing
>   Through the bright, celestial dome,
> When sweet angel voices, singing,
>   Gently bid us, " Welcome home,"

can we, O, can we, regret to go? Dear auntie, uncle Horace will be there, too. You say mother is like him. I shall know him — shall I not ?

> 'In that land of ancient story,
>   Where the spirit knows no care,
> In that world of light and glory,
>   Shall we know each other there?'

Yes, auntie, I feel that we shall."

She became exhausted, and, while Hester stroked gently the soft locks, which had regained something of their former brightness under her care, fell asleep.

Hester seized this opportunity to write a note to Mr. Lovering, and also one to Morgan, stating, in as few words as possible, her worst fears.

CHAPTER V.

Alone with the Dying and the Dead. — The sad Return.

That night and the next day passed slowly at the small house near the swamp. Harmony was sinking rapidly.

"I should like to see them once more," she said several times during the day, "if it could be so. But it is all right. Poor Morgan! what a disappointment! May God help him to bear it. Give my dying blessing to my dear parents, brothers, sisters, and friends. I love them all. Poor Morgan! what shall I say to him? O, if it could have been, if I could have lived to help and bless him, how happy we might have been yet! But it may not be. Tell them not to mourn for me. I'm going home. How sweet that word is — 'home'! How it rests me to think of it!"

"I hope, darling, that your husband and parents may arrive to-morrow. I have sent for them."

She smiled and said, "It would be pleasant, but it may not be. Tell my parents that, when left alone here to suffer those three dreadful nights, I felt willing to suffer it all, and more, to regain my husband's love and reformation; and God has given me my desire — blessed be his name! What more can I ask for myself? These children, too, I feel easy about them. How wonderful, wonderful it is!"

Towards night she became restless in body, but calm and triumphant in spirit. She kissed the children, saying, fervently, "Father, I commit them to thee; lead them not into temptation, but deliver them from evil, for thine is the kingdom, the power, and the glory. Amen."

Hester could not realize that the dark river was flowing even at the door; she could not hear the sturdy strokes of the boatman as he neared the "hither shore." She could not see the shining escort coming with songs of joy and great rejoicing to release the ransomed one, too early crushed by the sorrows and disappointments of earth. No, she could not see them, even when they folded their golden wings, and waited silently in the small house near the swamp. She did not hear their gentle whispers, or see their looks of heavenly sweetness; but she felt their presence, and grew strong in faith and love.

"Auntie," said the sick one, with a smile, "it is almost over, and the pain is gone. I am only waiting, and weary, weary. You will love my darlings, auntie, for my sake?"

"Yes, lamb, I will love them while I live. Even as I have loved you, will I love them," was the reply.

"And will you, can you, take my little baby, and shelter it in those strong, kind arms; will you? I remember now what its grandmother said. Will you take it? I would not have it left with her."

Hester took the little unconscious thing, and folded it to her breast, and then said, solemnly, "I will, if God permits it."

"He will," said the dying mother, "he will. Let me kiss you. I am happy, O, so happy! and God will see to them, and you will guide their young feet in the blessed path." She grew more and more restless. "I am twenty-six at twelve to-night, auntie," she said; "it don't seem but a little while since you used to rock me to sleep. Once again, auntie, once again let me lie in your bosom, and go, yes, go to sleep."

Hester raised her — O, how tenderly! The shining escort smiled approvingly as she folded her to her warm, full heart, and said, —

"Now, what shall I sing?"

"Sing,
> 'Rock of ages, cleft for me,
> Let me hide myself in thee.'

That is what I want now; but tell me first, auntie, what separated you and uncle Horace. Did we, our folks, do it, and make you unhappy?"

"No, darling, no; I never received anything but kindness from them. I cannot tell you how it happened now: it would distress you. It is all right, darling."

"Yes, it is all right," murmured the weary sick one; "sing now."

When the last stanza was finished, the little hand clasped in Hester's was cold and still, the eyes were closed, and weary little Harmony had *gone to sleep.*

"Asleep in Jesus," murmured Hester; "O, how sweet! My little lamb, you were led early, too early, to the slaughter. Why was it so? How willingly I would have shielded you! and yet I made a mistake. I should have given them the proofs of her perfidy, the reasons of her hatred to them; they would have acted differently then. "O Harmony, my beautiful, my precious! Why were all your beauty and sweetness wasted?

scattered by the foul breath of that envious, slanderous woman. Why was she permitted to pursue you even to the gates of death? But it is all over, darling, all over, now. Sleep on; she cannot wake or trouble you. I was mistaken; I should have given you the reasons for what I told you. I have kept my secret too well, far too well; may God forgive me."

She laid the little cast-off dress of the soul reverently on the bed, and knelt there alone with the dead, as she had knelt, more than thirty years before, with the cold clay of one dearer to her than life.

Again she is living over the agony of that night; again her strong form is bowed and quivering with the blast that then swept over her, and, as she thought, passed away forever, with its power broken.

"O God, open again that secret chamber," she prayed, "and bury again those dead, dead hopes, those crushing fears, that parting agony."

"Rock of ages, cleft for me,
Let me hide myself in thee."

As the Sea of Galilee was stilled, hushed to rest by a word from the lips of the blessed Master, so the soul of Hester Strong was calmed into trusting peace by the pitying One. She arose — prepared the dead for the silent grave.

How beautiful she was! the weary, sorrowing look all gone, the eyes closed as if in peaceful slumber. Hester could now look cheerfully on the lovely face; but as she turned away from the dead, she remembered the living.

The noble husband, who had been so near the very

brink of ruin, and returned to the threshold of reformation — what would be the result of this stunning blow on him, the absent parents, brothers, and sisters? The feeble mother, why could she not have died in her loving arms? Hester wept as she gazed on the sleeping children, and thought what might have been, and what might now come upon them. How should she tell them? She laid herself down by the helpless baby, and tried to rest; but her heart was too full for sleep.

A great murmur of indignation ran through the community the next morning after Harmony's death. The house was filled to overflowing; the little children could find no quiet place to weep only on the bosom and in the arms of dear auntie Hester.

"Who will take care of us now?" sobbed Wallace.

"Shall I have to go to grandma Lentell's?" whispered Winnie.

"Let me stay wis you," said Elida, clinging to her neck.

"God, our Father in heaven, will take care of us," was all Hester could say, for her own mind was sorely perplexed concerning them.

Many tears of pity and affection were shed by neighbors, and all seemed to vie with each other in kind offices now. Why could not some of those who might have known the circumstances, have come forward when a life might have been saved? It was the same old story — "I did not think;" "I was very busy;" "I wish I had known;" and some could say truly, "I did not know." All felt most keenly that there was one who did know — one who had promised to watch over the lonely wife in her husband's compelled and shameful absence. They knew that neglect and guilt lay at the door of the great house on the hill. Mrs. Bartlett kindly offered to take the infant to her own house, and care for it till it could be better provided for; which offer was gladly accepted.

Mrs. Mehitable was stunned by the news of Harmony's death. She had been sincere in thinking her not sick : she was never sick herself; why should others be? But death was a terror to her. The still small voice whispered unpleasant things in the soul's ear — truths which she hated, but could not shut out. She closed the door and made it fast, took two letters from their hiding-place, read them, and rocked the little, wiry, wizened form back and forth, back and forth, exclaiming bitterly, "O, hum! everything comes at once. If Morgan should go to law, as he promised her, the game will be up. But them Loverings won't have the handling on't now; that's a comfort. Hum, hum! I've played the wrong card this time, too; I might have let her have these, but I didn't think she'd die. Well, I hated her; she looked like the only man I ever loved, and he deserted me; yes, he deserted me after I had sold myself to the evil one, almost, to get him. Hester says them Loverings were not the cause on't. O, well, it can't be helped! Morgan mustn't know I didn't give her these; he mustn't know I left her alone so much. I wish I could still that tongue of Hester's; I hate her worse than ever. I'm glad she didn't marry Horace; she was a fool not to, though. O, hum! I don't know what to do first. I can't do nothing with Hester; and then them Loverings know all about it. Well, I must see Morgan first of any on um — that's all," she said as she arose, went to the stove, dropped the two letters into it, then called her son and bade him harness the smart horse, saying to Abigail, "I must bring Morgan myself, or the fat will all be in the fire. You'd better go over; it will look better."

"No, I shan't," was the prompt reply; "I don't go for looks."

Mrs. Mehitable was too late. Hester's note had informed him that Harmony was dying, and the friends he had made while there hastened his departure. Their hearts were filled with the deepest pity by his grief and remorse.

"It will be all over with me," he said, hopelessly, to the jailer's family, — "all over with me, if she dies. I shall be a murderer; I can't bear up under it. If I knew she was dead now, I would drown this misery in rum; yes, I couldn't help it. O, God! what a wretch I have been."

They saw that it would be useless to reason with him; they said kind, comforting words, and bade him a sad good by. Mr. Lovering had informed him of his mother's course towards Harmony; of her dismissal of Mr. Drake; neglecting to send for Hester; of the destitute, suffering condition in which he found her.

"And now if she should die before I reach her!" He shuddered to think of it.

With a heavy heart he turned his face homeward, and hurried on till he came in sight of Mr. Drake's.

"Stop here," he said to the driver, "just a moment."

He strode up to the door with a face so pale and haggard that his old friend scarcely knew him.

He caught him by the arm, and said, hoarsely and hurriedly, "Miller Drake, do you remember how I sacrificed the hard-earned wages of months to save you from imprisonment and dishonor? Do you remember it? What did you promise me then? O, what did you promise me when I went forth to pay a debt which was not mine? You have been false, false as — You knew my mother, or might have known her, better than I did. My wife is either dying or dead; your neglect helped to kill her. I called to curse you, and you will be cursed!"

He turned and went hastily back to the carriage, refusing to listen to Miller Drake's excuses, simply saying, "You were false — faithless and false."

Hester was terrified at the wild, hopeless face of Morgan, which peered in at the door about noon. He rested his eyes on his dead wife for a moment, and then disappeared with a stifled groan. Hester called to him, little Elida called, but on, on he went towards the great house on the hill. They were greatly perplexed, and a friendly neighbor went in pursuit of him. In a short time, grandpa Lovering and wife arrived. Calmly they looked upon the silent, upturned face; tearfully they listened to the story of her dying hours. And when Hester inquired if they had met Morgan on the way, they replied that a man, who might have been he, leaped over the wall and fled hurriedly out of sight.

"O, it was he!" said Hester; "he could not bear to meet you."

She showed them his letter to Harmony, which had been lying beneath the pillow. They read it, and wept afresh.

"O, if it might have been!" they said; "if she could

have lived to realize those bright, fond hopes we all indulged! all but you, Hester; you seemed to be clearer sighted than the rest of us."

"But I was once as blind as the blindest concerning Mrs. Lentell," she replied. "O, Mary, when this is over you shall know my secret, which I have so stubbornly kept. But think you Morgan will adhere to his good resolutions?"

"I cannot tell," said grandpa; "I fear not; but I must seek him and obtain permission to bury this dust with her kindred, and among those who knew and loved her. Twenty-six years old to-day! Ten years a wife, and four times a mother," he mused. "O that I could recall the past!"

Morgan arrived at the great house in a state bordering on insanity. Bending over the affrighted Abigail, he exclaimed, vehemently, "Murderer! where is your accomplice, your mother? Where, where is she? Tell me before I—"

Just then the friend who had followed him arrived, and answered the question Abigail was too much alarmed to answer.

"She has gone for you."

"She needn't," was the sharp reply; "the work is all done. She is dead; and now I shall drink, and drink, and drink, until I forget it all. That's what she herself has taught me. When Harmony used to plead with me not to drink the damning beverage, she used to say, 'Morgan, I would have my rum, in spite of her; you work hard and need it.' Didn't I mind her? didn't I?" he groaned. "Yes, I minded her, wretch that I was, and if there is a God in heaven, I'll mind her still. She shall eat her own words, and drink the bitter cup she meant for another. O, Harmony, my patient Harmony," he said, in a wild, despairing tone. "If I could have heard you say you forgave me, if I could have atoned for the past, I might have been a man again, a father to our children; but now it is no use, no use."

"But she did forgive you, and loved you to the last," said the friend who had followed him. "Come, go and see how peacefully she is sleeping, and receive her dying message."

He dropped into a chair, covered his face for a moment, and then said, mournfully, "I can't, I can't look at her. I helped to kill her. O, she was nothing but a child — a trusting, beautiful child — when I brought her here. I cannot see her, or meet her parents. They are there; how they must hate me! I hate myself, and God hates me! I must drink. I haven't tasted rum these three weeks, and never meant to again; but I must now," he said, fiercely.

He opened the closet, where the full decanters always stood, and drank like one determined to forget, in spite of his friend's remonstrances.

He reminded him of his children, of friends who loved him, of happiness, and respectability in the future.

"Friends!" he exclaimed, in a mocking tone. "If my own mother is so false, what can I expect of others? If she and Abigail would sacrifice my happiness to spite an innocent woman, where in the wide world, think you, can I find happiness? It is all a sham. No, they have helped me make this bed, and now they must lie in it."

He soon sank into a state of helpless intoxication, from which he could not be aroused.

Poor, miserable, mistaken mother! you have been playing a dangerous game. You commenced early in life to make false moves, regardless of the feelings or sufferings of others; you moved on, and now you must reap as you have sown. You gloried in the firm, steady reins with which you guided your family. You governed them by fear; they obeyed because it was more comfortable to do so. Selfishness was the groundwork of your power over them. You laid a sandy foundation to stand on in the decrepitude of old age; you forgot that any government based on fraud, deception, and ungodliness must perish; and that truth, justice, and humanity were the only firm foundations to build upon. You forgot that " righteousness exalteth," while " sin is a reproach." Alas! you will find that the way of the transgressor is hard. By the untimely death of your son's wife, and the terrible fall of your son into inebriety, you are left in possession of your ill-gotten property; but a curse is resting upon it, and in your own breast you have the witness of your wicked deeds. Yes, your conscience will ever accuse you, and your firmly *misguided* children will prove a terrible scourge.

Mr. Lovering was allowed to follow his own plans without molestation. Slowly the little procession moved along; sadly the friends of other days gathered around the sweet flower, so early faded. Tenderly they laid her in the bosom of mother earth, " under the sod."

> " O spirit, freed from bondage,
>   Rejoice; thy work is done!
> The weary world is 'neath thy feet,
>   Thou brighter than the sun!

" Awake, and breathe the living air
    Of our celestial clime;
Awake to love that knows no change,
    Thou who hast done with time.

" Awake! lift up thy joyful eyes;
    See! all heaven's host appears;
And be thou glad exceedingly,
    Thou who hast done with tears.

" Awake! ascend! Thou art not now
    With those of mortal birth;
The living God hath touched thy lips,
    Thou who hast done with earth."

CHAPTER VI.

What became of the Children. — The Midnight Call.

Harmony's death, and the trying circumstances attending it, hastened an event which had long been dreaded by the family. Consumption had been kept from fastening its fatal fangs upon Mrs. Lovering by the utmost care and vigilance.

Under the pressure of this great and peculiar trial, she failed very fast. The motherless children of her daughter she looked upon as worse than orphaned; she saw their father rushing down the awful precipice of inebriety; he would only be a shame to them — a terror, and not a protector.

She shuddered when she thought of them with their grandmother Lentell. Her own house was being filled with her son's children. The son's wife evidently thought Harmony's children intruders, and treated them as such. With the true instincts of a woman, she saw a life of suffering and danger before them; and the feeling that she was helpless — unable to save them from it — was depressing.

Again and again she was assured by her husband and children that they should be taken care of. She saw, better than they did, the difficulties in the way.

"If Hester was young," she used to say, "I should

feel easy about them. The remainder of Harmony's portion would support them until old enough to earn a living. If they could all be with her, I should feel satisfied. Old Mrs. Lentell would not trouble them, I think."

"Never fear for those children," Hester used to say, cheerfully; "their dying mother committed them to One who is strong and mighty — even the orphan's God. Can you not trust them in his hands? They will have trials, disappointments, and temptations, as who does not? but they will come off victors, every one of them. They will have to struggle with poverty and disgrace on their father's account; but it will make them strong and self-reliant. Have you forgotten how destitute I was left at an early age? Has my life been more dark and cheerless than that of thousands who started with brighter prospects? Do you suppose I have forgotten who it was that made my childhood like a summer's day? Believe me, Mary, I have a pleasure before me, and not a task. I wish I was young, for their sakes; but for myself, it seems good to near my glorious home. How often the sweet voice and dying words of our darling come back to me in the still watches of the night! O, Mary, she looked so much like Horace that it seemed like losing him again when she died. The sweet verses she repeated contained the very essence of our last conversation together. Let me repeat her words again, and then tell me, Mary, if we can regret to go when such blessedness is in store for us. We shall not only see our Lord, and be clothed in the brightness of his ineffable glory, but we shall meet the loved and lost. Ay, we shall *know* them, too; I feel assured of it. Yes,

those that are one in Christ on earth, shall be one in Christ in heaven.
'We shall know each other there.'"

"Your words comfort me," said Mrs. Lovering. "My faith grows brighter. Repeat that last verse again; yes, I think it will be so. We shall arrive there by many different roads, some dark and thorny, some on beds of down, some on straw, perchance; but it will be all the same when we reach the haven of rest, whether the voyage be rough and full of peril, or smooth and prosperous. Don't you think so?"

"No, not all the same, for the torn and tempest-tossed, the benighted traveller, will be filled with a fulness of joy and exultation which the peaceful, prosperous voyager can never know. Mary, we must be weary before we can fully appreciate rest; we must drink the bitter cup of sorrow before we can experience the fulness of heavenly bliss. It must be so, for 'He doeth all things well.'"

As yet all the children had remained at grandpa Lovering's. It was pitiful to see the little things trying to be so good and patient for fear of being sent to grandma Lentell's. They said but little about their mother, except at night, when auntie Hester put them to bed; then the pent-up feelings must find vent. Their artless talk often brought tears to those eyes which were wont to weep with those who weep, and sometimes, as the children knelt around her for their evening prayer, little Elida would say,—

"P'ease God, let me stay wis auntie ever so long, and don't die her, too, as mamma did. Dear God, don't, for Jesus' sake. Amen."

This simple prayer always seemed to send a wave of uncontrollable grief over Wallace and Winnie. It reminded them that the time was drawing near when they must be separated from her and from each other.

"O," said Winnie on such an occasion, "if God is so good, why didn't he let Wallace and I go to heaven with our sweet mamma when there was nobody to want us here? I heard aunt Judith say so to-day. She said she couldn't have us round in the way. O, I have tried to be so still and good, and play with her baby when I wanted to go out of doors! Don't you pity us, auntie?" she sobbed.

Hester moved the wondering baby, and took her in her arms to comfort her, while Wallace and Elida still knelt, weeping.

"Pity you? Yes, darling, and God pities you. He will make it all right, dear. He loves you, and we all love you. He has a nice, snug little nest for you somewhere. He wants you down here for something; perhaps it is to take care of me when I am old; perhaps it is to watch over this little kitten when I am gone home. Let me lay her in your arms; see, she is almost smiling at you!"

The children's attention was now turned upon baby. Soon Elida was seated on the other knee, playing with baby's tiny feet.

"I want a place, too," said Wallace.

"If auntie had two laps, you could has one," said Elida.

"He shall have my place," said Winnie; "he is the youngest."

Baby was delighted at the novelty, and watched the proceedings with her large, calm eyes, with quiet satisfaction.

When the children's minds were sufficiently diverted, Hester gave them their good-night kiss, and they retired to the sweet, refreshing sleep of childhood. Not so with Hester; the failing health of her dear friend, Mrs. Lovering, whom she had loved as a sister, together with the care and anxiety of providing suitable places for the two eldest children, weighed down even her elastic spirits. And then there were the little ones — her own peculiar charge — to care for. She wished, if possible, to secure them all against the interference and domination of Mrs. Lentell; but how that could be done was a question which had caused her many sleepless nights.

"She will not meddle with them till they are old enough to work," she used to say to Mr. Lovering; "but they must be placed entirely beyond her control, if possible."

As she sat revolving the matter over and over in her mind after the children were asleep, she could not refrain from weeping, until her broad chest shook with emotion. She had forgotten the little wise, old-fashioned baby in her lap, who had been looking on in blank amazement. At length she was aroused by a little frightened, quivering cry.

"Why, darling, darling pet," she said, softly, tenderly; "precious birdie, did she think her auntie was crazy? Did she, darling one?" said Hester, smiling through her tears. "Naughty little dirlie, not to let her auntie-mamma cry her cry out."

Thus she soothed and quieted the little thing, and then sung a gentle lullaby till baby was fast asleep.

Noble, conquering Hester! self-denying, loving Hester! Did you see the infant's angel smile, O, so sweetly! as he made the record of the day?

WHAT BECAME OF THE CHILDREN.

>Did you catch the faintest echo
> Of the music soft and clear,
>Floating round the sainted mother
> When you soothed her children's fear?
>Did you hear the glad hosannas
> When you kissed away the tear?
>Hester, there's a crown preparing;
> Many, many stars are there:
>In that crown shall shine those children,
> Bright, and beautiful, and fair.

O, Hester, you are rich in heaven. Yours are the gold-bearing bonds of loving words and deeds. There will be no discount on your treasures, Hester; they are secure in God's eternal safe. "Inasmuch as ye did it unto these little ones, ye did it unto me."

Open thine eye of faith, O, Hester, beloved of God, and chosen; for this thy last shall be thy crowning work. Only believe, and thou shalt see the desire of thy large, unselfish heart accomplished concerning these children, for thy prayers have been accepted in heaven, and even now the answer is at hand.

"Hester, Hester!" called Mr. Lovering, cheerfully, just as she was laying little Fostina in bed.

Hester's heart gave a bound, a throb, and then stood almost still, as she hastened down stairs.

"Here are the papers," said he, meeting her at the door; "they are ours, thank God!"

"Thank God!" ejaculated Hester, fervently; "then they are ours. Precious children! At this moment I would give a great deal to be young and rich. But riches often prove a snare, or take to themselves wings and fly away when most needed; youth soon passes away, and beauty is vain. The wise man says,—

  'All is vanity and vexation of spirit.'

But this is a happy hour for me. I must make the best use of my time while I stay here. Who knows but I may bring them a good piece on their way yet? How did you find Morgan?"

"O, don't ask me; it is too sad. He seems to have but one aim, or object, and that is to torment and punish his mother. The suit at law was stopped by their giving bonds for his support."

"Is that so?" said Hester, sadly. "Poor woman, she will reap a fearful reward for her life of sin and selfishness. Now, Mr. Lovering, my plans are all made. Don't oppose me — will you? I have thought it all over. I shall buy half of grandpa Manlie's house. They are upwards of ninety, you know, and cannot have much longer to stay here. They wish it, and say it will be a comfort to have me with them. Their daughter loves my children (don't be jealous now; you have lots besides these), or, if you choose, our children. Will that do better?"

"Yes," said grandpa; "I shall claim a share in them, and wish that I was situated so that two of them could stay here. But we have never quarrelled with Judith, and don't mean to; she has her good qualities, but patience and benevolence are not among them. If it were Edward's or Frank's wife, they could stay and welcome."

"Well," said Hester, "never mind. I know Judith; they can't stay here; besides, Mary is not able to have them; they must go as soon as possible. I want them all for a few months, until this great sorrow has worn off a little. So take us to the village to-morrow — won't you? Change of scene will do them good. It would have broken your heart to hear them talk to-night. They — that is, Wallace and Winnie — know they are not wanted by their aunt; they feel it."

"Poor lambs!" said grandpa. "But what shall we do without you, Hester? What will Mary do?"

"The girls must come home in turns," said Hester. "I should love to remain, but duty calls me away."

"But you can't think of keeping them all," persisted grandpa; "it is too much. Their uncles and aunts must take Wallace and Winnie."

"Yes," said Hester, "I do think of keeping them all for the present. Some time they may have to go, but not now. Don't urge; the little things have had as much suffering as they can bear. We will see what can be done for them in the spring."

Mrs. Lovering saw the wisdom of Hester's plan, and cheerfully submitted. It was pleasant to think that in all probability Hester would, after all, be with her aged parents to soothe their declining days. Horace, to be sure, would not be with her; but they would meet him on the other shore. Mr. Manlie refused to take a cent for the house, but said to her, solemnly, as he placed the deed of one half of it in her hand, —

"Take it; it should have been yours long ago, my daughter. God bless you, and spare you to bless others for a long time yet."

And so the children found a home for the time. Would that it could have been a permanent one for them all.

"Passing away" is written upon all things below; so, when the summer flowers departed, and the autumn leaves fluttered in the chilly wind, when the green grass lay crisp and silvered, Mary M. Lovering, the loving daughter, sister, wife, and mother, went to sleep on earth — to wake in heaven. None knew the hour of her departure. They came for her in the silent watches of the night, and bore her away without a sigh, a groan, or a sad farewell.

"You have rested nicely to-night, mother," said the tender husband; but no answer came. "Mother!" and the voice was slightly startled. "Mother!" — bending over her; but there was no voice — she was gone. O, yes, she had gone so quietly, so peacefully, she was resting so profoundly, that the tears and sighs of those who loved her did not disturb her rest. Dear weepers, would you have it otherwise? Would you call her back to buffet the turbulent waves of the dark river? Would you, for a few, last, gasping words, call her back to struggle with the mighty conqueror of life, and see her yield, reluctantly, perhaps, through fleshly fear?

O, no, you would not. Thank God, rather, that she is so safely through; that she is so soon with Christ, who careth for you.

"Weeping may endure for a night, but joy cometh in the morning."

"Weep on — and wait."

CHAPTER VII.

THE CHILDREN'S PRATTLE. — THE WIFE'S BURDEN, OR A SYNOPSIS OF MR. GILES.

LOOKING out of the window, watching the carriages, the school children, the girls from the mill as they went and came, went and came, six times a day, six days in the week, in sunshine and rain, was fine entertainment for the little country children.

It pleased them; it made the days seem short; it was something new. It is no use to chide these children for their love of novelty : we all love it.

"This is a nicer place than the country," said Wallace; "don't you think so, auntie Hester? There is more boys, and horses, and funny carts, and stores, and a factory with a bell to it. I should like to pull the rope and make the bell dingle. Say, auntie, isn't it nice?"

"Yes, dear, this is a pretty place, and there are a great many things to amuse children from the country. But don't you think you will miss the merry birds and flowers, the orchard and the berry pasture, the little brook where your water-wheel is?"

Wallace looked serious for a moment, and then said, —

"Poh! no, indeed! My water-wheel was a little thing; they've got a bigger stream here, with a water-wheel on it larger than our barn. The man let me see it the other day; he said it would smash me up though, if I went near it."

"That is so," said Hester. "You must not go near the mill without my permission. There was a little boy killed there once."

"Tell us about it," cried the children in chorus. "Tell us, auntie."

"O, he disobeyed his parents, and went in swimming, and was carried over the mill-dam and killed."

"O, dear me!" said Elida. "Wasn't he sorry he went and got in, and didn't mind better? Was he all dead when he got down to the bottom of the dam, auntie?"

"Yes, dear, and terribly bruised; it was a sad sight to see."

"Well," said Wallace, thoughtfully, "I'm glad it wasn't me. Can I play on the bridge sometimes, if I will be careful not to fall in the water, or tear my clothes?"

"Yes, dear," said Hester, smiling; "the bridge is below the dam. I think you may go there safely, provided you will be careful."

"The mill is a buzzing thing," said Winnie, very demurely. "If it would stop buzzing, I should like to work there; but the noise makes me crazy. Don't you think it is hateful, auntie? It keeps saying things."

"Does it, sister?" said Wallace; "what does it say?"

"Why, in the spin-room it says 'buzzy-uzzy, buzzy-uzzy' all the time; and in the weave-room it says 'clap-it-to-clap, clap-it-to-clap.' Why, the looms ain't a bit like grandma Lentell's; but I felt as if she was going to box my ears every minute while we staid there; and after we got home, I kept hearing it, and after I went to bed it was 'clap-it-to-clap' till I went to sleep; and in the morning my head felt sick."

"Well," said Elida, encouragingly, " 'haps it will be stiller when it grows older; then you can work there. I'se doin' to spin when I'se old, so I can have them pretty things they wind the thread on to play wis. Won't it be funny? And, Winnie, if you work in the weave-room, you can has some too: why, I seed a boy carry a bushel full up there; and, Wallace, when you's big enough to carry the basket, you can has some; and then we will bring some to totty mite, and aunty will let us play wis them. O, how funny!" and Elida laughed and clapped her chubby hands gleefully.

Baby jumped and crowed, which was always the prelude to a chorus of happy voices, and a good time generally.

Hester laughed heartily at Elida's concluding speech, though feeling somewhat sad. It grieved her to think that the children must soon be separated. The dear old people in the other part were kind and patient, but she knew they needed rest and quiet at their time of life; besides, she did not feel able or competent to look after them all.

She wished she could have kept Winnie instead of Elida, she would have been such a help about baby. Elida's disposition seemed to have caught the brightness of her mother's life, while living with her husband in the aged widow's family. Her heart was like a little fountain of sunshine and gladness. She would make friends more readily than Winnie, who was timid, caretaking, and sensitive, but amiable and unselfish. But her aunt Elevia Giles said her husband was unwilling she should take one of the children, unless she could have the eldest.

"He thinks I couldn't get along with the work; should have to hire washing, sewing, &c., for some time. He says Winnie could help a great deal now, and pretty soon she would be old enough to — "

"But he seems to be looking at only one side of the question," said Hester. "Now, I love all these children for their mother's sake, and presume you do; but if you go to making all those nice calculations about the probable benefit of adopting one of them, it will be a failure. Love, mutual love, and benevolence, must be the basis of such a relation, and not self-interest, or it will prove a bitter mockery, to the child at least. If you take one of them from good and noble motives, such as your grandparents had in adopting me in my infancy, why, a blessing will grow out of it; otherwise it will be a snare. Don't you think so, Levie?"

"Yes, Hester, I do; I am sure grandpa's adopting you has been a real blessing to us all. What should we have done without you? But Mason and I don't think alike about many things, and it don't do for me to oppose him since we were married, unless I wish to live in a quarrel. I should prefer Elida; there is just difference enough between her age and Unie's. They would soon be companions for each other, and we are abundantly able to bring them up. I wish Mason was different. Riches are worse than useless, unless they can be used without so much — " Here the young wife bowed her head and wept.

Hester was astonished. Elevia had not been two years married: she had supposed her very happily situated in all respects. True, she had noticed a change in her, — a care-worn, weary look, — and had attributed it to the responsibilities of housekeeping, or ill health. She had seen but little of Mason Giles, and thought him remarkably pleasant and perfectly devoted to his amiable wife. Hester thought a great deal in those few moments. She had known Elevia from her very birth; if there was trouble in her lot, she felt sure the fault was not hers. She had become so accustomed to human nature in all its moods and tenses, could read it so correctly that she did not hesitate mentally to pronounce Mason a mean, miserly, wilful, deceitful man. How could she let her little sensitive Winnie go into such an atmosphere?

"I am sorry for you, Levie," she said aloud. "So all is not gold that glitters. Poor child, then you have a skeleton in your nice home. Keep it out of sight as much as possible, darling. Never look at it when you can avoid doing so. Every look will make it more hideous. They have something of the kind everywhere, dear. I have learned a great deal going among the sick. Child, if we would be happy, it must be in spite of something. It must be by shutting our eyes upon some things, and resolutely fixing them upon others more pleasant and agreeable."

"But, auntie, you don't think a woman can be happy in spite of her husband — do you?" said Elevia, tearfully. "It seems monstrous to think of it; how can she?"

"In many ways," was the quiet reply. "If we

truly love God, and trust in Christ, no mortal can make us entirely miserable. There is a peace which the world can neither give nor take away, you know; and, as I said before, if you have a grief, don't nurse it, or it will become too mighty for you. If you have a cross, take it up bravely, or you will stumble over it; if a skeleton, shut it up, hide it, or with patient labor mould it into an image of beauty; or, if this cannot be done, cover it as much as possible under the beautiful mantle of charity, 'which suffereth long and is kind.' But don't try to do this in your own strength, dear; you cannot. But there is a promise, 'As thy day is, so shall thy strength be.' Lean upon it, Levie; trust in the 'elder Brother;' believe, and ye shall find rest."

"O," said Elevia, "I did not mean to speak of this. I have never spoken of it before; but I am so disappointed, so distressed, that it seems to me I can't bear it alone much longer. I know what you say about the promises of God is true, but I am not a Christian — I wish I was. But even then, I should need earthly friends to counsel and comfort me. Mother has been so feeble ever since my marriage, that I could never speak of it to her. It would have been such a comfort if I could!"

"Yes, dear, so it would; but I was your mother's friend, and yours too: speak to me freely and without reserve; perhaps I can help you. 'Bear one another's burdens,' is the injunction, you know."

"And you have done that most faithfully, auntie. I do wrong to burden you with my trouble; but it is so hard to bear it alone. To have Mr. Giles so pleasant and accommodating before folks, and then treat me like a hired servant or a slave when alone, is so cruel! I never do anything to suit him. The food is not just right; his linen is too stiff one week, and too limber the next; if a thing is faultless, he says nothing about it. If the pies are a little too sweet or sour, he talks about it continually till the last one is eaten, and often alludes to it afterwards to tease me. Baby has always been troublesome. And now, when I work hard all day, and am kept awake half the night with the poor little thing, he thinks it strange I should be tired. When I feel sad, he calls me cross. He never tries in any way to help me. This morning I felt sick and discouraged; little Unic was restless all night, and worrisome in the morning, so that, although I tried hard, I did not get breakfast on the table till five minutes after the usual time. He talked of it all meal-time; I told him how it was; he laughed, and said he knew women who had brought up ten children, and weren't dead yet. I told him my head ached; he laughed again, and said it always ached since I was married. O, auntie, that isn't half! I can't tell it. But the hardest thing of all is to have him so smooth and nice in company; that disgusts me. I am afraid I hate him for it. If he can be so pleasant and obliging in company, he can when alone with me. If he was always alike, I should think, with Mr. Phrenol, that it was his 'bumps,' and he couldn't help it. Now, tell me," sobbed the unhappy wife, "if you think I can enjoy much with my husband? Can I ever respect him, and be happy again?"

"I can't tell," said Hester; "I don't know him; if I did I could advise you. But all things are possible with God. If he is naturally affectionate, you may conquer him by kind, patient words and deeds; by mildly but firmly insisting upon having your rights respected; by letting him see that you mean to do right, the best you can, and all you can, and are determined that you will not be found fault with continually. Child, your situation is a trying one; you need that wisdom which cometh from above to direct you; seek to be reconciled to him first of all. You are suffering from two causes — overwork and disappointed affection. Now, if I understand the case, you do not need a little girl, but a large one, to do the heavy work and assist in tending the baby. Then you would be strong to contend with difficulties, and make a strenuous effort to remedy those things which annoy you so much. It vexes some men to see their wives always looking pale and sad; and yet they have not sense enough to know that they can't help it, when body and mind are overtaxed. They don't realize how hard it is to be broken of one's rest, or how much labor it is to do the work for a family. Now, if you could get a girl to relieve you some, and then apply yourself vigorously to correcting your own and your husband's faults, you might work wonders. Human nature is a strangely perverted thing, and terribly inconsistent; but patience and perseverance, it is said, will remove mountains. Will you try my remedy, Levie? or work out for yourself a better one?"

"O, auntie, I wish I could. Did you ever know any one so unhappy as I am to become happy again?"

"O, yes, child; a bad beginning sometimes ends well. You must labor, and wait, and pray."

"But, auntie, my face is such a tell-tale. When he says unkind things to me, I feel as if I should die, and

I show it. When he pats me on the cheek and pets me in company, I feel indignant, insulted, and disgusted; I can't help showing it, you see, and people think I am hateful, without affection or gratitude. I know it, I see it in their looks. And sometimes women who I know have kind, tender, thoughtful husbands, say to me, 'Why, your husband idolizes you, Mrs. Giles; I wish my husband thought as much of me,' &c. That cuts like a knife. My own sisters speak in that way. And then he loves to tease me before people, and will speak of my mistakes in housekeeping in such a pleasant, jocose way, that people think strange I cannot receive it in the same spirit. O, they don't know how often I have heard it at home, and how differently, until the mention of it chafes and galls my feelings. But I would be anything, and bear or do anything, if he only loved me. Then I might in some way work my way out of this darkness, and be happy yet."

"God can help you out of this trouble, my child; trust in him; do not despair. I have seen what promised to be very unhappy marriages turn out well. I have also seen what appeared to be very happy marriages become wretched ones by mismanagement and want of patience. Take courage, my child; be firm, gentle, and brave, and all will be well sometime."

Mason Giles had been a devoted lover; but when the prize was won, he threw off all disguise, and treated his wife according to the instincts of his sordid nature. Indeed, she became a kind of safety-valve, through which his selfishness escaped, and made him appear altogether better to neighbors and citizens. His farm was adjacent to the village, and Winnie would attend the village school, and could see her little sisters often. That was a strong inducement to Hester; but she saw great obstacles in the way of her going, and raised objections. But grandpa, uncles, and aunts were against her, and she consented on condition that at the end of the year she should return to her if she chose.

CHAPTER VIII.

A Tragic Scene in Village Life.

WALLACE saw and heard much to perplex him in village life.

"Why, auntie," he said one day, "there are a good many boys here that don't mind their mothers; and they say great, big, swear words, and fight. It isn't as nice here as I thought it was. The good boys do it, auntie."

"They do!" said Hester; "who are they?"

"Why, the minister's little boy swore; Jack Stillman told him what to say, and then all the boys laughed. Jack told him to say it to the *old man* when he got home. O, auntie, won't his father feel sorry?"

"Yes, dear, the boys were very wicked; but little Willie did not know what the words meant. His parents will tell him they are naughty, and he will never use them again. What makes you think the boys disobey their mothers, Wallace?"

Wallace hung his head, and blushed.

"Yous must tell auntie," said Elida, "or yous will be disobejent youself."

"Yes, tell auntie," said Winnie; "we ought to tell her everything, as we did mamma."

Hester waited, and after a few moments Wallace began.

"Well, auntie, you know you forbid my going to the

mill, and I haven't; but the boys tease me to all the time. I tell them you don't allow it; and they laugh, and call me 'baby' and you an 'old fuss.' I threw a stone at them, though, and I wish I had hit Jack, he is so mean."

"O, I am sorry you did that, Wallace," said Hester. "I knew a boy once that threw a stone when he was angry, and hit a good little girl, and put her eye out."

"O, dear!" said Winnie, covering her eyes. "Don't do it ever again, Wallace, will you?"

"Perhaps not; I guess not, if there is any good little girls round."

"Fro um easy, Wallace," said Elida, "so God won't know it."

"O," said Hester, "God is everywhere, and he knows everything. My dear boy, I hope you will remember this. Can't you find some good little boy to play with?"

"I know one," said the child, "but his clothes are ragged."

Hester told him that God did not look at the clothing of the body, but the state of the heart.

"A good child covered with rags is more pleasing in his sight than a wicked child clothed in velvet. God does not love disobedient children, for he has commanded them to obey."

"Has he, auntie?" said Elida. "Why, I never heard him speak 'bout it."

Hester smiled, took down the Bible, and said,—

"It is in this; I will read it to you."

"Well," said Wallace, "those boys don't keep the commandment."

"I am sorry," said Hester; "God will not bless them

if they do so; and they are on forbidden ground, and are in danger of becoming very wicked men, and may be left to commit some fearful crime, and pay the penalty with their lives."

"O, auntie, I am afraid somebody has committed one now," said Winnie, springing from the window. "See, they are carrying somebody into Mr. Gray's."

"O, that is where the ragged boy lives," said Wallace; "his mother drinks rum; the boys tease him about it."

"I hope you have not," said Hester, sorrowfully.

"Do she get intosticated?" said little Elida. "I didn't know mammas ever did so. O, how funny!"

Hester saw that people were coming and going — that a crowd was collecting around Mr. Gray's. She thought it must be something more than intoxication. Leaving the baby with the children, she went to see if her assistance was needed.

O, what a spectacle met her! Mrs. Gray, when alone with her baby, had emptied the contents of a tin pail, which the village demon had filled for her that morning, taking the very food from the little children's mouths in payment, immediately after the distressed husband had besought him not to furnish her with it.

"I want to get an honest living," was his reply. "It is my business to sell; if people make a bad use of it, why, it is their lookout, not mine. I have the law on my side, I believe."

"Yes," said the perplexed husband, "you have a wicked, perverse law on your side, made by wicked and perverse men, bound to live on the poor man's toil; but God's laws are against you, and he will vindicate my cause.

"You show no mercy to me, or my worse than motherless children; and if God is true, you will receive none. But I beg of you, Mr. Stillman, not to let her have any to-day; for I must leave home to work, or let them all starve. The children are not safe with her, especially the baby, for an hour, when she has it."

"Every one to his calling," was the unfeeling reply; and so she went again with her tin pail, and all the pork the house contained in it; and that hireling of Satan took it, and gave her the fatal draught which took away her reason, and made her an inanimate, loathsome thing.

She had fallen near the open fire, and the little innocent baby's face was buried in the hot embers, where its voice was soon hushed in death. Yes, it lay there, a naked, blighted little corpse.

Hester found it lying there. "Thank God," she said fervently, "that the angel of death was sent so swiftly to unlock the door of life for this little sufferer."

The inebriate mother, all unconscious of her own condition, or her baby's fate, lay there tossing her blistered, unsightly limbs hither and thither in mortal anguish. Her clothing had apparently taken fire from the infant's, but she felt not the scorching heat until it was nearly burned off.

Then her benumbed faculties were aroused sufficiently for her to arise and stagger towards the store, which was very near. She fell in a few moments, convulsed with agony. Kidder Stillman was the first to discover her terrible situation, and when a crowd gathered, he went also among them. Hester saw that she was not needed, and the scene was too appalling to gaze on from idle curiosity. Nothing could be done for Helen Gray: Her strong physical powers might enable her to struggle terrifically for an hour or two, but death was sure of its victim.

"Kidder Stillman," said Hester, mournfully, "you see what rum has done. Isn't it awful? Have you seen the innocent baby? Go look at it; what if it was yours? Look at that woman; she is a *wife;* what if it were your wife? It might have been. Helen was once fair, and bright, and strong. She has been ruined by a weapon *you* placed in her hand. Don't tell me it is your *calling:* I know it is. Satan called you to it, just the same as he calls the gambler to gamble, the thief to steal, the murderer to kill. Your calling is just as honest as theirs; not more so; you can't prosper in it always. O, let this most awful sight my eyes ever beheld be a warning to you, and cease from your work of death."

Hester returned home with an indescribable feeling of sadness. The children met her, eager to learn what had happened. She disliked to chill and sadden them with the recital of such a scene; she softened the circumstances as much as possible, and even then, they were very much shocked.

"Where did she put the baby when she fell down?" said Winnie.

"O, it has gone to sleep," said Hester.

"What will it do when it wakes up?" said Winnie; "won't it cry after its mother?"

"I guess not," said Hester; "God will take care of it."

"Isn't he dood, auntie? He takes care of all the children that hasn't got no mothers. O, he is *nice.* I love him," said Elida.

"Well," said Wallace, "Jack Stillman's father sold

the rum, I s'pose — didn't he? Jack drinks it. I mean to call him Jack *Kill*man now."

"And you t'row a 'tone at him," said little Elida, "when there ain't no dood girls round — won't you, Wallace? He is a naughty boy."

"My dear children," said Hester, "if you indulge in such things you will be on dangerous ground; and then you will go from one wrong act to another, from one sin to another, and perhaps you will become wicked enough to sell rum, or drink it. And then you won't know what you are about, and may do some awful deed, or come to a terrible end, as poor Mrs. Gray has. And be sure, Wallace, to avoid John Stillman as much as possible. He is a vile, bad boy."

"Yes, auntie, I will; and shouldn't you think he would be ashamed to tease us little boys so when he is such a great big boy?" said Wallace. "Shall I speak to that poor ragged boy, and take hold of his hand when the boys tease him, and lick um if they don't mind? That won't be wicked — will it, auntie?"

"I think it is wrong to fight," said Hester. "If he were insulted and abused, and you were strong enough to defend him, that would be right; but you are only a little boy, and must content yourself with kind words."

"Mayn't I give him my new picture-book, auntie — it will please him."

"Yes," said Hester, "I think that will be a good plan."

"And here's my baby-dollie," said Elida. "May I gis her to the 'ittle girl? You see her mother is all burned up amost, and can't make her any now, for Mr. Killman made her intosticated — all dead eny most. You can make me another some day."

"I don't know," said Hester, "that I shall have time; perhaps you had better keep that one."

Elida thought for a moment, looked at her baby, and finally concluded to give up her treasure.

"Well, I guess I'll gis it to her; I's got a 'ittle waked up sister to play wis me."

And the heroine folded her chubby hands, and gave a sigh of regret, or relief perhaps, that the deed was done.

"O, hum!" said the little thing. "I hope they won't gis my dollie any sugar wis rum to it over there, or she will be a 'nebraite. I shan't be there to shake my head and look sorry, as mamma used to. One time papa said, 'Sissy, take it, and papa will gis you a stick of candy.'"

"What did you do then, darling?"

"My mamma looked a 'ittle, and I runned and put my head in her lap, and said, 'Peep-boo, papa, peep-aboo!'"

"What did papa say then?"

"O, he laughed a 'ittle, and drinked it all up."

"But what is the matter, pet?" said Hester, as she observed Winnie weeping very quietly. "What is the matter, dear?"

"Why, auntie, I wish, O, I wish God would let me go to mamma, I feel so bad."

"Why, darling child, what makes you feel so? Don't you love me and little brother and sisters?"

"Yes, auntie, I love you all; but everybody dies so! My sweet mamma, my good, kind grandpa Lentell, and my grandma Lovering, have all died," sobbed the child; "and now somebody is wicked, and Mrs. Gray is burned. O, auntie, most everybody acts so that I want to die before I go to live with aunt Elevia."

Hester saw that the child had been looking too much at the dark side of life for her sensitive nature, and strove to turn her thoughts into a different channel.

Baby's wonderful perfections never failed to delight the children. She was "so cunning," "so sweet," "such a darling." There never was her equal, so they all thought; they loved her so Hester had only to hold her up, or let her jump and crow, and immediately sadness disappeared as if by magic.

"Do you know," said Hester, "that Christmas is coming by and by? Old St. Nicholas will be round with his bag full of presents. We must all have our stockings ready. I don't think he will pass us by — do you, Winnie?"

The child drew nearer to Hester, and taking baby's hand, smiled a sad, timid smile.

"He can't get much in her little bit of a sock — can he, auntie? Yours will hold the most — won't it?"

"Yes; and suppose we hang up a lot of mine? Perhaps the old gentleman won't notice the difference. How will that do?"

"I don't know," said Winnie, earnestly. "I should like a big stocking full; but then I shouldn't know which was mine, or yours, or Wallace's; and he would know that Elida and baby hadn't such big feet. Besides, I'm afraid he wouldn't have presents enough to go all 'round. No, auntie, the right way is the best."

"I shall hang up both of mine," said Wallace. "If he wants more room he can have it."

"I, too," echoed Elida. "If he wises to gis me a 'ittle pony, he can tie it to the table — can't he, auntie? and he can leave my candy on the top. O, dear me, hum! Won't it be funny?"

A TRAGIC SCENE IN VILLAGE LIFE.

"I wouldn't say 'hum!' darling," said Hester; "but I will tell you what we will do. We will spend the day at uncle Frank's, if it is pleasant, and leave our stockings hanging up."

"That will be funny," said little Sunshine, as Hester called her.

And so, with pleasant thoughts in their young minds, she listened to their evening prayer, and kissed them a sweet good night.

Winnie lingered.

"What is wanting?" said Hester, pleasantly.

"I want to know if my papa drinks rum now, auntie. He told ma, in the letter, he never would."

"I can't exactly tell," said Hester. "I haven't seen him, you know. I want my pet to look bright to-morrow, for I am going to let her visit Susie Trueman. So go to bed now."

"O, auntie, she won't want to play with me if my papa drinks rum. Let me stay with you all the time."

Hester was affected to tears by the sadness of the child. She was too young to taste the wormwood and the gall of life. She laid little Fostina in the cradle, took Winnie in her arms, and folded her to her bosom.

"What is it that troubles my pet so? Tell auntie all about it; auntie loves her."

"O, I miss my mamma so! I love you, too; but I want mamma. If I had a papa to love me, it would do," she sobbed; "but I am afraid he is on the forbidden ground, and will do something bad. O, auntie, if God would let me go to heaven, it would be so kind, or make me a Christian, like you."

Hester smoothed the bright brown hair tenderly, wondering what she should do to comfort her.

"Little one," she said, "did I ever tell you how my father and mother died when I was a little infant, leaving me without brother or sister, uncle or aunt?"

"No," said Winnie; "tell me about it."

So Hester began the oft-repeated tale, making it grow brighter and brighter as she proceeded.

"Hasn't God been good to me?" she said, in conclusion.

"Yes," said Winnie; "but you are good, too."

"Not very," said Hester; "but God will be good to you, my child. He wants you down here for something. You must ask him to make you willing to stay. Submission to God is what you need. You must pray to him, darling; ask him to help you be good and happy, and he will. That is the way I did. We must be willing to do just what God wants us to, and then he will be pleased with us and bless us. He says, 'Those that seek me early shall find me.' Now go to sleep, dear, and auntie will rock you, just as I do my little bit of a pet."

CHAPTER IX.

Mr. Trueman's Family. — Pleasant Memories.

"Alonzo," said Mrs. Trueman, "you remember Harmony Lovering?"

"Yes; she married that famous Mr. Lentell, I believe."

"Did you know she was dead, and that her four children are living at Mr. Manlie's with Hester Strong?"

"No, indeed; is that so? Where is her husband?"

"Worse than dead. They tell me he has become a real sot, and that Harmony died of neglect. I hear a great deal said about old Mrs. Lentell; I don't know how much truth there is in it; but if half is true, she is a monster of selfishness, and as different from your mother as sin from holiness. I mean to see Hester soon, and know the truth of these stories, and see if I cannot help her in some way. Only think of it! At her time of life, with four children, and one a baby!"

"Well, I wish you would go over, Linnie," said Mr. Trueman, thoughtfully. "We owe Hester a great debt of gratitude. Do you know I think she saved your life when you were so sick, after Georgie and Freddie died?"

"No, I did not know you thought me in danger; but it did seem to me that I could not have lived without her. I never shall forget the restful feeling which came over me after she came; and I cannot tell any one how tired and restless I was before. It did seem as if I could never rest again on earth, and I felt willing to die even, and leave you and all, if I could only rest. I never can describe the feeling of relief I experienced when Hester put her arms around me and kissed me, saying, 'Poor child, I know it all. There, now you can cry all you wish to; it will relieve you. Jesus wept at the grave of a friend.' O, it was so different from what others said! Even you, dear, thought it would hurt me to weep, and never spoke of the children in my presence; so my grief lay like a mountain of lead on my heart; it was crushing, crushing the life out of me. Hester seemed, in some way, to put her strong, loving soul next to mine, and lift the mighty burden, so that I could rest and sleep. She did not talk much at first, but allowed me to, until my feelings were relieved. Then I seemed to doze for a long time. I couldn't feel the burden; I only realized that I was weary, O, so weary! and that Hester was tending me — watching me — loving me. What is it, Alonzo, that makes Hester so acceptable to the sick and afflicted?"

"I do not know, unless it is religion. She is a person of strong, decided character, but perfectly under the influence of the law of love to God and love to man. She comes the nearest to my standard of Christian character of any one I know."

"Yes, I think so; but all Christians cannot minister to the sick and suffering as she does. It seems to me she is especially set apart for that peculiar work. She must have received a baptism of suffering herself."

"Possibly it may be so," was the reply. "I think I used to hear father and mother speak of a disappointment she met with when young; and then it is evident her heart has always been in her work. She has made it the study of her life to be useful, and has fairly earned the reputation she enjoys. I wonder what the sick will do now?"

"Some one will be raised up to fill her place, I presume. I hope those children will find homes soon, for her sake."

"She is sixty, I believe; but it doesn't seem possible. Her heart never will grow old. I can't understand it; she has worked hard. It must be one of the mysteries of godliness, I think. But I wish you would go and see her, and find out in what way we can help her bear her burdens."

"I will go this afternoon, and to-night we will talk it over, if alone; and I hope we may be, for it seems a long time since we have had an evening all to ourselves."

After tea, Mr. Trueman inquired, —

"How did you find Hester and the babies, Linnie?"

"I found them well and happy. Why, Hester has adopted the two youngest; the others are going to their new homes in the spring. I think it is a real trial to Hester to let them go."

"How about Harmony and her husband, and the old lady that rumor brands as a monster?"

"O, it is all true, and the half had not been told me. Do you know I love and venerate the memory of your dear parents more than ever since hearing Hester's story? What a happy lot mine has been! I don't suppose I know any more about work than Harmony did; but your mother didn't seem to expect me to know everything about housekeeping. She used to praise and encourage me all the time. When I made a mistake, and felt badly, she used to tell of one she made when she commenced housekeeping in such a funny way that I couldn't help laughing, and that made it easy, you see."

"Well, did you find out anything we could do to help Hester?"

"Yes; I brought home a lot of sewing for the children. And when I urged Hester to let me do more, she intimated that Christmas presents would be acceptable. We are to leave them at Mr. Manlie's. They are pretty children — all of them. I wish I could have the baby. She is not a beauty, in one sense, and yet she is strangely fascinating. Her eyes are like her mother's, only more beautiful, with a peculiar expression — half sad, half mirthful. She seemed to read my face very attentively, and then reached out her arms to me with so much quiet confidence that she fairly won my heart. I could not help weeping when Hester told me how sad little Winnie is at times. She is more thoughtful than most children, and very sensitive. I told Susie to invite her to spend the day with her, but Hester could not prevail on her to come. She said Susie wouldn't want to play with her, because her father drank rum. Isn't it a shame, Alonzo, this whole liquor business? Can't something be done to stop this nefarious traffic? Only think of Mrs. Gray! How awful! O, how I pity her husband and children! There is no end to the misery it brings upon mankind. I should like to sink every still-house and dram-shop down into the bottomless pit. There! now I'll stop, or I fear I shall want to pitch the rum-sellers after them, and do wicked things to fathers who fill the hearts of their children with sorrow and shame."

"Then you didn't mean Kidder Stillman," said Mr. Trueman. "I have something of that feeling towards him since that terrible tragedy. It seems worse for a woman to die in that way."

"Yes, it does seem worse. I am thankful it is not very common, for I really think that, bad as it is for husbands and fathers to become brute beasts, the children suffer less than when the mother pursues the same wretched course. I do wish something could be done to stop the sale of the poison stuff. It makes me wicked to think of it. I didn't think of Kidder when I spoke; but I own that, as I went past there to-day, I fairly loathed the sight of him. I confess, I compared him to a certain cloven-footed character we read of, and the store to his den."

"Why, Linnie," said Mr. Trueman, "is it possible? I thought I was alone in that feeling. But it does exasperate me exceedingly to see such miserly selfishness. There is no help for it, though, while man remains a depraved being, unless the strong arm of the law can be brought to bear on one side, and Christian courage and fortitude on the other. But you must try to make Winnie feel that we respect her in spite of her misfortunes. It is one of the saddest features of intemperance that innocent women and children suffer more than the guilty subjects."

"Yes, I shall try to. I have invited her to spend the day after Christmas with us, and I shall invite a number of little girls in the afternoon, so that she may become acquainted. She is going to live with her aunt Elevia in the spring, and will attend our school."

"That is right; do what you can for her," said Mr. Trueman. "I am glad she is going there; Mr. Giles is very much of a gentleman, and wealthy. She will be well cared for."

"I fear not," was the reply. "Hester does not feel so. She intimated that he is not what he seems to be; but pray don't speak of it; it may not be so. And yet Hester is seldom wrong, you know. But don't forget the presents."

CHAPTER X.

MR. AND MRS. STILLMAN. — A DOMESTIC SCENE.

"MARIA," said Mr. Stillman, "I want you to go to the city to-morrow, and get a new velvet bonnet, and a cloak of some kind. Mind, now, you get something that will put Mrs. Trueman and Mrs. Steele all in the shade. I am doing more business than their husbands are, — that is, in some branches, — and I want people to know it. Don't mind expense. I want you to look better than any one at church. John and Clara look first rate in their winter suits. That Trueman is a mean puppy, croaking round about temperance. This is a free country, I want him to understand. But sometimes I wish it wasn't; for I would like to stop some of this noise about the sin of rum-selling. That mean, contemptible Steele is trying to undersell me; but we'll see," — snapping his fingers. "I know a trick worth two of that. Water is cheap."

"Yes, we *shall* see," sighed Mrs. Stillman. "Kidder, I begin to see now, and feel too, that rum-selling is a sin — an abominable sin. I wish from the bottom of my heart you had never engaged in it. I wish you would give it up. It is a curse to us, and always will be."

"Well, now," said Mr. Stillman, starting up and walking round the room resolutely. "Maria, what's to pay? I thought you had got rid of those whims and notions. Has the parson been talking to you? Say, what's the matter?"

"No," said Maria, emphatically, "he hasn't; but I begin to see for myself. I don't know how I can help it. John is being ruined by the influence of rum, and the company it draws to the store. You must be blind, or you would see that he is."

"I can't, then; but I hope I haven't got to hear temperance at home, as well as abroad. I won't have it, Maria. Why, that canting hypocrite Trueman called at the store to-day, and tried to induce me to give up selling liquor. The dog! he knows I get other custom by keeping it."

"Yes, and lose some. Kidder, we are disgraced forever by that affair of Mrs. Gray's. How came you to let her have it? Why, I am so mortified I don't want to meet anybody. How could you take that little piece of pork? It was a shame. It is all over town. The children sing out, 'Pork, pork' to John. They call him Jack Killman now; and Clara says the girls whisper and draw back when she comes near them: it is awful."

"They are envious, I suppose," was the curt reply, "because my family dress better than they. Trading is my business, Maria. I am not to inquire into the peculiar circumstances of my customers. I should like to see myself doing it. How did I know Lot earned that pork doing chores for Mr. Manlie? How did I know they hadn't a barrel full?"

"Why, Kidder Stillman, you *did* know they hadn't a barrel of pork, nor anything like it. You might have known it was all they had. And they say Mr. Gray called on you that morning, and begged of you not to let her have any. Was that so? Tell me, Kidder; did he?"

"Well, what if he did? I tell you it is my business to sell, and ask no questions. I paid for a license; and how did I know she would get in the fire? She was a nuisance, any way."

"How came she to be a nuisance, Kidder Stillman? That is the question. You can't deny that Helen Gray was a nice, respectable woman when you came to the village. Hasn't she bought all she drank of you? You can't deny that, either. I don't think there is another store in the place where she could have bought it. I, for one, am heartily ashamed of you."

"There now, that is what I get for working to dress you and the children in fine clothes. But I tell you to stop your lecturing, Maria; I can't hear it."

"But you will have to hear it. I have lain awake half the night ever since I saw that little burned infant and its mother. O, mercy, what a sight! They are right before me all the time. O, Kidder, I felt like a guilty accomplice in the horrid deed; you don't know what I have suffered ever since. Why, I had rather be clothed in rags the rest of my life than to wear the price of so much sin, and misery, and death. I never saw the business in its true light before — never. I only looked at the beautiful things it purchased for me and mine — blindly, foolishly. I have now looked at the wretchedness and rags, the poverty and shame, it brings to the consumer; and now my nice house, my beautiful dresses, everything we have, is stained all over with guilt. Wherever I look, I see something like the terrible hand on the wall, writing, 'This is the price of tears, of misery, of hunger, ay, of blood.' I can't bear it, Kidder; you must stop, or I shall be insane."

Mr. Stillman began to be alarmed at his wife's state of mind.

"Well, well, Maria, don't talk about it now; you are nervous. You ought not to have gone over to Mrs. Gray's. It almost undid me. I had to be resolute, and drive the subject out of mind. I thought I'd give up the business right off; but what's the use, Maria? There is Steele and others; they'd sell it if I didn't. I might as well have the profits as any one; but I shall look out not to sell it to a foolish woman with a baby to burn up again. Trust me for that. Steele may have that kind of customers for all I care. Come, you'd better go to the city, and buy those things; it will take up your mind."

"But I don't want my mind taken up; I am satisfied it is wrong to sell rum. My eyes are opened; I don't want to have them closed again by gewgaws. I have thought altogether too much of dress and show. My love of them has almost blinded me to the evils of intemperance; and yet I never thought it was right to sell it. I have had my secret fears for John; and now I see plainly that, unless something is done immediately, he is a ruined boy. He is rude and coarse at home, and is continually repeating some low vulgarism he has heard at the store. And Clara is ashamed of him when they are out together. Poor child! he is becoming a town's talk; good children shun him."

"O, come, Maria, you are nervous. John will do well enough — sowing wild oats you see. He is smart; that's all; none of your milk-and-water folks. He will come out right; don't worry. Come now, don't act so. Here, I will give you some money, and you go in to-morrow and buy what you need. I don't want you to go looking shabbily; it will injure my trade."

"I don't wish for any money; I can't think of going, and I don't need anything but a clear conscience to make me happy. You are a kind husband; we have been happy together, and may be again if you will give up selling liquor; we can live comfortably without the profits, and I shall be a thousand times happier."

"Why, Maria, you talk foolishly. We couldn't half live if I were to give that up."

"We don't more than half live now, and never have; I mean as we ought to," said the dejected wife, still weeping. "But I had rather die than live by cursing and killing others. Come, Kidder, do please, now, give it up. We shall never be prosperous and happy till you do. I fear I have been as much to blame in the past as you have; but I can't sustain you in it after this, and I shall never consent to spend a cent of money obtained in this way again. Won't you promise me?" She laid her hand upon his shoulder, and looked tearfully into his face.

"I can't promise, Maria; I will think of it. I couldn't bear to see my family poor, or meanly dressed. I am sorry you feel so; but my stopping would make no difference; somebody'll sell it; they'll get it somewhere. I'll see about it."

"Never mind, Kidder; let others sell it if they will, and reap the reward; but promise me that you won't," persisted the awakened wife.

"Perhaps I will, when I sell out what I have on hand. I must go now; you are making too serious a matter of this."

And the unhappy wife was left alone with her sad reflections. Clara was out spending the afternoon. John was — she knew not where. She had little expectation that her husband would ever think as she did. And O, she trembled, as she thought how often she had detected the fatal smell in his breath recently, and an unnatural hilarity in his manner. She wept and sighed in turn, until John, a boy of sixteen, entered the room noisily, saying, —

"Come, old woman, hand over some money. The old man is mighty crusty to-night; can't get a cent from him. I tell you, fork over. Jim Steele and I are going over to North End, to a ringtum with two of the handsomest girls out."

Mrs. Stillman was exceedingly shocked. She saw that her son was in the first stage of drunkenness, and perfectly reckless.

"I have no money, Johnnie; come, stay at home with me this evening; I am lonesome," she said, in as quiet a voice as she could command.

"Well, I guess so; pretty likely I shall — isn't it? when Jim and the girls are waiting down by the corner. Come, trump up something; your watch'll do."

He seized it, held it up for a moment defiantly, and rushed from the room, saying, —

"Tell the old man to hand over the real shin-plasters next time."

Mrs. Stillman hurried to the store as fast as her trembling limbs could carry her, and entered it just in time to hear Mr. Crafty say, in a sarcastic tone, —

A DOMESTIC SCENE.

"I thought you were more of a man, Mr. Stillman, than to be nosed round by a woman. Now, I tell my wife that it is nothing to her how I make my money, or spend it either, so long as she is well supplied."

"What is it?" said Mr. Stillman, alarmed by the appearance of his wife. She told him in as few words as possible, and disappeared.

Mr. Stillman spoke hurriedly to his clerk, and excused himself to the company by saying, —

"I have an engagement down at the corner, and ought to have been there before," and went in pursuit of his son, — so young in years, so old in vice. Of course the counsels of Mr. Crafty and his compeers, backed up by love of gain, and the cravings of a young and growing appetite, prevailed; and the casks were emptied and filled, emptied and filled. Mrs. Stillman became very reserved; but people called her haughty, and wondered what she had to be proud of. She ceased to dress as much as formerly; they supposed it was because Jack cost them so much in drunken riots. They didn't pity her; didn't she know it was no worse for her husband and son to drink than for other people's husbands and sons?

CHAPTER XI.

Christmas Morning. — Reminiscences of the Past.

"It has happened just right — hasn't it, aunt Hester? Now I am glad it snowed so fast, if I couldn't go skating. Uncle Frank will come in his big sleigh. O, won't it be fun to see the horse go and make the bells jingle!" said Wallace, on Christmas morning.

"O, funny, funny!" shouted little Elida.

"It will be nice," said Winnie, "if we don't tip over in the big piles of snow."

"We shan't tip over," said Hester, tossing the baby. "Uncle Frank is used to snow, and old Charlie is kind and careful."

"Isn't she pretty, with her new frock? How nice Mrs. Trueman has fixed it, with the blue ribbon and edging," said Winnie, as Hester held little Fostina up to the admiring gaze of the children, and turned her round and round, so that they could have a full view of the bow on the back, and see how cunning she was all over.

"Pretty!" said Hester; "yes, indeed, and as sweet as a pink. She is a darling, every bit of her, and just as good as can be."

"Don't you wish father could see her?" said Winnie, sadly.

"Yes, and grandma Lentell, too," said Wallace, triumphantly. "Poh! *a monkey!* I should think she

CHRISTMAS MORNING.   107

looked more like a little beauty — shouldn't you, auntie? I don't love grandma much; she says 'Hum!' all the time. She's real homely, and I think she looks like a —"

"Your grandmother is not as good and lovely as I wish she was, but you had better not speak disrespectfully of her. It will do no good, and will be sure to injure you," said Hester, quietly.

"How will it, auntie?"

"Well, I don't know as I can make you understand what I mean; but here is a pail of nice, clean, fresh water. Now, if I were to pour in a few drops of vinegar every now and then, it would soon grow sour; or a little wormwood, it would be bitter — would it not?"

"Why, yes, of course it would," said Wallace.

"But suppose I should drop in a lump of sugar now and then?"

"Why, it would be sweetened water then," said the children, in concert.

"It would be dood," said Elida. "We'd drink it all up, and gis you and totty sister some."

"Well," said Hester, smiling, "when God makes us little innocent babies, at first we are good, and fresh, and pure, and sweet, like little birdie, here; and when we are old enough to think, and talk, and act, if we are careful to think good, and pure, and loving thoughts, we shall remain more pure and lovely than we shall if we indulge in bitter, unkind, envious feelings. Or, in other words, kind, loving, tender thoughts, words, and deeds make us better, and those around us; but cross, unkind, selfish thoughts, words, and deeds injure us, and those with whom we associate. Do you understand me, children?"

"Why, you mean, if I tell about grandma's badness,

and say she looks like a monkey," said Wallace, rapidly, "it will make me, and us, bitter, or sour, or bad. And if I talk about somebody's goodness, it will make me, and us, better."

"That is it," said Hester, encouragingly. " But we must hang up our stockings. Uncle Frank will be here soon. There he comes, now."

" O, dear !" said Martha Manlie, to her parents; "I should think Hester would be distracted, with all those children to fix off. I declare I thought I should be crazy the little time I staid there; but Hester seemed to enjoy it. They are as good as kittens, all of them; but there would be too many for me, and Hester is ten years older."

"La, sakes, child," said grandma, "you ain't used to children, and Hester is. You'd get used to it after a while. I never enjoyed myself better in my life than I did when I had my seven around me; and my mother used to say the same of her ten. There they go. Hester is a dear good girl. She seems as young as ever she did. God bless 'em."

"I wish 'em all a merry Christmas, from the bottom of my heart," said grandpa, looking up from his paper. "God bless 'em."

"Wallace looks like your brother Horace, child—don't you think so?" said grandma.

"Yes, mother, and Winnie like our Mary, only not as cheerful. She is rightly named *Winnie*. I wish she was going to stay here, instead of Elida; her quiet, thoughtful ways suit me exactly. Elida is a dear little thing too, and baby is a remarkable child. I don't know what to think of her. She is the wisest little thing I ever saw. She is getting acquainted with me, and I am glad. I mean to tend her half a day Sunday, and let Hester go to church, she enjoys it so much."

"That is right, Martha; your poor brother set his life by Hester; and wasn't she worthy of it too? O, how that wicked Mehitable Sharp made them suffer! I can't bear to think of it. I always blamed Horace, though, for going off without knowing the truth of the matter. But la, it is all over; I didn't never mean to think of it again. But I am glad them children didn't take after her. I couldn't love them if they did. Their grandpa Lentell was as nice a man as ever lived. He waited upon me to a horseback ride once. He was a handsome fellow: folks teased me about him considerable. But I liked your father the best," looking over to the corner where he sat, fondly. "I was fortunate, Martha. I hope you will do as well some day."

Martha smiled as she said, "Why, mother, don't you see I am away beyond the matrimonial corner?"

"You ain't, child; you are young enough, and good enough, to be married any day, and might have been long ago, if your father and I could have spared you."

"God will bless you, Martha," said grandpa, smiling.

O, how those few childish words of the mother wakened thoughts in the heart of the devoted daughter, of the long-ago love, which burned brightly on the heart's altar for a few brief months, making the bright and beautiful things of earth more bright and beautiful, causing all nature to smile with gladness, and life seem like a pure, sweet reality, which it would be blessed to live.

Yes, she thought of that time for a moment, and smiled — a little patient smile. And then came thoughts of another time, so full of blighted hopes and withered expectations, so full of chilly dreariness and desolation, that she instinctively bowed her head over the Blessed Book, which lay on her knee, and pressed her hand to her throbbing temples, as if she could thus stop the tide of mournful memories, and drink in peace from the sacred pages before her.

But her soul's eyes were fast riveted on memory's blotted page. Thus she sat, while before her passed, in panoramic view, the manly form of her affianced husband.

Now he was sitting by her side, holding her hand, telling her honestly, frankly, tenderly, all his love. How pure it seemed! How she loved him in return! She felt ennobled and elevated by his love, by her love. It was a blessed moment, but it passed. Another scene. How could she look at it? She shrank nearer to the Holy Word of promise, the hands clasped painfully over the throbbing temples, the head bowed lower and lower, as if to let the dreadful wave pass over.

O, it came, it came, and was past. She was well nigh stunned by the mighty shock. The beautiful things of life were veiled in sadness, earth draped in mourning, and the light of heaven very dim, in the presence of this sudden darkness, which extinguished forever a pure, true, and beautiful love.

No, not forever! It will live and burn on, brighter, purer, and holier, in the kingdom of heaven.

"Martha," said the aged mother, "why don't you read, child? I knit into the middle of my needle long ago, and have been waitin'. Read 'The Lord is my Shepherd; I shall not want.'"

"Yes, mother, I will read in a moment. I want to run up stairs first."

She came back, and read calmly, *very calmly*, page after page of the Holy Word, to the aged listeners, and her soul grew strong. She took up again, hopefully, the broken threads of life, and went on her way cheerfully.

CHAPTER XII.

THE CHRISTMAS PARTY. — MISS PATTY STEARNS.

"O, HERE you are," said Emma Lovering. "Why aunt Hester, you look as motherly! Give me baby, while you take off your things."

"She is asleep, the darling," said Hester. "Let me lay her away in a quiet place, and she won't wake till dinner time."

"Why, how good she is! Weren't you cold? How did you like your ride, children?" said aunt Emma.

"It was nice," said Elida.

"Splendid," said the others.

"We's didn't be spilled a mite in the snow," said Sunshine, smiling all over her face.

"Has you got a puddin' wis plums in it, auntie?"

"Yes, pinky, I have; and mince pies too, and little cakes for boys and girls that are good, and lots of sweet things."

"I's dood, auntie, and I likes them things: may I has some?"

"I guess so," lifting her up and kissing the dimpled cheek. "Now I want you to have a good time, and be very happy. Georgy and Fanny have been talking of this visit for a month or more. Now let us see which of all the children will behave best. Let us try to please each other."

Hester took the children into the large, old-fashioned parlor, where the great logs crackled and sparkled, and sent out a perfect flood of warmth and comfort to the chilly ones around.

Grandpa Lovering was there, trying to look cheerful; but thinking, thinking all the time of Mary, the love of his youth, the light of his home, the mother of his children, the companion and friend he had lost.

"I will not sadden them still more by my sadness," he thought.

The brothers and sisters were struggling bravely to bear their own burdens, and help the others in their painful task. The last time they had met was at mother's funeral; and Harmony, their gentle sister, too, had gone; her place was vacant. They missed them so! O, they felt more lonely than ever, now that they were all together.

They saw the pain in each other's faces, they heard it in each other's voices, and felt it in the earnest, silent clasping of the hands. After the first greetings were over, the children took possession of the porch, which had been made warm, and trimmed with evergreens for the occasion.

"There was a baker's dozen," uncle Frank said.

But things moved slowly at first, for the children, some of them, had been deeply wounded by the two deaths in the family circle. All felt the influence of the sad hearts around them, until uncle Frank led aunt Hester among them, blindfolded. First came a smile, then a shout.

"Now, children," said Hester, as she went cautiously along, reaching out her arms, "I'll catch you, if you'll let me. But mind now, we must be — O, who is this?" feeling all over the head, rubbing the ears and pinching them, but no sound. "Well, I guess it is Master George Lovering." (A great laugh.) "Am I right?"

"Yes, yes; 'tis he," shouted the children.

"And here is my Sunshine," said Hester, catching Elida, who had been saying, —

"Here I be, here I be, auntie."

"Well," said Hester, taking off the bandage and tying it over Georgy's eyes, "I was going to say you must try to play as quietly as you can, for baby is asleep, and grandma Stearns isn't far off."

"I wish she was farther off, though," said George; "she'll think we ought to be set down in a row, learning the Catechism." And several others said, —

"So do I, so do I. She isn't a bit like you, auntie Hester. O, won't you stay and play with us?"

"Do," echoed from all parts of the room.

"No, dears, I can't; I want to see grandpa. He is lonely. See how good you can be, and take care of the little ones," she said, disappearing.

"Why, I would give more for one of our aunt Hester's little fingers than I would for Patty Stearns, and all the money and things the cross old thing has got in the world," said Fanny.

"If I hear her old crutches a coming, I'll hold the door. She thinks it is wicked to laugh," said George, as he began to dive this way, duck that way, stoop over, and walk with his arms stretched out this way and that. Such a diving, ducking, dodging, scampering time as there was for a few moments! the little ones pleading to be caught.

"There, now," said George, with a flourish, "I've got somebody. 'Tis Fanny, I know by her wig." And so it went on, game after game, until joy sparkled in every eye, when suddenly the door flew open, and there stood Miss Stearns, leaning on her crutches, and looking mournfully, ay, sternly, over her brass-bowed specs.

"I shouldn't thought you'd felt like making all this noise," she said, dolefully, "when your poor grandmother and aunt Harmony are both dead. Death is a solemn thing, and you've got to die, all of you, some time. You'd better be larnin' the Catechism, or some of Watts' hymns."

The children were as silent as if death in all its grimness stood before them, all but Fanny, the oldest.

"Why?" said she; "have we waked the baby? Aunt Hester told us to play; she played with us at first."

"Mercy, mercy! Did I iver hear the like of that? Well, go on; destruction's before you."

"Didn't you love to play when you were young?" inquired Fanny.

"Not after my grandmother and aunt died — not I," was the slow, solemn reply, with a mournful shake of the head.

"How old were you then?" persisted Fanny.

"Well, it's no matter now; I was thirty or up'ards. I've seen the emptiness of earthly things, and I hope you will before long." She turned slowly away, with a sigh, saying, "Mercy, mercy! how depraved human natur' is!" The door was closed as soon as it was safe.

"There, now," said George, sticking his jackknife over the latch, "I hope somebody else will die soon."

"O, I wouldn't," said Winnie, fearfully.

"Yes, you would," said George, "if you were as tired

of her droning, croaking voice as we are. Why, Sis and Bub get just as far from her as they can."

"Yes," said Fanny, "she thinks it is foolish and wicked for mother, or any of us, to say 'darling,' or 'birdie,' or 'Lizzie,' or 'Willie.' She always says 'William,' and 'Elizabeth,' to those little things."

Fanny's perfect imitation of Miss Stearns' voice and manner caused a hearty laugh.

"Hush! hush!" said several voices; "she will come again."

"No she won't," said Fanny; "the door is fast."

"What makes your folks keep her?" inquired several of the cousins.

"Because she can't stay anywhere else, I suppose," was the reply. "Mother pities her. Why, we can't have company, young or old, without her hobbling in with her crutches, looking like a fright; and she has real nice clothes laid away. And then, nobody must speak, unless spoken to by herself, because she happens to be eighty. This is the way she begins," said Fanny, settling her face, and changing her tone:—

"'George, bring the cricket. My limb it pains me desput. It's thirteen years and up'ards since I fell and broke it. Fanny, it 'pears to me there's a stitch down. I ain't a bit well,' addressing the company. 'My eyes pain me, and I rested poorly last night, too. The doctor left me some trade for um, but they ain't a mite better.' A little pause. 'I was sayin' it's up'ards of thirteen years since I fell and broke my limb, and I hain't stepped a step since.'

"By and by the company gets to talking, and grows lively. She frowns, moves her crutches, and plunges into us again. 'Let's see,' very dolefully addressing some one who has buried a friend some time, ; 'I believe it's ten years the 10th day of March since your sister died. I remember it as plain as day,' shaking her head mournfully."

"That is a way she has of extinguishing mirthfulness, father says," said George. "He says she can tell the year, the month, the day, and the hour of every death in town for the last forty years."

"She likes funerals," said Fanny, "and it's the only thing she does like, except good living. Last Thanksgiving morning she complained of being sick, and mother made her a quart of milk porridge. She crumbed it full of bread, and then, when dinner was ready, she wanted a lot of turkey, saying, 'I niver tasted a mouthful of breakfast.' 'Didn't you eat a bowlful of bread and porridge?' said mother. She looked up with an injured, indignant look, and said, 'I niver heard porridge called victuals — niver.' I can tell you, the turkey and fixins, pudding and pies, melted away like snow forts before the sun, if her appetite was poor."

"She isn't willing we should laugh or play," said Fanny, "or read anything but the Bible, Pilgrim's Progress, Watts' Hymns, or the Catechism."

"You have forgotten the 'ivery-day book' and the letters she makes everybody read," said George. "She looks indignant enough if we read a word to ourselves."

"We shall turn sour, or bitter, or bad," said Wallace, uneasily, "if we keep on. Hasn't somebody got some sugar to put in?"

The children laughed, looked at each other, and inquired, —

"What do you mean?"

Winnie told aunt Hester's morning illustration.

"There isn't much danger of our being sweetened — is there, Fan," said George, "while that vinegar jug is round? She ought to have been a frog, she loves croaking so well."

"Come, come," said Fanny, "let's play 'puss, puss in the corner,' or 'forfeits.' Aunt Hester is right. The more I talk about her, the worse I hate her; so I shall stop."

After the children left the parlor, grandpa said, making a great effort to speak cheerfully, —

"We miss them — don't we, children? we miss them. But we shouldn't be willing to call them back — should we?"

A long pause. Elevia arose, sat down on a cricket at her father's feet, and laid her head wearily on his knee. Silently he placed his arm over her neck for a moment, drew his hand over the bowed head, caressingly, and said, "My child, would you call them back?"

"No, father," was the earnest reply. "I would rather go to them."

Hester, as usual, came to the rescue. She talked of the absent ones so hopefully that the mourners could almost rejoice that they were not here, bearing the burdens and sorrows of life.

"God help us to be ready when we are called to go," she said.

Here Miss Stearns entered.

Every one knew what to expect. It was the old story. Self was the beginning, the middle, and the end; so the company resigned themselves to the infliction as best they could.

"Miss Strong," she began, "I shouldn't thought you'd felt like playing with um. I'm astonished that you sanction the follies of youth so. I'm surprised and shocked, I say, to find them children a-playing so soon; and you begun it. Christ's kingdom niver will be established while his professed followers are —"

"Cross and ugly," said uncle Frank, laughing.

"Mercy, mercy! You are too light," — with a sigh. "He was a man of sorrows, and acquainted with grief. We ought to follow his example in those things."

"Yes," said Hester, reverently, "we ought to follow his example in all things. He was kind, and tender, and loving. He was meek and lowly, full of pity, gentle and forgiving. He was perfect in holiness. O, we ought to imitate him in all things, especially in his self-denying love; for love is the bond of perfection."

"It was in July, I believe, Mr. Lovering, that your daughter died; the 28th day of the month; and your wife, November 7. Well, there is enough to keep us from frivolity. I've seen the emptiness of earthly things."

Here dinner was announced. After some waiting, the crutches were adjusted on a chair brought for that purpose. Grace was said, and the business of the hour went on as briskly and quietly as could be expected, considering that twenty-eight hungry people were seated around the table. The children were radiant with delight and expectation.

"I likes puddin' wis plums in it," said little Elida.

The company smiled, all but Miss Stearns; she was shocked.

"Children should be seen, and not heard, was the rule

in my day," she sighed; "but now they are heard first. That child needs a mother,"—looking at Hester.

"O, come, Miss Stearns," said uncle Frank; "this is a Christmas dinner, or supper, whichever you please, and not a funeral, nor a lecture. Let us be thankful for our blessings, and show it by being cheerful. There is a time for everything, you know. Let me give you a generous piece of turkey, or chicken, or whatever you like."

"I likes baked roosters, I does," said little Willie, with a flourish.

"Wis a wis bone on it?" said Elida.

"Yes," said Willie, "and some 'tato and graby on it."

All smiled but the chagrined and solemn Miss Stearns. It was funny to see the little piles of plums on the children's plates — pleasant to see them count their treasures, and divide, so as to share equally.

"Well, we've had a nice time — haven't we?" said Fanny. "I was afraid Miss Stearns would spoil all; but she hasn't."

All expressed satisfaction, and the company dispersed.

"I think you do wrong to keep Patty Stearns here," said Hester, aside. "It will have a bad influence on the children; prejudice their minds against religion, &c."

"I fear it will," said Emma. "Frank threatens to send her off. She is terribly stingy, too, and frets about the price of board. Why, she wouldn't eat a meal away on any account. If invited, she declines, saying, 'I pay my board at Mr. Lovering's.' Yet she will invite company to eat here. Did you see that bag on her arm? She always brings it to the table, and if there is cake, or anything better than common, she drops some in slyly.

Queer — isn't it? And the other day her brother, an old man, came to see her. She wanted to comb his hair, and actually came to me for a comb. 'Why,' said I, 'where is yours?' 'I don't want to use mine,' was her reply. 'Well, I don't want you to use mine, neither,' said I. She seemed quite offended. I think we shall have to let her go; but I am sure I don't know where she will find a place. Nobody wants her."

When Hester went to Miss Stearns' room to say good night, she could scarcely help smiling at the sight that met her. She found her sitting in one corner, a comical-looking hood on, her head bowed so that the bow on the pointed top stood erect, " meditatin'," as she called it, and saying over her Catechism, hymns, &c., out aloud.

Hester heard

"Hark! from the tombs a doleful sound,"

and closed the door sadly, saying to herself, "There are other doleful things besides tombs. I wish she could learn to praise, as well as mourn. She has more cause for gratitude than many others I know of."

CHAPTER XIII.

WHAT SANTA CLAUS LEFT. — JUDITH LOVERING'S ADVICE.

MARTHA MANLIE had kindled a good warm fire, and was waiting to help Hester unpack her precious freight.

"This is thoughtful in you," said Hester; "I meant to have asked you to do just this thing. You take Sunshine. Wallace and Winnie can scrabble out themselves. Pet is fast asleep. She is a darling, auntie Martha. There, it is nice to have this warm room to come into. The folks all sent love to you and the dear old folks. How have you enjoyed the day?"

"O, very well. I have thought of you a good deal. I expected you and the little ones would come home tired out. Aren't you half crazy with the confusion?" said Martha, as she went on quietly unwrapping the children, who were trying to wait patiently for an opportunity to explore the stockings.

"I's had the *bestest* time," said Sunshine. "O, I's never seen such nice plums on a puddin' in all your life, aunt Martha. I brought one to you, and my grandpa, and his mother. Be she waked up?"

"May we look and see if he has been here?" asked Winnie and Wallace, in a breath.

"O, yes," said Hester, "I forgot you were expecting the old man with the bag. Have you seen him, Martha?"

"Yes, I think he has called," said Martha, opening

the bed-room door, and exposing five stockings pinned to the bed-quilt.

"Mercy sakes!" said Winnie; "why, they are all full, and running over. I'm afraid he won't have enough to go round."

"Yes, he will," said Wallace; "he makes such things, and has a store full of um."

"O, good, good! Here is a sled for me; and here is a little pony; that is for me; and here—"

"You mustn't claim everything," said Hester. "We will see whom the things are for soon. We shall find the names attached to them. Let's see: the sled is for Wallace, the book for Winnie, the pony for Elida. And now you may see what the stockings contain."

The merry voices were hushed for a moment, while childish hands pulled out one thing after another, until the last was extracted, and then,—

"See! see!" shouted the children.

"I've got a jackknife, and lots of peppermints," said Wallace. "Hurrah! I'll cut up your kindlings now, auntie."

"Mine is a baby, a mite of a dolly, that he brought me," said Sunshine, "and some sugar things. I'll gis you some, aunties."

"That is a darling," said the two aunties. "But what has Winnie got? Isn't she pleased with the old gentleman's gifts?"

"O, yes, indeed; but I am confounded, auntie. I didn't expect half so much. Here is a beauty thimble and scissors, and comb, and such a lot of candy, besides the darling book. O, I didn't expect *so much*." And little sensitive Winnie fairly cried with the surprise and joy.

"You will have one of those books every month, darling," said Hester.

"Who do you suppose it is?" said Martha, stroking the child's head.

"Why, it is God, I think. He told somebody to do it, because we are orphans. Aunt Judith told me I was worse than an orphan. Are orphans *bad*, auntie?" sobbed the child.

"Bad? No," said Hester, cheerfully. "They are the sweetest, darlingest little things in the world. I think they are nearer and dearer to the dear God Father than children who have earthly parents. Don't you, Martha?"

"Yes, indeed," said Martha; "and all God's people love little motherless children better than any others, if they are good."

"Do you suppose that God thought anything about telling him to give us these?" asked Wallace, thoughtfully. "Why, he is away up in heaven."

"Yes, dear," said Hester. "God reigneth in heaven and on earth, too. He is everywhere, beholding the evil and the good. He will punish our evil, wicked deeds, and reward the good. I want you to remember the verse, 'Thou, God, seest me,' for he is always looking on. When you desire to do wrong, think of God, and be afraid to sin; when you desire to do right, be sure God put the thought in your heart; and He will help you, and bless and love you if you obey."

"But who tells us to do wicked things, auntie?"

"Satan, who is a very wicked, cruel spirit; he hates God, and —"

"Poh, auntie! I shan't mind *him*. He is a hateful old fellow. I heard a dressed-up man say on the street, the other day, that Jack Stillman and his father acted like the devil. He is Satan — isn't he? Poh! he is mean."

"But, my dear child, Satan is a very powerful spirit. There is only one Being stronger than he."

"Who is that, auntie? God?"

"Yes, dear. God can help you resist this malicious being, and when you pray, 'Lead us not into temptation, deliver us from evil,' that is what you mean. You must not forget to ask God to take care of you, my dear children, every day; neither must you forget to thank him for all his blessings."

"These are blessings, I suppose," said Wallace, pointing at his sled.

"Yes, dear."

"Well, I thank him for all mine, and I mean to be good, and love him."

"Who, do you suppose, did it, auntie?" said Winnie, smiling. "I guess they wanted to put some sugar in our lives — didn't they? I wish I knew who, so that I could love them."

Hester and Martha looked at each other, and smiled.

"Why, St. Nicholas, of course," said Wallace; "he is always doing such things at Christmas time. He is a funny old man, and slept between two feather beds, one night, when he didn't want to go out. Don't you remember, mamma used to tell us?"

"Yes, he be funny," said Sunshine, who had finished the last peppermint, and commenced a stick of molasses candy. "Yes, he is a kind old San Dicolas — isn't he, auntie? He gis my 'ittle beauty sister a cunning rattle. Mayn't I gis it to her, when she wakes up?"

"Yes, dear; but auntie cannot let you eat any more candy to-night. It will make darling sick, and auntie will have to give her bitter medicine."

"I likes bitter things, auntie," said the child, demurely; "let me eat it all up."

"No, dear," said Hester, decidedly; "give it to me, now; in the morning you shall have it."

"No, no," persisted the child. "Santa Dicolas told somebody I might eat it all up. He wants to sweeten me all sweet, he do. Now I'll tell him," she said, pouting out the red lips, and crying.

"He won't bring naughty folks any, next time."

"O, sissy, sissy," said Winnie, hurriedly, "he won't bring you any more if you talk so. Aunt Judith says we must be good all the time, and never say things, because we are orphans. She says we must be still, and never get in the way, nor anything, or folks won't have us round. O, dear! won't you stop crying?"

Hester and Martha gave each other a sharp, quick, indignant look.

"When did she tell you all that?" said Hester.

"Out in the porch, auntie, when I was playing; it made me cry. She told me not to laugh so loud, for I was worse than an orphan, and it didn't look well. But Fanny told me orphans were good as anybody. She said I might laugh as loud as I pleased, for I wasn't half as much in the way as aunt Judith."

"Well," said Hester to Martha, "I shall have to talk to that woman. I didn't mean to, but I must. Mary always stood between us when she was alive."

Martha nodded assent, and said, "Father and mother wanted to have the children come in a little while."

Elida was as sunny as ever by this time.

" O, funny ! " she shouted ; " now I'll gis the plums."

" There," said Hester, when the children had left the room, "I am glad they are gone, for I am bursting almost with indignation, and I feel like crying, too. What a strange woman that Judith Lovering is! Only think of it. Trying to dampen and darken the little bit of enjoyment the poor child was having. There are dark shadows enough around her now, without her throwing any. Why, Mr. Lovering will find it hard to get a housekeeper, on her account. I don't think he knows her yet. Mary, our angel Mary, took all her poison shafts into her own tender bosom. O, she hid them away there, and they killed her ; I don't hesitate to say it. She didn't let her husband know what she had to endure. She tried to hide her meanness from him, from every one. Yes, she bore it silently and alone, and it killed her. I have seen things there that would make a saint ' angry, and sin not ; ' and sometimes I wanted to tell her what I thought of her ; but Mary would beg so, that I desisted. But Winnie is a sensitive child, and I shall talk with Judith, for — "

" Ah," said Martha, " she was rightly named Judith Small. I wish she had never changed it, for Mary did fail so fast after she went there, that I feel as you do."

CHAPTER XIV.

Winnie's Visit, and the Party.

Hester exhausted her ingenuity in preparing Winnie for her visit at Mr. Trueman's. She dressed her in her very best, and took her into grandpa's, that they might help her fortify the shrinking child for the events of the day.

"Now, praise her all you can truthfully," said Hester aside; "it won't hurt a child like her."

"You look like a posy," said grandpa, "just picked out of the garden, with the dew all on."

"She is as comely as her mother," said grandma; "and that is saying a good deal. How curious you are, Hester! She looks well enough to go to the parson's, or anywhere else, as to that matter. She makes me think of the old adage, — 'Pretty is that pretty does.' She looks like a modest little violet with that blue dress on." And grandma stroked the child's smooth hair with her wrinkled hand, and smiled, until Winnie thought she, too, was beautiful, and wondered why grandma Lintell was so different.

Martha said her dress was neat and becoming; and hoped she would enjoy the day. They all sent kind regards to Mr. and Mrs. Trueman.

"Shall I say, 'Grandpa and grandma sent their love to you, and my aunt Hester and aunt Martha, too?' Is that right?" said Winnie, hesitatingly.

"Yes, that will do nicely," said Hester.

"Very nicely," said the rest.

She kissed baby and Elida, said good morning cheerfully, and went forth to find that every cup of happiness contained a little drop of something "bitter, or sour, or bad," as Wallace said, dropped into it sometimes wickedly, sometimes thoughtlessly, sometimes accidentally. She spent the morning pleasantly, playing with Susie and her dollies, dressing and undressing them, rocking them to sleep, &c., until Susie said, —

"Did you have some at your house, Winnie?"

"Once," was the reply; "but they wasn't like these. My mamma made them," — with a little sigh.

"O, I forgot; mother told me not to ask you," she said, apologetically. "Of course they were pretty if your dear mother made them. She isn't dead, — is she, Winnie? She is up in heaven with God and my darling brothers, that went before I was born. But I shall know them. Grandpa and grandma went since I was a big girl. They will know them, and find them for me. O, you are crying! what makes you? You will see her again. Mother says she was good. Don't cry; I am sorry I speaked about it, if it makes you feel bad. I didn't mean to; mother said I mustn't unless you did. Come, don't cry, and I will give you old Hagar; you liked her best. Mother will be willing. She wants you to love us, because — " Susie stammered; she was afraid to say "because you are a poor motherless child, with a drunken father;" so she put her arms around her neck, almost crying herself, and said, —

"I am real sorry I said it."

"O, it wasn't you that made me cry," said Winnie,

returning the caress. "I like you, and your papa and mamma. I remember the Christmas presents; they were so beautiful! But when I think of my dead mamma, I always cry. I don't mean to, but I do. O, I wanted her to stay with me, but she couldn't; and most all the time I want to go to her; but aunt Hester says God wants me down here for something. There, I won't cry any more; it makes you feel bad; but I want something. I want to love Jesus." And Winnie wiped and wiped the little red eyes. But they wouldn't stay dry.

"No, I ain't crying about that," said Susie; "but I was thinking what if God should take my mamma, and leave me. I should cry all the time then, I believe."

"No, you wouldn't *all* the time," said Winnie; "God would help you forget it. Haven't you got some books with pictures in them?"

"Yes, a whole lot; come into the library, and I'll show you."

Before dinner the little girls were very happy, and the best of friends.

Mr. and Mrs. Trueman succeeded in diverting Winnie's mind from painful thoughts during the dinner hour. The children vied with each other in showing her kind attentions.

"Be you got a brother?" said Walter.

"Yes, and two sisters; one little baby sister, and another about as big as you. I think you would love them," said Winnie, glancing up at Mr. and Mrs. Trueman.

"O, yes, I know we shall. When it is warm weather, we are going to bring Miss Hester and her pets over here to spend several weeks. Do you like cherries?"

"Yes'm," was the reply; "but I shan't be there then," — drawing a long breath. "I'm going to aunt Elevia's."

"O, well, that isn't far off," said Mr. Trueman, cheerfully. "Your uncle trades at my store, and I will ask him to bring you over when they are here."

"Yes," said Mrs. Trueman, "you will go to school with Susie; and, as I think you are a good, truthful girl, I shall ask your aunt to let you come often and spend the night with us. Would you like to?"

"O, yes'm;" and Winnie gave a quick glance at Susie, who met her look with a bright, broad smile. She smiled cordially in return. The shadows faded from her heart, the sadness from her face. Mr. and Mrs. Trueman looked at each other significantly, well pleased with the result of their efforts to cheer this, Christ's little one; when little Walter, wishing to occupy a silent moment, said to Winnie, —

"Do your father be in the naughty jail-house now?"

The parents tried to check the unfortunate question, but too late. Winnie blushed, gave a quick glance around the table, looked down, and burst into tears.

With the thoughtfulness of mature age, Susie arose and said, —

"Come and see my birdies. I'll give you something to feed them with."

As the children left the room, Mr. Trueman said, —

"Walter, don't speak to the little girl about her father or mother again — will you? It makes her feel badly. Linnie, we shall have to be more guarded in speaking before the children. I would rather have given a great deal than to have had this happen."

"I's sorry Walter made the little lady cry, papa. Walter sorry; never do it another time, papa."

"It is a pity that she is so sensitive," said Mr. Trueman. "Situated as she is, life will be full of pain. I wonder what can be done to help her overcome it."

"Kind treatment and time will do something for her," was the reply. "Only think what she has seen and suffered in the last few months. What would become of our Susie, or Lucy even?"

"It is a hard case, Linnie. I am so outraged with our law-makers, that I can't sit down quietly any longer. Such a child needs a father, and so do all children; and yet the law, which claims to guard the rights of the people so very humanely, sanctions a traffic which, I should think, a demon would be ashamed to engage in.

"I tell you, Linnie, the more I come in contact with mankind, the more I see of life, the more I am convinced of the depravity of the race; you may call it total, if you like. And that there is a wicked, malignant spirit, full of all manner of evil, and cruel as death, is just as plain to my mind as that there is a God.

"There is our hope. There is a God, perfect in all his attributes; infinite in power, as well as holiness. Some time he will overthrow this whole scheme of wickedness, and cause that truth and justice shall prevail."

He paused a moment, and then said, "I called on Stillman, and talked as kindly as I could, and made about as much impression on him as I should in talking to a worm. But I'll have it yet; see if I don't."

"What do you refer to, dear?" said his wife.

"Why, the liquor law. It has got to come, let them rage as much as they please."

"Then you think it will be passed?"

"Yes, I do. It may not this year, but it must eventually. The right must prevail. Lucy, you had better stay in the parlor, and help the children along. Keep them at play, and see that no one slights Lottie Gray or Winnie Lentell; that is a good girl."

"I think I shall go in, too," said Mrs. Trueman; "and we can keep them busy — can't we, Lucy?"

"Yes, mother, I shall like it, if you go; I'm afraid they wouldn't mind me."

"Lucy," said Mrs. Trueman, "several of the little girls are coming; wait on them into the nursery. Let us be careful not to slight any, nor make 'lions' of them, but treat them as nearly alike as possible. But if any among them seem bashful, or sad, or timid, we must take extra pains to make them feel at ease. They are our guests, you know."

"Yes, mother, I'll remember. I have noticed how you manage."

There was a little reserve at first; Lottie Gray was painfully embarrassed, though very well dressed, thanks to Mrs. Stillman. She saw Clara whisper to Regena Steele, and felt sure she was telling her, "That is my dress," &c. She shrank away in one corner, and wished she was at home. But Lucy's quick eye detected the trouble in a moment, and she took vigorous measures to remedy the evil.

"Come, girls," said she, "let us play 'Button.' Who will go round first? Well, I will begin at Clara. Susie, you and Winnie come over here and sit by Lottie; she is a little stranger to most of us. I am glad you could come to-day, Lottie; mother wants you to get acquainted."

"Choose me for your judge," whispered Lucy to Winnie and Lottie. They did so, and she was sure to make their penalties as light as could be, so that they need not feel embarrassed.

"O, you are having a nice time," said Mrs. Trueman. "When you are tired of that, you can play 'Hunt the squirrel.' You all know how to play it, I presume."

"O, that will be nice," said Susie. "Come, Winnie and Lottie."

"Suppose you stay and hide the squirrel, Regena," said Lucy.

And so the plays "Hunt the squirrel," "Dress the lady," "Magic music," &c., went on briskly till nearly tea time. Then Mrs. Trueman played and sang.

Lottie entirely forgot herself and her misfortunes. She had a natural passion for music, and a fine voice. But the supper — that surpassed anything she had ever seen.

Mrs. Trueman was amused to see her give a quick glance of pleased surprise, and then apparently remain as unobservant as those always accustomed to such things. Evidently she was learning.

"The party was an entire success, Lucy," said Mrs. Trueman. "I was pleased with you — very much so; and Susie, here, was a very good girl. I think our visitors were pleased with us, too, with themselves, and with each other."

"That is the greatest possible compliment to their entertainers," said Mr. Trueman, smiling. "You both look as if you needed rest. I think you have spent the afternoon profitably. It is a grand, a noble work, to help bring out and cultivate the affections of the young, and promote a friendly, cheerful, loving spirit among them.

There is where our forefathers failed; don't you think so, Linnie?"

"Yes, I think that was one of their greatest mistakes. The emotional nature was sometimes smothered by the sterner qualities, and life robbed of half its beauty and brightness. But I fear the next generation will go to the other extreme."

CHAPTER XV.

Making Calls here and there.

We will take a peep at Mr. and Mrs. Stillman. They are at breakfast. The table looks inviting, but the faces around it sorrowful, or forbidding.

John's name is seldom spoken there; but he is often thought of — with painful forebodings by the mother; with undefined fears by the sister. Mr. Stillman was absorbed, most of the time, in his *lawful calling* — dealing out liquid poison — taking just enough to drown the still small voice within. John had shown himself so apt a scholar, and seemed so mature in wickedness, made the golden profits of the rum casks disappear so strangely, that Mr. Stillman thought the safest course was to send him to a reform school.

"Well, Maria," said Mr. Stillman, "so you have taken up the hatchet, and mean to withstand me — do you? We'll see. You shall go looking decently, or not go at all."

"I should like to see you prevent it," she said, defiantly; "but as to decency, I think I dress far more decently now than I have done in the past, considering," — bending over towards him, and fixing her eyes steadily upon his face, speaking very slowly and impressively, — "considering where the money comes from. Isn't it so, Kidder? I tell you, if an angel should engage in that business, it would make a demon of him after a while. Well, it is no use to talk; while you continue in that business you are nothing to me but a shame. The sooner I die the better for me."

"And for me, too," said the enraged husband, mockingly.

Ah, well, you have seen enough of this family to give you an insight into their lives. Maria was right in her opposition. She was fighting on the right side, and against the common enemy.

Let us go with her to Mr. Gray's. She has been there before since the awful tragedy we have mentioned. She was met at first suspiciously. Was she not the wife of the man who had blighted their lives, blasted all their happiness? Why had she come? To look at their poverty and destitution? They were both embarrassed.

"I called," she said, "to see if I could not do something for you."

She broke down, and wept. That was after the funeral. Those tears opened the bleeding hearts of the family; they wept together, and then talked it all over, and from that day were fast friends. As she heard Mr. Gray's honest, manly statement of facts, she was mortified, distressed, and indignant, in turn. O, what a revelation that was to her!

"This distresses you," said Mr. Gray. "I will stop; it will do no good."

"Yes, it will," was the reply; "I ought to know it. It seems like some awful story I have read; and yet all this has happened at my very door. How could I have been kept in ignorance? So poor Mrs. Gray inherited one of those morbid appetites for such things. You told Mr. Stillman of her weakness, and yet he —" She remained silent a few moments, and then continued: " I shall do what I can to repair the injury; but I cannot raise the dead. But as fast as I can, I shall buy back the articles of furniture, and return them to you. The looking-glass is in my spare chamber, I should think, by your description."

"O," said Mr. Gray, much affected, "I cannot ask, or expect, that. If you will be a friend to my children, and show Lottie a little about housekeeping, it will be a great kindness."

"That I will do with pleasure; and if you won't be offended, I have garments, which my children have outgrown, that I should like to bring over."

"Persons in our circumstances must conquer their pride," was the reply. "We should be glad of them."

As Mrs. Stillman left the house, she thrust a little wad of something into Lottie's hand, and disappeared.

Lottie spread it out.

"Ten dollars!" she exclaimed. "What does she mean, father? Why, she has made a mistake."

"I guess not, my daughter; God has put it in her heart to give it. This will enable me to pay for the coffin and the shroud, dear."

Mr. Gray sighed deeply as he thought of the past; a tear crept very silently down his prematurely wrinkled cheek as he took the wife's offering, and went on thinking thoughts which cut and lacerated his soul whichever way he turned them. O, sometimes God cannot bestow a greater blessing than forgetfulness; and sometimes it is inexpressibly blessed to remember. Mrs. Stillman proved invaluable to the afflicted family.

To-day, as she left her house to call on them, — a bag of sugar, tea, and other necessaries on her arm, a large, gilt mirror in them, — her tall form looked queenly, in spite of last year's cloak and bonnet. She did not do this stealthily, but openly and by much personal sacrifice.

"Father thanks you, and we all thank you very much for the money," said Lottie, meeting her at the door. "It helped him pay for mother's coffin and things."

"Don't mention it, dear child, to me or any one. I wish it had been ten times as much. I am only doing for you what I ought to do; and yet I cannot undo the past," she said, mournfully.

"O, don't feel so badly, dear Mrs. Stillman," said Lottie, affectionately; "you didn't do it; we don't blame you."

Mrs. Stillman was weeping; she must speak to some one, or her heart would break. She looked up into the sweet, pitying face of the child before her, and said, —

"Lottie, you cannot understand how much this terrible business of liquor selling has cost me. It has robbed your poor father of that which was very dear; it has killed your mother and the baby, and stripped your house of every comfort; and when I think who furnished it, I tremble; for there is an avenging God."

"O, but father says God loves and pities us, too," said Lottie. "He forgives us when we are sorry. I know he loves you, Mrs. Stillman, you are so good to us. Father prays for you every day, and asks him to lead you into the kingdom of grace, and give you rest."

"Dear Lottie," said Mrs. Stillman, taking her hand, "you comfort me. If your father can pray for me, I surely ought to pray for myself. You think I am much better off than you are — don't you?"

"Why, yes, I thought so," was the reply. "Your house is nice, and you have everything — don't you?"

Mrs. Stillman smiled sadly as she replied, —

"Yes, I have a great many beautiful things; but these cannot make us happy. I have been robbed as much as you have, dear, but not in the same way. O, I would change places with you this moment, if I could."

Lottie was perplexed.

"Your mother loved you to the last — did she not?"

"O, yes; when she was sober she loved us; she was never cross."

"And your father is an honest Christian man; that is much to be thankful for. But how are you getting along? Can I help you about anything to-day?"

"Father told me to ask you how I should cook this veal."

Lottie listened attentively, like one determined to profit by instruction.

"It is a real pleasure to instruct you," said Mrs. Stillman, "you are so teachable. You must come over when you want advice; looking after you is one of the greatest comforts of my life."

"I am glad," said the simple-hearted child; "for I don't know what I should do if you didn't help me."

"I hadn't thought of that before," mused Mrs. Stillman, as she went to her home of plenty — of everything but peace and comfort. "I never thought of that. God is a loving, pitying Father, as well as a just, avenging Judge. O, yes, Jesus was a man of sorrows, and acquainted with grief. I cannot live so. I wonder what Lottie thought of me. Dear child, she cannot know how awful it is to have the heart's best treasures stolen, and the soul stripped of love and respect for one's companion in life, and filled with contempt and scorn. Truly, I have seen my idol shattered, my poor boy ruined, and my pleasant things laid waste. Lord, pity me!"

Now that Mrs. Stillman has turned her thoughts heavenward, let us leave her, and call at Mr. Trueman's. Mrs. Trueman, Lucy, and Susie are preparing for a walk. They look odd enough with their baskets, bundles, and pails — all they can possibly carry. Lucy laughed heartily as she surveyed the company.

"I chose evening," said Mrs. Trueman, "because it would look ostentatious to carry all this in the daytime, and injure their feelings. In assisting the poor and needy, we should do it as delicately as possible; otherwise it will leave a sense of shame and degradation which is injurious to proper self-respect. We will wait a moment for papa; he would not miss going. He will take that bundle of clothing for Mr. Gray and Albert. Lucy, you may take Lottie's new dress and cape; Susie, the bonnet and gloves. I want her to forget her sorrow as much as possible. She is a noble little girl; these new things will make her think of our love and respect."

"Walter wants something — take it," grieved the child. "Walter wants to go, too."

"Darling child," said mamma, stooping and kissing him; "he cannot go with mamma to-night. Father will let us ride some day with him, and we will call and see the little girl and her brother Albert; that will do — won't it, darling?"

"Next day — to-morrow — mamma," said the child, pleasantly, "Walter and mamma go to ride with papa. That do, mamma."

"God is blessing us far beyond our deserts," said Mr. Gray. "Let us thank him for his goodness in the past, and trust him in the future, my children."

The Trueman family returned home that night realizing fully that "it is more blessed to give than to receive."

CHAPTER XVI.

The Separation. — The Aged Christian's Death-bed.

Wallace came bounding into the room one day, saying, —

"See, auntie, see! Albert and I have found these," holding up some trailing arbutus.

"O, yes," said Hester, "that looks like spring — doesn't it?"

" O, dear me!" said Sunshine; " dey's my 'ittle sweet springs! O, funny, funny!"

"I didn't want to see them," said Winnie, timidly.

"Didn't you, dear? Why not?" said Hester, who guessed the reason.

"Why, they say things, auntie; everything talks to me."

"Why, dese don't talk," said Sunshine; "don't you love my springs?"

"What do they say?" said Hester. "Tell auntie about it."

"O, they say, 'Winnie, it is May now; you must go to aunt Elevia's, and leave auntie and Wallace, Elida and baby.'"

"What else talks?" said Wallace.

"Everything; the chimney on the large house away over the woods talks, too. It looks like papa's house, where grandma Lentell lives."

"What do it say?" said Elida, with wondering eyes.

"She means that these things remind her of other things, or make her remember them," said Hester. "My dear child, you must not let things talk to you so much; that is, you must not look at things that make you feel unhappy — remind you of unpleasant events. But you must look at things that remind you of the goodness of God and the kindness of friends."

"What things are those?" said Wallace.

"Why, little brother and sisters, the nice presents from grandpa, and kind Mr. Trueman's folks," said Hester.

"And at my darling dear auntie," said Winnie, cheerfully. "If I could always look at you, auntie, things wouldn't talk so sadly to me. But this baby almost always makes me think of mamma. And then I think how papa, and mamma, and Elida, all went down to grandpa Lovering's, in the winter before mamma died; and how they were coming home that very night, but a great big snow came, and the wind blew, and piled it all up so they couldn't get home for one, two, three — four days, wasn't it, Wallace? And we hadn't anything but potatoes to eat, for papa left us with grandma Lentell till he came home; but aunt Abigail and grandma acted so we wouldn't stay. We ran home in the snow before night, for we thought they'd come; but they didn't. O, it was such a long night! Wallace went to sleep, but I couldn't; for I thought papa and mamma would get into the deep snow, in the dark; and when the wind made a noise, I thought it was them. O, dear, dear! it makes me shiver now."

"What did grandma do, that you disliked so much?" said Hester.

"Why, she said I looked like the Loverings too much; and when I said, 'No, I thank you,' she and Abigail laughed so loud, and said, 'That's Lovering all over.' And they kept doing so, and saying my mamma was slack, until I was just as mad!"

"I wouldn't say 'mad,' dear," said Hester; "you felt indignant, I suppose; I should, I am sure."

"Yes, that was the way I felt; and I told Wallace we would run home when they didn't know it, and stay till the folks came."

"Did any one come to see where you were?"

"Yes, uncle Simeon came, just before it was dark, and wanted us to go home with him. I said I couldn't, for grandma didn't love us. He laughed, and said I was a little goose to mind her, for she didn't love anybody. But I couldn't go; I thought they'd come. He said he'd stay, but mother would storm worse than the snow if he did. So the next day after one he came and brought us something in a pail, and said, 'Mother says you deserve to starve for running home; but she has sent you something, little spunk.' I was real glad; for I thought, now we'll have some nice doughnuts, or pancakes, or pie, or something good. So I got a tin pan to put them in, and he just took out some dry pieces of bread, most all crust, and some pieces of cheese. Uncle Simeon said an awful thing then, auntie; he said she was 'a mean old cuss.'"

"My dear children," said Hester, "I dislike to have you repeat such language. You will try to avoid it in the future — won't you? Didn't you have anything but potatoes all that time?"

"O, yes, auntie; at first there was some bread and meat; but we ate that up pretty soon."

10

"What did your father say, when he came?"

"Why, he"—Winnie hesitated—"why, he said just as uncle Simeon did."

"Did he say *old tuss?*" said Elida.

"There," said Hester, "you see how quickly the little ones catch such words. So you must be careful not to speak them."

"Yes," said Winnie, "I will. But after father went over there, he said she served us right; we ought to have staid where he left us. They brought lots of nice things from grandpa Lovering's. I was glad I was like them, for I think they are the best—don't you, auntie?"

"Yes, dear, I do; and I like to have you resemble them, for I love them very much."

After a few moments' silence, Winnie said,—

"How long is a year, auntie?"

"It is twelve months, darling."

"Well, how many weeks are there in a year?"

"Fifty-two."

"O, that is a great many," sighed Winnie. "Well, how many days, auntie?"

"Three hundred and—"

"O, auntie, don't say any more. It never will be over."

"Of what are you thinking now, dear?"

"Why, I am to stay with aunt Elevia a year; and it is so very long."

Hester saw her mistake in specifying any time in the child's hearing. She hardly knew what to say. She reflected a moment, and then said, cheerfully,—

"Perhaps they won't want you so long, or perhaps you will want to stay always. There come your uncle and aunt this moment. Now, see what a brave little girl you can be."

Winnie turned pale, and Hester herself felt strangely agitated. She, too, had to be brave. When Winnie was prepared to go, she went in to take leave of grandpa Manlie's family.

"God bless you, my dear little girl," said grandpa, "and keep you, and bring you into the kingdom at last."

Grandma laid her hand on the child's head, prayed silently for a moment, and then said,—

"Kiss me, little Winnie, good by."

"You must come and see us often," said Martha, striving to hide her emotion. Something in her mother's voice and manner affected her. Winnie kissed the children, calling the baby many pet names; but when she came to Hester, she threw her arms convulsively around her neck, overcome with suppressed emotion.

Hester allowed her to weep a few moments, simply drawing her close to her bosom, and motioning the others to be silent. She then led her into another room, and said,—

"Our Father in heaven has ordered it so, darling. He knows what is best for us — don't you think so?"

"Yes, auntie; but I am so wicked I can't get near enough to him. He is away off. And Jesus is good, and wants to comfort me; but I am so naughty I want to stay with you, — I love you best, — or go to mamma. I wish I could love Jesus best."

Hester talked very kindly to the child, and then, kneeling down by her, prayed that God would bless little Winnie, and forgive her sins for Jesus' sake; that the Blessed Spirit would teach her to be good and happy —

teach her to cast all her sorrows upon Jesus, who loved her and died to redeem her. "Dear Father," she prayed, "wilt thou pity and love her, and help her to love and trust in thee!—Now, dear," said she, "I want you to promise me that you won't talk with things that make you sad, but when you are lonesome and feel badly, go and tell Jesus. He alone can make you happy. He will draw you so near to him that you will feel safe. Good by, dear—be brave."

When Winnie had left the room, grandma said, with a smile on her wrinkled face,—

"Martha, it is the last time. I shan't see her here again. I shall take that kiss to Harmony and Mary soon."

Grandpa arose, went to the bed where she had been lying several weeks, took her hand as tenderly as he had taken it more than sixty years before, when he said, "Mary, will you be mine—take me for better and for worse?" and said,—

"Mary, are you tired? Are you going home to leave me? O, Mary, I hoped we should go together—can't we?" bursting into tears.

"Sit down near me, father; I want to talk about this. I have been lingering on the shore some time; I wasn't willing to go over alone, dear. I have waited for you. We have travelled a long, long way together, and the road has been rough sometimes; sickness and death have met us on the way; but you have been true, dear—true as the needle to the pole, and kind as a mother could be to the child at her breast.

'We have borne each other's sorrows,
And shared each other's joys,'—

haven't we, dear? Don't weep so; it will break my heart. It is only a little while and you will be called; Jesus will come over with you. Martha will be a tender nurse, dear; comfort her when I am gone. She will miss us less if we go one at a time. By and by we shall all get home. Glory be to God and the Lamb!"

"But, mother," said Martha, "what shall we do without you? What makes you think you are going? You were as feeble as this last spring. O, we can't spare you."

"O, yes, you can, child: 'As thy day, so shall thy strength be.' God will support you: hasn't he always? Are you not willing I should enter into rest, my child? I shall have an abundant entrance. I hear my Saviour calling, and I long to go. Remember that 'he doeth all things well,' and bless the hand that leads me to my Father's house."

The voice faltered; she fell into a gentle, quiet sleep, never speaking again on earth. She lingered several days, knew them, and smiled faintly when they talked to her of Jesus and heaven. She motioned Hester to sing, and looked serenely happy while she sang, —

> "'What's this that steals, that steals upon me now?
> Is it death? is it death?
> If this be death, I soon shall be
> From every sin and sorrow free;
> I shall the King of Glory see!
> All is well! all is well!'"

Grandpa said but little. He sat by the bed, holding the faded hand as if it had been an infant's, kissing the wrinkled cheek reverently. Thus they waited and watched, cheering each other by speaking of the better land.

"O, Hester," said Martha, leaning on her broad shoulder, "you comfort and sustain me in this trying hour. I would not hold her back, but I dread to have her go."

"You will be willing when the time comes," said Hester. "But we must restrain our grief for grandpa's sake," she whispered. "Their souls are so knit together that when one is loosed the other will feel it deeply. I fear for him."

O, how eagerly he watched the flickering light! placed his trembling finger on the feeble pulse! He groaned a deep, inward groan when the light went out and the pulses stopped.

"Rejoice," said Hester; "she is with the angels! Rejoice; she has entered into rest! The Lord reigneth; he doeth all things well. Let us pray."

She stepped lightly, she walked softly with God, praying that the Spirit might indite her petitions, comfort and heal these bleeding hearts. They were comforted and sustained, and blessed anew the Father of all mercies for giving them Hester Strong.

CHAPTER XVII.

THE NEW HOME AND ITS TRIALS. — MR. WILEY'S FAMILY.

"THIS is a much more desirable home, Winnie, than the one you have left," said Mr. Giles. "I hope you will try to deserve it, and be so obedient and industrious that I shall be willing to let you stay. It isn't every destitute child that is so fortunate. Don't you think this is a nice house?" he inquired. "Were you ever in one like it before?"

Winnie was embarrassed; grandpa Manlie's old-fashioned house was much more desirable to her. She was longing for the dear home left, its dusky walls, and the dear faces around the capacious hearth.

"I think this is a pretty house," she said, timidly; "it is something like the one papa built."

Mr. Giles gave a low whistle, and remarked to his wife, —

"She's got the Lovering pride; will never be grateful, do what you will for her."

"Gratitude is a rare virtue," said Elevia, quietly; it thrives best in an atmosphere of unselfish love. I think my dear little niece has proved conclusively that she has a loving, grateful heart. I shouldn't wish to have her manifest more feeling, than she did when leaving Hester."

"She had better have staid with her, then, in that dingy old house. I dare say it is more like home to her than this," was the cutting reply. Winnie turned red, then pale, as she thought, —

"Then *they* don't want me, either."

Elevia read her thoughts. Calling her into the nursery, where Unie was sleeping, she gave her a pretty, entertaining book to read, and requested her to sit by baby and keep her asleep. She returned to the room where her husband was sitting, went up to him, and spoke his name softly, but sadly.

"What now?" was the ungracious reply; "another scene? I am sick of them."

"I don't wish for another scene," was the reply; "the one on hand is to be my theme. I am sorry you should wound the child's feelings so. I told you before she came, that I should not let her come to be abused. She had far better go to the workhouse. I told you I would try to get along with her assistance, if you would treat her kindly. Otherwise, she shall not stay and you will be under the necessity of hiring help."

"Whew!" said Mr. Giles. "That is rule No. 4 — isn't it? First, I am to treat you just the same at home as abroad, alone and in company. A capital joke! Then I am to give you money to keep by you, without asking you to account for it. Good! Then I am to replenish the family larder without comment — that's it, I believe. And now I am to treat a beggar like a princess. Am I correct, Lev?"

Mr. Giles whistled "Moll Brooks," &c. Elevia stood there waiting, very calmly, to all appearance, but her heart beat painfully.

"Mason," she said, choking down her emotion, "you treat these things lightly. I, at least, am serious and in earnest. I was never more so in my life. I cannot, and I will not, bear these insults. I shall not live a year in this way; and on my own account I do not wish to."

"You needn't live on my account," was the mocking reply. "Don't, I beg of you. There are plenty of handsome girls waiting and wishing to become Mrs. Giles second; so don't put yourself out." He laughed as only such persons can laugh.

"Defeated again," sighed Elevia. "O God, there is nothing left for me but misery or death. But that child's life shall not be blasted in this house. I might have known it would be so. Why could he not have told me frankly that he should treat her like a bond-girl, before she came? I told him I should receive her as a beloved child, and that he must not go for her unless he was willing to do the same. He made no objections. How foolish I am to expect anything better of him!"

Winnie laid the pretty book in her lap unread. She was thinking. Child as she was, what she had seen and heard in her new home filled her with sadness. She felt that this would never, never seem like home. She felt sure her aunt was not happy, and wondered why it was. Her house was very nice, and all the things in it were new and beautiful. Her mind was sorely perplexed. She did not think it strange her uncle did not want her; no one did; and the old wish to die and go to mamma came back with overpowering force. She began to weep violently. Baby stirred; she stifled the bitter sobs nobly, saying, —

"O, dear! I am always doing something. There, I

mustn't cry now; it will wake the baby. To-night, when they are all asleep, I'll cry. No, I guess I will tell Jesus about it; auntie said I must. O, mother, mother," she cried, "your little girl is sad."

Thus Winnie rocked the cradle, and talked with her own thoughts, till baby awoke. This was the longest half day she had ever seen.

"Three hundred and sixty-four and a half more of them!" she mused, clasping her small hands tightly. Mrs. Giles exerted herself very much to banish the unfavorable impressions of the afternoon from Winnie's mind, and partially succeeded. She went to her room with her when she retired.

"You shall go to see aunt Hester and the children every week," she said, "and carry the milk over to Mr. Wiley's every pleasant morning. Envena is about your age."

"Who is Mr. Wiley?" inquired Winnie.

"O, he married your uncle Mason's sister. They live in the large white house over there," pointing in the direction.

"Please, what dress shall I put on in the morning, auntie?"

"O, your red one, I guess, for you are a stranger in this neighborhood." Winnie was pleased with the novelty of carrying the milk, and wondered what they would say to her, till her aunt took the light, kissed her, and said good night.

Now, she was left up stairs alone for the first time in her life. She had nearly always fallen asleep amid the hum of voices, or while listening to mother or aunt Hester singing to the children. A feeling of indescribable loneliness, amounting to fear, crept over her. She covered her face.

"I didn't pray," she whispered, "that is the reason I feel so. But I am afraid to get up in the dark. I wonder if God won't hear me if I pray in bed." She crawled away down under the clothes, listening for she knew not what. Remembering that her mother prayed when she was so very sick, and that she seemed easier afterwards, Winnie resolved to pray. She tried to think of the words aunt Hester used in the morning, but could not. "O God, my Father in heaven," was all she could say for some time. This she repeated over and over, with sobs and tears. "Dear Jesus, I am a poor little girl that nobody wants, because there are so many of us. Do, Jesus, let me go to mamma; there is room there. O, let me come to you, dear Jesus; let me come to you. Help me to submit." Thus she prayed and wept, until, relieved, she fell asleep.

O, ye of little faith, can ye not believe that Jesus, the loving, pitying Jesus, sent the Comforter to that lonely, suffering one, in answer to that feeble, broken prayer? Verily so it was. Winnie arose, with a calm, peaceful feeling, in the morning. She did not forget to thank God for all his goodness, and ask him to give her a new heart.

"O, I know now what my Father in heaven wants of me," she mused. "He wants me to comfort aunt Elevia, she is so sad. I guess her husband don't love her much. She looks like my dear mamma. She used to fold me in her arms, and say, 'You are mother's comfort, darling.' How happy that used to make me! Nothing can ever make me very happy again, I think; but aunt Hester says I shall be happier than ever before, when this cloud passes over, if I trust in Jesus, and live to make others happy.

"Dear Jesus, I want to love you more, and trust you, and be like you. Won't you teach me, and help me to do right?— O, I forgot to ask God to bless anybody but myself." She knelt again, to invoke the blessing of God upon the dear ones at home, not forgetting her earthly parent, and then hurried down to see what she could do for her aunt.

"I must look cheerful," she thought. "Aunt Hester says that is one way to do good."

Mrs. Giles met her with a kind good morning, inquired how she had rested, &c.; but Winnie saw at a glance that she was sad and weary; so she did not say, "What can I do for you?" but looked sharp to see where she was most needed. Baby was sitting in the cradle, reaching out its arms to its weary mother, and moaning piteously. Winnie was a skilful little general in baby tactics; so she took advantage of her position, and very soon baby forgot its aching teeth, and was having a nice frolic.

Mamma forgot her weariness as she listened to the jubilant children. The breakfast was ready in season, and Mr. Giles was at a loss to find fault with anything. His wife began to take courage.

"Elevia, I think you use more coffee than you need to. Now, it isn't a mite better for being too strong. I have told you so a great many times. I do wish you would pay attention to what I say. Coffee costs money." He waited for a reply. Elevia was silent.

"Why don't you answer me?" he inquired, indignantly.

"What was your question?" was the reply; "I heard none."

"There it comes, the real Lovering pride and stubbornness. I say the coffee is too strong."

"Yes, I heard you say that. I have heard you say it several times lately. Day before yesterday it was too weak. About half the time it is too weak, and the other half too strong; and yet for the last few weeks I have been particular to put in just the quantity you specified. Now, if you will tell me just how much less to put in, I will try to suit you. But I tell you plainly that I will not submit to so much unreasonable fault-finding."

Elevia broke down, as she always did; and the tears came trickling slowly down her cheeks, which were really very pale and thin.

"O, well, you needn't cry; I am used to that," was the insulting reply. "Your tears move me about as much as your threats. You 'will not submit;' 'will not'—that is getting to be a common expression with you. I should like to know what you will do about it. If a man can't have his way in his own house, where upon earth can he? If a man can't be master in his own family, he isn't a man."

"I agree with you, Mr. Giles. I never objected to your being master here." She spoke calmly, looking him steadily in the face. "I claim to be the mistress in this house; if I am not, what am I? You didn't *buy* me of my father—did you?"

"No; but I wish I had," was the cool reply. "I would break that stubborn will, or *worse* than that," with a look so full of bitter scorn and hate, that Winnie became alarmed. Thus the meal ended, and Mr. Giles went to his daily labor, much to her relief. She pitied her aunt more than ever, and sought for opportunities to cheer and help her; wishing all the time that she could tell her of Jesus, and the way to be happy.

"Now you can go and carry the milk to Mr. Wiley's," said her aunt, "and invite Envena to come over this afternoon, and go out a little while with you to search for May-flowers. Should you like to?"

"Yes, auntie, very much; but you are almost sick. I should rather stay and play with Unic, and let you rest." Elevia was so unused to kindness or consideration recently, that this thoughtfulness affected her. She stooped and kissed the upturned mouth, saying,—

"You are a darling child; auntie loves you very much."

"That sounds like my mamma," said Winnie, smiling through the tears which just then sprang unbidden to her eyes. "I am glad you love me, and I want you to tell me of it a good many times, because I forget; and I am so naughty, I think nobody can love me much. Aunt Hester says everybody loves me, and I think they do; but I shouldn't think they could. But there is somebody else I want you to love, auntie," she said, timidly.

"Who is it, dear? Aunt Hester and the children? I love them ever so much."

"No, auntie; I want you to love our Father in heaven, and Jesus. Mother used to call him the sinner's Friend. She loved him, and I am trying to love him; and to-day I think he loves me. I feel as if I just wanted him to take my hand and lead me; and when I cry, I would love to have him wipe the tears away, as mamma did; and when I am sick, I want to lay my head on his bosom and rest. God don't seem so far off as he did. O, auntie, do you think I have really found him?"

"I hope so, dear; I should think so. How long have you felt in that way?"

"O, only this morning. Last night I felt so bad I wanted to die; but I was afraid of God, and so I prayed as fast as I could, and by and by I felt better, and began to say mamma's hymn, —

'Jesus, Lover of my soul,
Let me to thy bosom fly.'

It seemed to me as if he did open his arms wide, and I crept in, and didn't feel alone. And then I went to sleep, and never waked up till morning. And this morning I feel so different I don't want to go to mamma, but stay to comfort you. Mamma is just as happy as she can be without us — isn't she, auntie?"

Elevia hardly knew what to say.

"O that I, too, could find Jesus!" she thought. "I need him. Perhaps this darling child has come to lead me to him."

"Yes, dear," she replied, "I think your mother is supremely happy, and I believe you have become a Christian, one of Christ's little ones. I hope it is so; and now you shall be my teacher."

"O, not your teacher, auntie; the Holy Spirit must be your Teacher; mother used to say so, and auntie Hester says so. Let me be your comforter; that is what mother called me." Winnie thought, as she tripped lightly along, —

"'Tis beautiful out here. I never was in such a lovely place before. The willows are so pretty, shaking their leaves in the sun! How fresh the grass is! it looks as if God had kissed it in the night. I guess the birdies love him better than they did, they sing so sweetly. I wonder if I can sing any better than I could before. I'll sing aunt Hester's hymn : —

'Rejoice! rejoice! the promised day is coming;
Rejoice! rejoice! the wilderness shall bloom,'"

sang the youthful disciple, with great satisfaction, little thinking that the change, the beautiful, sublime change, was in her own soul, wrought there by the transforming grace of God.

"Aunt Elevia, let me bring the milk this morning," said Winnie, when Mr. Wiley had opened the door.

"Well, come in," was the reply. "Envena has been wanting to come over and see you. "Here, Venie, here is the little girl you are so curious to see. She looks like any other child — don't she?" Envena received her very cordially, smiled, and said many pleasant things. She praised her hair, wished hers was as pretty; praised her dress, and wished she could have one like it. Winnie was delighted with her new friend. She longed to tell her of Jesus, but dared not. She invited her to come over and play with her and the baby, after dinner.

"I should like to come," said Envena, as she walked a little piece with Winnie; " but I shouldn't think my aunt Elevia would keep you cooped up in the house this pleasant day. I run out of doors all the time; it is more healthy."

"O, she wants me to go out; but she is almost sick, and I'd rather stay in and tend the baby."

"She isn't very sick," said Envena, in a soft, loving tone; "I wouldn't wait upon her, if I were you; but perhaps you are used to working hard, and don't care to play. Did your father buy that dress for you? My father is able, but mother says he is stingy. O, now I've hurt your feelings. I'm sorry; forgive me — wont you? I am real glad you have come to live here; we can go to school together, and have nice times."

Winnie brightened up; she didn't like some things her new friend had said; but she was so pleasant, so gentle and affectionate, that she was, on the whole, quite sure she was a good little girl, and didn't mean any harm.

CHAPTER XVIII.

The Good Shepherd's Watchfulness. — The Disclosure. — The Burial.

Winnie was beginning to feel quite at home in her uncle's house. She had something to do; she was needed. Mrs. Giles was becoming so feeble that her time was all occupied in useful, loving labor. She saw Envena daily; was fascinated with her, she was so thoughtful, so tender, and loving; but somehow there was a little tinge of unhappiness left in her mind after every interview — something of regret or mortification — — something which made her feel that her lot was hard, that her aunt was just the least bit to be blamed for something, that the baby was troublesome, &c. And so the child-Christian had to flee to Christ often, and on her bended knees, with clasped hands, beseech him to give her a submissive heart. She remembered aunt Hester's motto — "Submission to God is a sure and safe passport to peace and happiness." And the good Shepherd, true to his promise, always gave her an answer of peace, and extracted the little poison arrows which had been so naturally and skilfully sent into her sensitive soul by one perfectly qualified by nature and education to deceive and wound without disgusting or alienating the victim.

Elevia saw daily new evidence that Winnie was indeed a Christian. She herself felt an indescribable yearning after something to lean upon — some place to rest — a refuge from the storms of life. Both mind and body were weak; she could not grasp the strong, safe anchor of hope which was just in sight. She was faint and weary with the conflict in her own soul, and the unjust treatment of her husband.

The week had passed, yet Winnie had not visited or heard from her old home. She was longing to go and tell them what Christ had done for her; but her aunt seemed so unwell and sad, that she was not willing to leave her.

Just then grandpa Lovering drove up to the door. She was delighted, for "now," she thought, "I shall hear all about them, and he will see how sick and unhappy auntie is, and he will do something for her.

"O, grandpa," she exclaimed, rushing out to meet him, "I am so glad you've come! Auntie is sick, and I am so different! I want to tell you."

"Why," said he, in surprise, "is Elevia sick? I saw Mason yesterday; he did not speak of it. But what has come over my little girl?" taking her hand and starting for the house.

"O, I am a great deal happier than I was. I hope I have learned to submit. God is very near, and I love him. I don't want to go to mamma. Jesus is my Saviour, and I want to serve him here."

Tears came into grandpa's eyes as he patted the upturned cheek and said, —

"I thank God that my little Winnie has chosen that better part, which shall not be taken from her."

He was grieved to see Elevia looking so pale and thin, so weary and hopeless.

"Elevia, child, come here and sit on father's knee; perhaps it will do us both good. How long have you been so weak, dear? Does Mason know how ill you are? I inquired yesterday; he said you were well."

"O, father, father," sobbed Elevia, overcome by those few tender words, "take me home with you. O, take me somewhere; I cannot breathe here. *He* hates me; he has told me so, many, many times."

Mr. Lovering folded his strong arms around the shrinking wife, and said, —

"If that is true, my daughter, you shall go. Thank God, I have a home for you. But you are sick and sensitive — nervous, perhaps. Poor child, you need your mother. What a loss she was to us all! There, lie on father's breast; I know it isn't as soft as hers, but it is *true*, Levie."

She wept on. Now that the gates were open, it was hard to close them.

"Impossible," mused grandpa, aloud, "impossible. How pleasant he seemed yesterday! and yet I have felt at times that all was not quite right. Winnie, don't you think uncle Mason loves my little Levie here, and means to be kind to her?"

"I don't know what he does mean, grandpa," was the simple, honest reply; "but he don't act as if he loved her. He scolds awfully when he is alone with her, and doesn't behave a bit good. He pushed her this morning because she couldn't fix his collar right."

Mr. Lovering was shocked and confounded by the child's reply. He could not speak for several moments. He then said, —

"What did your aunt say, Winnie?"

"O, she cried, and went up stairs. Uncle Mason was real pleasant to me when she was gone; said I was beautiful, and could do things better than my aunt. He tried to give me some raisins, but I couldn't take them, I felt so; and then he went out."

"Where is he now?" he inquired. "I must see and converse with him. But I came to carry you over to mother Manlie's funeral."

"Why, is she dead?" asked Elevia and Winnie in a breath.

"Yes; didn't Mason tell you? I asked him to bring you, but he said his engagements were such that he could not; so I concluded to come myself."

"He didn't mention it," said Elevia, forgetting to weep. "Poor grandfather and aunt Martha, how they will miss her!"

"Yes," was the reply, "but Hester is there, like a tower of strength for them to lean on; and they have an Almighty Friend, who sticketh closer than a brother, you know. O, my daughter, why will you not make him your Friend also? You need religion; why will you not come to Christ? He will give you rest and peace."

"I am trying, father; but I am so unworthy! I was so thoughtless about these things when I was happy at home; and when I was married, then I thought I was happy enough without religion. I worshipped Mason. But I must see grandma again before they bury her. How often she has tried to lead me to Christ! O, I must see her."

"Do you feel strong enough to go, dear?" asked Mr. Lovering.

"Yes, I think I am. I must go; I want to see Hester and all of them so much."

"Well, my daughter, I think you had better go. I will find Mason and talk with him while you are getting ready."

"O, father, if he knows I have told you anything, how shall I stay here?" she said, with a startled look.

"What, Elevia, *afraid* of your husband! *afraid of him!* Has it come to this? Rest easy, my dear child. I will wait, and be very wise."

Elevia was reassured. Winnie was very quiet and helpful. She anticipated all her aunt's wishes, and did all in her power to help her.

"You are such a comfort, Winnie!" she said; "so different from what I was at your age! I don't know what I should do without you."

Winnie smiled through her tears, feeling amply paid for her efforts.

"I am so glad I can help you!" she said; "it makes me happy. I thought when mamma died I should never be a comfort to anybody again. God is very good, and grandma Manlie has gone to live with him, and before this she has found my sweet mamma. O, they are so joyful up there! I can almost hear them sing. Now mamma will hear from us. I wish, O, I wish she could know I have found the way."

"She will know it, dear; the angels rejoice when sinners repent; she will know it."

Mr. Lovering tried to banish all coldness from his manner when he met his son-in-law, and treat him with cordiality.

"I came over to take your family to the funeral," said

he. "I wish you could go. You forgot to mention it to Elevia."

"Yes, I declare it slipped my mind. Is Levie going? She don't seem well to-day. I am afraid the excitement will be too much for her."

"O, I guess it won't hurt her," said Mr. Lovering, clinching the right hand into his hair. "No, I guess it won't hurt her to go. She looks feeble — very. I fear she is going the way of Harmony and her mother. Have you consulted a physician?"

"No, I haven't; she isn't willing to do anything for herself. She wouldn't take medicine if she had it."

"I think she needs rest more than anything," said Mr. Lovering. "The babe is fretful. If you could bring her, and the baby, and Winnie, over to my house for a few weeks, it would be a good thing. I'm thinking you'll have to hire a nurse soon if you don't."

"O, I have no idea she would be willing to go," was the reply; "and as to hiring help, she preferred the little girl Winnie. I couldn't think of having two."

"O, ah," said Mr. Lovering, almost losing command of himself; "O, I guess she would come if you wished it. But Winnie is to go to school, you remember; that was the condition — wasn't it? You told me your property amounted to fifteen thousand, I believe, when you asked for my daughter. I should think that would enable you to keep help when your wife is sick," he said, in a jocose way. "But I must go; the funeral is at two. Come over; I have an excellent housekeeper now, and have been making some alterations in my house. Judith is rather troublesome, and I have a very summary way of getting along with such folks without quarrelling.

You see, when folks can't live without a perpetual quarrel, they had better be separated — don't you think so?"

"Why, yes, I suppose that is the best way," stammered Mr. Giles.

"Well, I have closed all doors between the two families. O, if I had known how it was I should have saved my wife some vexatious things. I mean to treat Judith well; she has her good qualities, but she is stingy and selfish. Bring Levie over soon. Good by."

There was a great gathering at the funeral; children and grandchildren, friends and neighbors, came to sympathize with the mourners, and pay a last tribute of respect to Mrs. Manlie, who was loved and esteemed for her many virtues. Hester, by common consent, led the aged mourner to the coffin, and supported his tottering steps, in company with the weeping Martha, to the village graveyard, which was close at hand.

"Lean hard as you please, father," she whispered, as they neared the spot, and her eye fell upon a marble slab with this inscription: —

To the Memory of

HORACE L. MANLIE,

Who Died in 1829, Aged 28.

As she stood there waiting, she glanced back for a moment, sighed deeply, and then looked steadily into the future. Faith arose triumphant. She felt like joining in the exultant song of triumph with the redeemed beyond the veil. The harsh rattling of the falling earth upon the coffin disturbed the glorious vision. The aged pilgrim leaned heavily upon her arm. She felt the bowed form shrink and tremble at every grating sound.

"Shall we go?" she whispered. "They are not here — 'dust to dust' — but they are among the angels, and near the throne. O, they cannot come to us; thank God, we can go to them. What a joyful meeting!"

"Hester," said grandpa Manlie, after the funeral, "Horace could not have comforted me, supported my feeble steps, and cared for me, more tenderly than you have. They should have named you 'Comfort.' Let us have but one table, one home, after this. I need you, and Martha needs you."

"It is a great happiness to me," said Hester, "to be able to fill Horace's place to you in a small degree. But won't the children trouble you?"

"No; they will be a blessing. I will keep our room — Mary's and mine — just the same. We will have a common sitting-room — all things common but that room. When I feel like seeing any one in there, I will say so."

Martha joined in his request, and Hester gave a cheerful consent.

"We shan't quarrel," said Martha, "unless Hester claims more than her share of the work."

"Well," said Hester, "you must let me do just all I please. I am *strong*, both by name and nature. But I see another difficulty — Martha will be claiming a full share of the care of the children, and their affections, too."

"The baby is to be my especial charge," said grandpa. "I want to call her 'Mary.'"

"Mary Fostina isn't a bad name," said Hester. "I like it. We will call her that."

It was affecting to witness his watchful tenderness of the little one. Her cradle was admitted to the room of sacred memories. There she took her daily naps undisturbed by noise, and not a fly or mosquito dared approach the little sleeper.

"My Mary!" he spoke it often, and lingered lovingly over the sound. "My Mary!" how he loved to speak it! It became a household word. Winnie and Wallace liked the change; said it looked better spelled on paper — "Mary F. Leutell."

"Write a Mary to my name, too," said Elida; "then you will has two 'ittle sweet springs," alluding to what she had called the May-flowers. "I spects God isn't very dood" she said, sadly, one day.

"What makes you think so?" said Hester.

"'Cause he died poor grandpa's mother, and let the naughty man plant her in the ground. I saw um; it is all dark down there. Will she come up when it is warm, auntie?"

Hester explained the solemn mystery as well as she could, and told her the story of the infant Jesus, which called forth many loving expressions from the affectionate, impulsive child.

"But I's happy 'nuff now, auntie. You tell God, so he won't die me, and send me up to heaven. I's your 'ittle Sunshine; so you couldn't spare me a bit — could you, auntie?" caressing her.

"I love to keep you, darling," said Hester, kissing the soft, fair cheek.

Wallace took his departure for uncle Frank's in high glee.

"It will be splendid to drive the cows and ride the horse to plough, and rake hay, over to uncle Frank's — won't it, auntie? I mean to study hard when I go to school, so as to get into the same class with George next winter."

"I hope you will be a diligent scholar, and a good boy, and enjoy yourself," said Hester. "Perhaps uncle Edward will want you to study medicine with him when you are old enough. Your uncle Horace, you remember, was a doctor. I am pleased with your spending a year at uncle Frank's. Your aunt Emma is a dear, kind woman, and will treat you as she does her own children. O, Wallace, try to please them all, and do not forget that 'thou, God, seest me.'"

CHAPTER XIX.

MORGAN LENTELL, OR THE BROKEN WEB.—THE ACCIDENT.

It is only seven or eight miles from Mr. Maulic's to Mrs. Mehitable Lentell's; just a pleasant ride: let us go. She is weaving most heroically, and talking to herself. Listen.

"O, hum! I wish I knew how about that 'hereafter' that the priest preached about last Sunday. When Nabby gits me there agin, she'll know it; that's all. It's proper warm to-day;" wiping the perspiration from the wrinkled brow. "But if that sermon is true, I hain't seen the wust on't yet. Hum, hum! I wish I was as innocent as I was when I stole that letter from the office, an' laid awake all night to cut an' contrive how to deceive her. 'Pears to me the Evil One helped me. O, well! I've had the wust eend o' the bargain. W'at's the use to bother? It's done,"—bringing her foot down forcibly,—"and can't be undone; an' I've suffered for it. I shall git along well enough, I guess. I wish the parson—"

"What are you grumbling about, old woman?" muttered Morgan, as he staggered into the room. "Can't I help you weave? Harmony couldn't, you know;" and he plunged his still brawny arm through the slender threads, leaving a discouraging hole.

"There!" he growled, "that is what you did to the beautiful web of my life; only worse, a—sight worse.

I tell you, I've seen her to-day; she sent you this;" raising his hand to strike a blow. "O, no," he stammered, "that wouldn't be like her;" drawing the hand back; "no, it is I that give you this;" striking her a blow on the face. "That is to pay you for the blows I got when a boy. Ah, well! I never meant to strike a woman;" turning away.

"And she your mother," sighed Mrs. Mehitable. "Morgan, I shall have you taken care on, if you ever strike me agin."

"Well," said he, turning and looking her full in the face, "isn't that what you pledged yourself to do, if I would stop the lawsuit? Ha, ha! mother! A precious mother you proved yourself. Didn't you send me to jail? and murder the best and loveliest woman I ever saw? My God! my God! Drake and you, and Nab and the devil, conspired against me," he said, in a frenzy of passion. "The hottest place in — is too good for any of you; or me either," he groaned, shrinking away to his room.

Such scenes as this were not uncommon in the great house on the hill. And yet, Morgan, true to former habits, still performed a great deal of labor. But at times a sort of insanity took possession of him; then he was a perfect terror to them all. He would not venture to the small house near the swamp, feeling sure it was haunted. They are reaping as they have sown. But we will leave them for the present, and call at uncle Frank Lovering's. Things have changed, you will see, since Christmas.

Are you surprised to find Patty Stearns there yet? I will tell you how it happened. She found it impossible to get any one near by to take her. Some made one excuse, some another. Some told her plainly why they would not take her; and finally Hester Strong, while there spending the day, told her where her life had been a failure, and why she was not loved. She was quite indignant at first.

"I think," said Hester, "that your circumstances early in life had something to do with making you sad; I may say, soured your disposition. And then, as you grew older, and your sick, irritable parents died, and you commenced teaching school, you made the mistake of thinking true dignity was a reserved, distant stateliness; religion a sanctimonious austerity; that your office entitled you to great respect and consideration. You neglected to cultivate the affections, and strive, by kindness and conciliation, to win the esteem and confidence of those you met, but laid claim to that which cannot be bought or sold, except by paying in the same coin. 'Love begets love,' it is said. Love is the all-conquering power, which shall finally triumph over sin. God is love. You have seemed to forget that, and dwell upon his justice and severity, losing sight of his loving-kindness and tender mercy. Others make the fatal mistake of trusting to his merciful attributes, leaving justice and judgment out of the question."

Hester said all this, and very much more, in a kind, sympathizing way, which was irresistible. A tear glistened in Miss Stearns' eye, as she replied, —

"Perhaps you are right, Miss Strong. I have thought a sight about what you said, last Christmas, of the character and life of Christ. I think I have failed there. I remember my parents always looked on the dark side of iverything; and they had an uncommon sight of trouble. I thought iverything they said or did was right. But we are poor creatures, all of us; they might have been wrong in that. I niver remember seeing them laugh in my life. They said there was no mention of Christ's iver laughing; he wept often, fasted and prayed in the midnight air, and on the mountains."

"Yes," said Hester, "I know that is true. But it was not for himself he wept, fasted, and prayed. The burden of our guilt was laid upon him; by his stripes we are healed. His was not a selfish sorrow; and the wise man says, 'There is a time to laugh' — a time for everything. I think we dishonor God by looking on the dark side altogether. We must accept our blessings thankfully, and make the best of our misfortunes and trials; for if we are the children of God, all things shall work together for our good."

This plain, Christian talk had a decided effect upon Miss Patty, and prepared her, in a measure, for a new affliction. George was appalled, one day soon after this, to hear his mother call to his father, —

"O, dear! what shall we do? Miss Stearns has fallen, and broken her other limb, I fear. She can't stir." Several men came and assisted in getting her up, for she was very large and heavy. Dr. Edward Lovering was soon there, and, much to the consternation of the family, decided that her hip was broken just below the joint. He remarked to Mrs. Lovering, as he left, —

"I think the old lady won't hold out long. She is injured internally, and is so fleshy and aged, it will go hard with her."

"Poor thing," said Emma Lovering, "I am glad she

is here. We will try to be patient with her. She had a hard time when young. I am told she was a faithful daughter."

George and Fanny thought of their rash wishes, and felt sorry.

"We don't know what we shall be, when we are eighty," said Fanny, "with a lame leg and nobody to love us. Let's be real kind to her now. She may live a long time, but she can't ever sit up again, uncle Edward says."

"Well," said George, "I'll go for the men to help move her; it will be awful to lie there so, and go to the 'poticary shot,' as Willie calls it, for medicine."

"O, don't say anything funny now," said Fanny; "only think what mother has got to go through, and father too."

"O, I know it," said George; "I am doing what father calls 'taking things by the smooth handle.'"

And so Miss Patty has been lying on that bed of pain three months. She has changed in every respect; comparatively speaking, she is patient and grateful. She is apparently failing. Uncle Frank thinks she must have been a Christian; that the pure gold was there, only crusted over by mistaken notions.

"I am really afraid I shall wear you all out," she says frequently, "I am so heavy to lift, and need so much done. Move me just a mite — won't you? I suffer so. Thank you; you are all kind. The Lord will reward you. There, I feel easier; I ought to be patient; our blessed Master suffered more than mortal agony, and all for us. O, I've been a poor servant, unfaithful and unworthy. If I could live my life over, I would look more on the cheerful side of things."

And now the whole family, Wallace included, love to wait on her, notwithstanding her faults, for she is trying to imitate the Master. On our way back to the village, we will step into grandpa Lovering's. Rumor whispers that matrimony will be committed there soon. He tried to persuade Martha Manlie to become the mistress of his house, but she firmly, though gently, declined.

Charles Lovering was surprised when his father told him, one day, many circumstances which had happened in the family.

"I don't want to prejudice you against your wife," said Mr. Lovering; "she is a good wife and mother to you and your children, an excellent housekeeper, a good nurse, &c.; but she worried your mother constantly by suggesting that you did more than your share of the work, that we used the most meat, &c. She objected to my having the children and grandchildren at home so often, said hard things about my doing so much for Harmony, and didn't want the children here after their mother died. I didn't know much about it when mother was here to bear it, though I used to overhear some things. She seems worried all the time, for fear I shall defraud or overreach you. But since I have had a housekeeper, I have known all. Now, don't get angry, my son, but hear me out. You know Judith don't want me in her family; she has told you so often. What am I to do? I can't get any one to stay while things remain as they are. I don't want to distress you, or injure you in any way; but there must be a change." And the son knew his father was in earnest, when he saw the good right hand clinched firmly in the thin gray locks.

"Well, what do you propose to do, father?" he inquired.

"Do? Why, what I always wanted to do, but you thought it unnecessary labor — divide the produce, potatoes, apples, pork, butter, all — everything. I shall close the doors between the two tenements. Understand me, my son; my heart is all right, my affection for your family the same; but I want to remove all reason for complaint. I want peace. Judith will see her mistake some time. I shan't hold any ill will towards her, and your children are as my children. But I must keep a home for the rest of them."

"I want you to, father. I don't think Judith means half what she seems to."

"Perhaps not," said grandpa. "I shall build a new wood shed at my end of the house. It will be all ready for some one of your children when I am gone. I am conscious that no two families ought to be mixed up; they will be happier by themselves."

"I hope you will stay a long, long time, to use the house, father," said Charles, fervently. "Judith is over-anxious about me and the children."

"That accounts for her mistake," said grandpa; "we all have to live and learn. I am glad you have so good a wife, and think, when we get fixed right, and begin all new, we shall get along nicely." And they did. The nature of the woman was not changed, only her surroundings were different.

CHAPTER XX.

Mrs. Giles' Sickness. — Miss Ann Thropee, or Sympathy Wasted.

Hester is at Mr. Trueman's, spending a few days with her adopted children. A stranger would suppose her to be a real mother of about forty-five. She is in earnest conversation with a member of the family not yet introduced to the reader — a modest, intelligent youth of about sixteen, the eldest son by the first wife, and own brother to Lucy. Reader, you are surprised to learn that Mrs. Trueman is a step-mother. Listen, and you will see that I am correct.

"Do you think you shall study theology?" said Hester.

"Yes," was the earnest reply, "I desire to, if father and mother think it best. I know that it is a high and holy calling, and feel unworthy; but the promise is, 'Those that seek me early shall find me;' and if God is with me, I can do all things — even conquer my easily besetting sins, and preach the glorious gospel acceptably."

"I am sure," said Hester, "your mother will not oppose you in that, for she has expressed the wish to me that it might be so; and your own mother would have desired it above all things. You hardly remember her, I suppose."

"Yes, I remember her as a pleasant, beautiful dream. I felt angry with God because they told me he had taken her, until you came, and then you talked to me about God and heaven, and how mother was sitting beside the clear, bright fountain of life, listening to the music, and eating the delicious fruit from the tree in the midst of the garden, until I felt sorry for my anger, and you asked God to forgive me."

"I remember it," said Hester; "my heart ached for you. I did not suppose it would be possible for any one to fill that mother's place so faithfully as this dear mother has. You have been truly blessed."

"I know it; the boys at school think she is my own mother: I know no difference. Did you ever know that I date my conversion from that terrible sickness she had after my little brothers died? My dear friend, I owe you a lasting debt of gratitude for saving my mother's life, and calling my childish attention to serious things. I had thought religion a gloomy subject, fit only for the sick and aged; but your cheerfulness removed that prejudice, and made me desire to be a Christian."

"Howard," said Mrs. Trueman, opening the door, "I wish you would take the carriage and your sisters, and drive over to Mr. Giles', and bring little Winnie over to spend the day. She is such a sweet child, such a trusting Christian, and we all love her so much, that I want you to see her. Father says you can have the horse two hours; so give them all a drive, and get back by dinner time."

"Yes, mother," said the boy, rising and bowing very graciously, "I am happy to be your obedient servant in such a mission."

"Well, do not forget to inquire for Mrs. Giles, if Winnie cannot come. I fear the dear child is confining herself too much to her aunt. She hasn't been to school a day yet."

"No," said Hester; "I was afraid it would be so. I wish you would send for her to spend the night."

"By all means," was the reply. "Children, try to persuade her to come prepared."

They found Winnie shut up in the nursery, singing baby to sleep.

"Let's listen a moment," said Lucy; "isn't it sweet? Why, it is a hymn! I thought it must be some new song."

"Yes, it is a hymn," said Howard — "one of the sweetest and best: I know it."

> 'Praise ye the Lord! My heart shall join
> In work so pleasant, so divine;
> My days of praise shall ne'er be past
> While life, and thought, and being last.'

If Winnie can praise God, surely we, who are older and so much more highly favored, ought to," he said. By this time a cold, hard, stern-looking face appeared at the door.

"Is Mrs. Giles at home?" said Howard.

"Yes," was the blunt reply, "and like to be for the present."

"Is she very sick?" said Lucy.

"Yes, I s'pose so; she thinks she is, an' the doctor says so. He's her brother, you see."

"I am sorry she is sick," said Susie; "we wanted Winnie to go to our house to spend the day and night. Aunt Hester, and the baby, and Elida are there, and we want her ever so much."

"You can't have her, I s'pose; I've got my hands full, doin' the work, without lookin' arter young ones." Winnie sang on, unconscious of the great pleasure which was being denied her.

"Can't I see her?" said Lucy.

"S'pose so; go into that room over there, if ye've a mind to. Who be ye, at any rate?" said she, looking at the carriage.

"We are Mr. Trueman's children," said Howard, as the girls stepped into the nursery.

"O, I know; you're a stuck-up family. Yer father's wiser'n Holy Writ; that says, 'Take a little wine for yer stomach's sake;' he thinks it's wrong to use it, sick or well, rain or shine. I'd like to have 'im driv to work, out in the hot sun, hayin' or suthin'. Tell 'im so. Better men 'an he is use it, an' are likely to, for all 'im. You're the fust wife's boy, I s'pose. Wal, I pity ye, or any other young one that's got a step-mother, or father either; that's a fact."

"You needn't pity me," said Howard; "nobody ever had a better mother than ours. I never should think of her being a step-mother if people were not so fond of telling me of it."

"That shows yer depravity," was the insulting reply. "Ye think it is smart, do ye, to forgit the mother that bore ye? Ye'll see the day that ye'll feel yer loss; an' ye orter."

"I won't detain you," said Howard. "If you please, I will sit on the piazza until my sisters return."

"One on um ain't yer sister; she's yer half-sister; better call things by their name."

Howard walked away, instead of sitting down, wondering who their new acquaintance was, and how she could spend time to say such disagreeable things, if her hands were so full. It occurred to him that Winnie might, perhaps, take her little charge, and ride a while with them. He walked up to the nursery door, and tapped lightly. Susie opened it.

"Ask the little girl," he was about to say; but as his eye fell on Winnie, her occupation, position, and the expression of her face caused him to recall the words. "She doesn't look like a child," he thought; "what a sweet face! Walter was right when he called her 'little lady.'" Lucy introduced her brother with evident satisfaction.

"I thought," he said, looking at his sister, "that perhaps Miss Lentell could take her little charge and ride with us for an hour." Winnie blushed; she had never been called "Miss" Lentell before.

"Call me 'Winnie,' please," she stammered; "I want Lucy's and Susie's brother to call me 'Winnie.'"

"That I will do," said Howard, laughing; "we ought to be well acquainted, I hear so much of you at home, and my letters have been so full of you of late."

"I feel acquainted," said Winnie — "don't I?" looking at the girls. "They speak of you so often, I know just how you looked."

"Can't you go?" said Lucy. "I can take Unic in my lap."

"I will ask auntie," said Winnie. She came back, in a few moments, with baby's wrappings and a beaming face. "She says I can go, and she thanks you very much for calling for me. She wants me to go home with you."

"O, I am so glad!" said Susie; "won't we have a nice time?"

"But I can't go," said Winnie, cheerfully; "auntie is so sick I couldn't leave her for anything. She can't sit up a moment. I wish I could; I would like to. I want to see all the folks. But if I could only see aunt Hester just a moment," she said, looking timidly at Howard.

"You can," said he; "we can drive there and back twice in an hour. Yes, you shall go and stay half an hour. But who was that woman that let us in? I should think you would want to go somewhere, and stay there, if she treats you as she did us."

"O, that was uncle Giles' half-sister, Miss Ann Thropee."

"Miss Ann Thropee," said Howard; "it sounds familiar; but I can't think I ever knew any one by that name. How can you live with her? Does your aunt like her?"

"O, we just *submit* to it!" said Winnie. "I want to see auntie Hester about some things. I am ready." Baby Unie was delighted with the ride.

"Let us take the whole care of her," said Lucy, "and you sit on the front seat with Howard; it will rest you." Winnie had a keen relish for the beautiful in nature. She was drinking in fresh draughts of happiness with every breath.

"The world never looked so pretty to me as it does this summer," she said. "I seem to see God in everything. I am not afraid of him now, Susie. You remember I used to be."

"Why are you not afraid of him?" inquired Howard.

"O, because I love him. He is my Father and my Friend now. Why, have we got here so soon?"

"Yes, and now you run in," said Lucy. "I will keep baby out here. Don't let them eat you up, Winnie."

"O, no danger!" said Winnie, as she went hastily in, and spent several precious moments answering questions as to why the rest did not come in, and why she herself could not stay longer. At the earliest moment when it would be proper to do so, Winnie said, "I want to see you alone, auntie, a little while."

"Mrs. Trueman will excuse us," said Hester, "and we will step into the parlor."

"Yes," said Mrs. Trueman, "I am sorry we cannot keep you, Winnie, but glad to see you give up so cheerfully, what I think would be a great pleasure to you, for the comfort of your aunt."

"She calls me her comfort," said Winnie; "and that makes me happy, because mother used to call me so."

Winnie hesitated when they were alone.

"What is it, dear?" said Hester; "speak right out; you know time is passing."

"I know it," said Winnie; "that is the reason I can't think what to say."

"Who is taking care of your aunt?" said Hester.

"Miss Ann," said Winnie, "that is one thing I wanted to tell you. Auntie will die if somebody don't do something."

"Do tell me, Winnie, if she is there," said Hester, thoughtfully. "Well, I am sorry. Is your uncle kind to auntie, now she is sick?"

"I don't call him so. He don't go near her, and Miss

Ann don't, either, only when she wants to say something ugly: I make her bed when Unic is asleep, comb her hair, and carry her a piece of bread and cup of tea, when there are any. Auntie cries often, and says nobody cares for her but me, now. She wanted uncle Giles to send for you, just for one day; but he wouldn't."

"What did he say?"

"Why, he said he wouldn't have you there with your pauper young ones. His sisters were enough sight better than you. But, auntie, you must come right off. I am afraid to stay there."

"Afraid of whom, Winnie? Afraid of what, child?"

"Well," said Winnie, "I don't really know. I feel so, that is all. Uncle Mason is real good to me now; buys me candy and nuts."

Hester was silent for a moment, and then said, "I suppose you must go now, dear; take this note to auntie."

"I thank you for taking me here," said Winnie. "I feel rested; now I shall be able to cheer auntie; and I have got a note for her from aunt Hester: that will make her feel better."

She went immediately to her aunt's room, gave her Hester's note, and told her about her ride. Let us peep over her shoulder.

"Darling," wrote Hester, "cheer up; it is always darkest just before day. I shall see your father before I sleep, or write to him. You must go home. Be quiet. We will manage it all. Aunt Hester."

The sick one smiled languidly, and hid the letter in her bosom.

"Winnie, how came you to think of going to Hester?"

she said. "You could not have done better. You are, indeed, my comforter, my good angel."

"O, no, not that," said Winnie; "angels are holy; I am sinful."

"Well," said Elevia, "couldn't you leave baby with me, and make me a cup of tea? I feel like eating now; things don't look so dark to me."

"I guess so," said Winnie. "Couldn't I boil you an egg? Grandma Manlie almost lived on them. I know how; let them boil three minutes and a half. It will make you strong. And shan't I toast you a piece of bread on a fork? Aunt Hester says that is the best way," said Winnie, with great animation.

"Why, yes," said Elevia; "I think I should like to have you. I want to get strong."

Winnie met with various rebuffs while getting her aunt's tea.

"I would like an egg," she said to Miss Ann.

"Well, what of it? What do ye want of an egg?"

"I want it for my aunt; it will strengthen her."

"Strengthen a fiddlestick," was the ungracious reply.

"Well," said Winnie, "shall I take the key and get one?"

"No, not for her. She's as well able to come out and eat as I am."

"She isn't," said Winnie, her indignation getting the better of her discretion. "I want an egg." Winnie dropped her head, put her middle finger in her mouth a moment, and thought.

"O!" said she, and started for the barn. Uncle Mason was at work there. She hurried past him to the nest on the hay, caught up two eggs, and was returning, when he met her in the path, saying, —

"What's your hurry, Winnie? I want to see you. Should you like a hat like Susie Trueman's?"

"No," said Winnie; "it would cost too much. Mine will do for me." She tried to pass him.

"Don't be in such a hurry, puss. I want you to have one. You are far the prettier girl. Come, give me a kiss; you know you are our little girl now. Your aunt wants me to treat you like a child."

"Please let me go," said Winnie, as she slipped past him, and ran swiftly to the house.

"I shall have to be cautious," mused Mr. Giles, as he looked after her. "She is a pretty little thing; looks as her aunt used to. Wasn't I proud of her? She was so brilliant and spicy, as well as handsome! La! a man don't know what he's getting when he marries. She is as wilted and faded now as a flower nipped by the frost; moves about like a ghost. I thought she loved me, and would keep her place. She will find out who is master. Heigh-ho! I wish Lev would get well, or—"

CHAPTER XXI.

WINNIE'S THOUGHTFULNESS. — SUNSHINE AND HER FREAK.

WINNIE found her aunt quite weary and faint from the care of Unie. The desire to eat had ceased.

"I have been gone too long," said Winnie. "I had to go to the barn for eggs, and the water wouldn't boil; now I'm afraid you can't eat."

"I will try in a moment," said Elevia. "It looks nice."

"I will set it here, and take baby out," said Winnie.

Elevia read Hester's note again, took courage, ate a little, and then lay back wearily, closing her eyes.

"I shall never, never be happy again in this world," she thought. "It cannot be. These bitter memories will follow me to the grave. This terrible disappointment has cast a gloom upon my spirits which religion, I think, cannot wholly dissipate. My God, lead me in the way everlasting, so that death may bring the relief I seek in vain on earth." A new thought took possession of her. "Will he let me keep the baby? He don't love it; thinks it more plague than profit. But won't he take it away to tantalize me? O, if he should take it, Miss Ann or Mrs. Wiley would have it." She covered her face, and wept. "There," said she, "I forget what Hester wrote." She read again, "'Keep quiet. We will manage it all.' Of course Hester will think of that the first thing. I wonder what Mrs. Payson will think of me, and of my coming home. They say she is a kind-hearted woman. If mother, my dear, lost mother, were there, what a difference it would make! There, I must stop thinking, and try to sleep. O for a place to rest! Little Winnie, I wish I could learn to submit and trust, as you have," she said, as the thoughtful child came in to see if she was sleeping.

"O, you will," said she, "when you are better. Aunt Hester says folks can't be hopeful in some kinds of sickness. Unie is asleep, and I want to comb your hair, as I did mamma's when she was sick; it used to get her her to sleep in a minute, sometimes."

Winnie combed gently for a while, here and there, until the invalid slept. Then she crept back to the cradle to keep baby sleeping. Thus several days passed. Miss Ann fretted, scolded, and mourned in turn.

Hester had a long, confidential talk with Mrs. Trueman while the children were absent, which resulted in another drive for Howard, in company with aunt Hester and Sunshine.

"O, dear me, hum!" said the little thing. "I hasn't rided a bit on a carriage wis a cloth over it this long time ago" (meaning a covered carriage). "Don't you 'member the sligh, and the bills, and the horse we rided on when we went to Kistmas? O, funny, funny! Don't you 'member the plums, and old Santa Dicolas, that brought the candy? I some naughty; I spects he won't gis me any more."

Howard laughed, and aunt Hester smiled.

"Who used to say 'Hum,' darling?" she inquired.

"Why, don't you 'member?" said the child with

evident surprise. "It was my other grandmother, up to where I used to live. She weaved and spun, and said 'Hum.'"

Hester smiled.

"Yes, I remember her; what was her name?"

"I guess I don't know," said the child.

"What is your father's name?" said Howard.

"O, his name be Morgan," said she; but no amount of coaxing could induce her to repeat her grandmother's name.

"Well, what is your name?" asked Howard.

"I's Mary Elida, I is."

"Well, haven't you another name?" said Howard.

"I dess not, only I's auntie's 'ittle Sunshine."

Hester was at a loss what to think. It was possible the volatile child had forgotten, having heard the name so seldom, and perhaps not at all for a year; so she resolved to wait for further developments. She took Mrs. Payson aside, and gave her a fair, condensed statement of facts concerning Mason Giles' character, of Elevia's state of health, and who was housekeeper.

"Don't tell me any more," said Mrs. Payson; "I know that woman. She hates the very ground she walks on. Why don't Mr. Lovering bring her home immediately? I hope I don't stand in the way. I want the children and grandchildren to feel just as much at home here as ever. If I am not suited, why, I can leave — that's all. I dislike to see a man neglect his children, just because his wife is dead."

"Well," said Hester, "it hasn't been so bad long. The right time hadn't come. Elevia wished to try in every possible way to please him, and win back the love she imagined she had lost."

"Love! I don't believe he ever loved a living soul, except himself, in his life," said the ardent Mrs. Payson. She could submit to injury, ay, insult and wrong herself, but had no patience when others were oppressed and abused.

"Mr. Lovering isn't the man," said Hester, "to neglect one of his children. I call him a pattern father, and a pattern man. I wish there were more like him."

"So do I," said the widow, enthusiastically; "I know him; there isn't a better man. He's down in the field. Just you let me blow this horn, and he'll be up in no time. I'm so indignant at what you've told me that I can't wait for him to go after her."

"How does Judith get along since things were straightened out?" inquired Hester.

"O, nicely. She takes every convenient opportunity to tell me what a fine woman Mrs. Lovering was; how prudent, &c.; how much they thought of each other, and so on; intimating that I am rather extravagant."

Mr. Lovering listened to Hester's story, Mrs. Payson putting in a word now and then, until Hester mentioned that Mr. Giles' half sister, Miss Ann Thropee, was housekeeper, and Winnie nurse both for baby and its sick mother.

"Zounds!" said the good man, starting up and plunging the strong right hand into the gray locks. "If that don't beat the horned mice and the leather-billed chickens! There, I shall make a fool of myself," said he, calming down. "But candidly, I had rather have a bear, robbed of her whelps, round, than her; and Mason isn't much better behind the scenes. Mrs. Payson, can you make room for her here?"

"Make room for her? If I can't," was the reply, "it is time for me to leave — that's all."

"Well, Hester," said he, "the thing must be done, but not hastily or shabbily; it will take some time to manage it. The poor child may die first. Can't you go over and spend the day to-morrow? Carry her some oranges, and what she needs, and put some of your hopefulness into her, and relieve Winnie, while I call a council of war, and see what can be done."

"Yes," said Hester, "I'll do it. I'll leave Mary Fostina with Martha and grandpa. Did you know we had changed her name?"

"No," was the reply; "but I am glad of it. I never liked the name. But what will you do with Elida? Won't you stay with grandpa?" said he.

"No, dess not," was the reply. "I spects auntie wants me all along."

"I will leave her at Mr. Trueman's," said Hester.

On their way back, Hester spoke purposely of Mrs. Lentell, of Morgan Lentell.

"And this is my little Elida Lentell," she said, speaking to Howard.

"O, is that your name?" said he, looking at the child.

"No, dess not," was the reply. "I's 'ittle Sunshine Strong, I is. Auntie's 'ittle girl. Santa Dicolas, he brought me a pony and a dolly. When I come again I'll show it to you."

"But what is your grandmother's name — the one that weaves?"

"I dess it is Hum," said the child, again changing the subject.

"No," said Hester, "that isn't it. Now tell me what

it is, dear, or I can't allow you to be my Sunshine, or my darling; and perhaps I shall have to send you to live with Mrs. Lentell."

"Hers name isn't like mine, I spects; hers is a bad, naughty name — isn't it?"

"O, well, if little Elida doesn't love auntie, I must send her back to grandma Lentell's to live," said Hester.

"O, I don't want to go to grandmother Lentell's," she said, flinging her arms lovingly around Hester. "I can say it — Miss Kittybill Hum Lentell. There, auntie, isn't I your 'ittle Sunshine now? I spects I is."

Hester was silent.

"Auntie, isn't I your darling?" pleaded the child. "I is dood, I is," tears starting into her eyes.

"Yes," said Hester, "you shall be my darling Sunshine if you will tell auntie why you were unwilling to speak the name 'Lentell' when I hear your prayers to-night. But you have found several new words lately — 'dess' and 'spect': where did you learn them?"

"O, my Walter say so," said the child.

CHAPTER XXII.

Hester's Visit to Mrs. Giles. — Little Johnnie's Death. — Removal of Mrs. Giles to her Father's House.

Hester took an early start next morning. Martha and grandpa were delighted to receive their Mary again.

"Father is very uneasy without her," said Martha. "I shan't consent to her going away again. The little precious birdie girl! You see I am learning to talk 'babified.' I used to think it was silly." Baby seemed pleased to get home. She toddled up to grandpa's door, and pounded with her tiny fist, saying, "Ope–e–do — ope–e–do."

Grandpa started with joyful alacrity.

"Birdie bird," he murmured, "did you fly to grandpa — did you? Well, well, truly glad am I."

"Su, su!" said baby, holding up her dress, and pointing at the red slippers which Susie Trueman had given her. Hester and Martha looked on, and laughed.

"I am glad," said Martha, "that father's sight and hearing are so much better — he enjoys seeing and hearing baby so well!"

"O, pretty, pretty!" said grandpa. "Come in, little Mary — *my* Mary, come and sit on grandpa's knee, and tell him where away ye went, little Mary."

"'Ide – e – 'ide," said the child — 'ide – 'ide away," as she pointed at the cradle, and smiled one of those wondrous smiles. She smoothed the thin white locks, stroked the wrinkled cheek, and manifested her joy and affection in every possible way.

"That is truly an interesting sight," said Hester. "O, if we could get their pictures just as they sit now! — the two extremes of life meeting and blending in such trusting love: it is beautiful! Why, Martha, these children are a blessing to us all."

"Indeed they are," was the reply. "When is Mr. Trueman going to call for you?"

"O, as soon as he has seen to the opening of the store! He is a noble, generous man!"

"Yes," said Martha; "but I think he is a little too fast about temperance. Because some people abuse a good thing, it does not prove it to be bad, you know. Now father couldn't get along without his eleven-o'clock dram, I am sure."

"Perhaps not," said Hester; "habit has become second nature. But I don't think Adam took a dram daily: I never have. I was born a teetotaler. I am just as well off—better, I think. The apostle says, 'If meat cause my brother to offend, I will eat no meat while the world standeth.' I say Amen to that, and apply it to all kinds of liquors."

"Don't you think it is good for a medicine?" said Martha.

"It may have been," said Hester, "when it was pure and unadulterated; so is meat good; but if it cause my brother to offend, it must be sacrificed: that is all. O, Martha, it pains me to see so much stubborn resistance, I call it, to the cause of temperance and humanity, among good, well-meaning people. It is owing to ignorance of the tremendous evils of drinking. I have been situated so that I could see the sin, misery, poverty, and cruelty it brings in its train. You have not seen much of it. I tell you it is the curse of the age. Think of Morgan, of Mrs. Gray, and a host of others. O, there he comes; success to the prohibitory law. If I were a man I'd fight to extinguish the evil by burning every still-house in the land. O, haven't you a loaf of your light, sweet bread, that I can take to Elevia?"

"Yes, indeed, and a glass of jelly, too. Isn't there something else I can send her?"

"No, I can't think of anything. Mr. Trueman has some oranges for her. But suppose I should want to stay all night?"

"You could, and longer, if needed; we can get along nicely. Mary isn't a bit of trouble."

"Good by; send for me, if you need me."

"I have been having a terrible *dressing down*," said Mr. Trueman, as they rode along. "Mr. Wiley thinks I am 'meaner than dirt,' to use his expression."

"No bones broken, I hope," said Hester, smiling. "Dirt isn't mean, unless it comes in contact with something mean. What is the matter with him? Can't he get rum enough at Stillman's?"

"Yes, but he don't want to go there! He says it is too bad to compel respectable people to go there for it."

"Let them go without it, then; there is no compulsion about it, I suppose," said Hester, indignantly.

"That is what I tried to make him believe; but he thinks it is one of the essentials of life; said he would as soon go without bread as spirits of some kind. He says he will have some for haying, by fair means or foul. He wished me anything but success, threatened to injure my trade all he could, &c. I confess my business has diminished since I stopped selling it, and commenced agitating this question, and that, too, in a quarter where I least expected it. There are not a half dozen real temperance men in the village. A great many call themselves so, but they are not. I don't understand it. Why, I thought the Loverings would stand by me."

"Haven't they?" said Hester. "Well, there is no accounting for the inconsistencies of good people. But they will come out right; all such folks need is more light. Habit is strong. There has never been a drunkard in the family until Harmony's husband. They don't realize what a common curse it is. But you won't lose anything, Mr. Trueman, in the long run; there must be pioneers in every good cause. God is on your side. Soon every house will have its drunkard, every home its broken hearts; for drunkenness is increasing fearfully. Then the evils of drinking will be appreciated."

"When shall I come for you?" Mr. Trueman inquired, as he left her at the door.

"O, I won't trouble you to do that!" was the reply. "Mr. Giles will be perfectly willing to carry me home, I think." Winnie was feeling discouraged and sad when Hester opened the door and stepped in.

"Why, aunt Hester! Where did you come from? I do believe God sent you. Auntie is worse, and baby is sick. O, dear! I haven't slept all night."

"Of course he did," said Hester, cheerfully. "Now you shall rest a little. I will go in and see Elevia, and then you must go to bed." When Hester opened the door, Elevia reached out her arms, much as little Unie was in the habit of doing, to her, and began to cry. She could not speak.

"There," said Hester, cheerfully, "you may cry just five minutes by the clock, and then wipe up, for I have a bundle of news for you as big as Bunyan's pack." Hester went on talking, quietly stroking Elevia's hair, and before the five minutes expired she was listening attentively, only sobbing now and then.

"I am so thankful you have come," she said; "poor baby is sick, and Winnie is worn out. They don't help the child a mite."

"We can always find something to be thankful for if we look sharp," said Hester. "Here is cause number two," taking out the oranges; "number three," holding up the jelly; "number four," displaying the bread.

"That looks like aunt Martha," said Elevia, smiling. "Give the largest orange to Winnie, right off; and can't you bring the cradle in here, and let the child go to bed?"

"Yes, indeed," said Hester; "I am glad your trouble doesn't make you selfish."

"I am selfish enough," she sighed, "and wicked as need be; but Winnie is so self-sacrificing! She never thinks of self." Hester cut up one of the best-looking oranges, quietly gave it to Elevia, and took one to Winnie, who was suffering sadly for sleep.

"There, Winnie, now go to bed, darling, and sleep; that is a good girl."

"Kiss me, auntie," said Winnie; "I feel more like my other self to-day, I miss mother so. Do Christians ever feel sad, auntie?"

"O, yes, dear; you know we are only pilgrims and strangers here. The spirit may be willing when the flesh is weak. You are very tired; but remember this, dear — God is the same yesterday, to-day, and forever; and Jesus is always watching over his disciples, in sunshine and in shade. Believe this, Winnie, and you will have a calm, restful feeling even when under a cloud."

Hester told Elevia of her visit to her father's, and its results.

"Mrs. Payson is all eagerness to get you away. You will have to get used to her bustling ways. She is good and kind, but not so quiet as I should like."

"Then she will not think me a burden?"

"No, not in the least. I am more afraid she will kill you with kindness than any other way."

"O, if mother were there," whispered Elevia, "this would not be such a terrible cross. I long to go, but I tremble when I think what the result may be. Will he see his fault and do better? or will he hate me worse than ever? These questions have caused me many sleepless nights. If I should never return here, will he take my baby from me? He neglects it sadly now I am sick; and Miss Ann hates young ones, she says."

"I know it is a trying case," said Hester, "and no one can advise you. Ask counsel of God. He will help you decide. If you think you can endure the yoke, be a benefit to your husband, and bring up your child right, here you ought to stay. But if your health and spirits utterly fail, as they now have, then you can do no good by staying, and self-preservation demands that you go. But let us leave this subject; wait and see what your father and brothers think. Mr. Gray is going to be married," said Hester; "there is quite a romance about it. He marries a lady he was partial to when young, but was too late; she was engaged to a man at the West. She married, and went out there. They had not heard from each other since until last April, when they met in the stage; she returning a rich widow, with one son, to her friends in this region; he going to the same town to offer his hand to a maiden lady, a distant connection. They recognized each other, and a spark of the old flame seemed to have lingered in one corner of Mr. Gray's heart. He told the sad story of his life, and then listened to hers, which had been bright until the death of her husband. And then and there, in the stage, amid the whirl and rattle, he offered his hand a second time, and was accepted. 'When you offered yourself before,' said the widow, 'you were well off, I was poor. Things have been reversed. You are poor, you say; but I have enough for comfort.'"

"That was a strange coincidence — wasn't it?" said Elevia, forgetting her trouble. "How are they getting along? Has Lottie kept house all this time?"

"No," said Hester; "the oldest girl, who worked in a factory in the city, learned a dress-maker's trade, and came home to keep house, so that Lottie could go to school; and Lucy Trueman is giving her lessons in music. Lottie has a splendid voice. Hattie isn't more than eighteen; has been in the factory a long time. Poor child! she has had a hard time; but her prospects brighten. I believe they buried two little ones between her and Lottie."

"Jack Stillman is at the Reform School, I suppose," said Elevia. "I pity his mother. How does she appear? As proud as ever?"

"No; she is a changed woman. She has not professed religion, but we all think she is a Christian. She has done nobly in Mr. Gray's case; bought back, by personal sacrifice, nearly all the furniture that poor, deluded Helen mortgaged, and by kindness quite won the hearts of the whole family. The girls go to her as they would to a mother. She has joined our new Temperance Society, and is very active, doing all she can to induce her husband to stop selling liquor. But she will never succeed —never; at least, I think so. He isn't far from a drunkard now."

"I should think intemperance was on the increase," said Elevia; "we didn't use to hear much said about it. Mr. Giles and Mr. Wiley lay it all to the temperance folks. They think it is impossible to get along without it in haying time, raisings, &c."

"It is on the increase," said Hester; "evil is self-propagating, as well as good, only more so. Let them lay it to the temperance folks, if they will. They know better, as well as I do. It is the increase of intemperance that has stirred up thinking temperance people to do something. Our young men are falling victims to it, their families to them. — What a long nap Unie is having! and you must rest now."

"She didn't sleep much last night," said Elevia; "you always carry rest wherever you go."

"Don't flatter me," said Hester, smiling; "give all the praise to God. I want you to try Martha's bread when you have rested a little. I suppose I must beard the lion, and make you a cup of tea."

"She won't do anything but growl," said Elevia; "she tries to make herself appear worse than she really is. It is unpleasant to have her here. She and Mason don't agree about anything. She seems to be afraid that she shall do a kind act. I verily believe she would be as much ashamed to speak a kind word, or do a loving deed, as you would not to."

"Quite likely," said Hester; "I have seen such folks."

"Good morning, Miss Thropee."

"Mornin'," was the gruff reply.

"How is your health?" said Hester.

"Good 'nuff, I s'pose; it ought to be in this 'ouse."

"There is a good deal to do, I know," said Hester. "Elevia is all worn out doing the work and being broken of her rest with the babe."

"Fudge! She didn't 'ave anybody in bed to wait on."

"No," said Hester; "it is a good deal of care and labor to look after sick persons as they should be. I thought you must be all tired out, and so I came over to take care of baby and Elevia a day or two, and relieve you of that trouble."

Miss Ann was cornered. She grumbled over something which Hester did not stop to understand.

"I'll trouble you to show me where the tea and sugar are," said Hester. "Elevia must take a good deal of nourishment."

"In there, I s'pose; find it, an' ye will. When I lay in bed I don't eat."

"Well," said Hester, "doctor says she has a low nervous fever, and that baby must be weaned, and she have great care, or she will go in a decline. Where did you say the sugar was?"

"I didn't say," laughed Miss Ann. "I had to hunt for it, an' you kin."

"O, well, I'll find it; never mind."

Hester went to a closet, found a very little in a bowl, made her tea, and hurried from the room.

"Bread in there somewhere," said Miss Ann.

"I don't wish any," said Hester. "I brought some." She did not stop to hear the reply.

"O, yes, ye thought mine warn't good 'nuff, I s'pose. I kin make as good bread as you kin."

Mr. Giles said, "Whew!" when he found Hester there, but was as polite as ever when they met; "was glad she could come," &c.

"She loves good living," said he. "Ann, starve her out."

"I'll fix 'er," was the reply.

"I can stand it a day or two," thought Hester, as she saw the starved-looking table. Dr. Edward took Mr. Giles aside, told him that his wife was in danger (which was really true), and that she must have the best of care, or she would die.

"She will be sick a long time at best," said he; "perhaps you had better call in another physician; I should prefer to have you."

"O, I don't wish to do that; but it seems to me, if Elevia would arouse herself, she might get up sooner."

"But, my dear man," said the doctor, "that is impossible; we must get her up. This nervous prostration is the worst disease in the world: there is nothing to build upon. By the way, sometimes change of scene will work wonders — rouse up the dormant energies, and set things right. If they would take her home a few weeks, she might rally. Don't you think they would?" he inquired.

"I don't know, I am sure," said Mr. Giles. He was thinking what a saving it would be — what a fuss it was to have a sick wife.

"I think father would like to have her come; she would be welcome there. I'll speak to him, and let you know in a day or two. She is growing weaker, and will not be able to ride there soon."

"Well," said Mr. Giles, "I'd like to have you ask him. As you say, change may do her good. Ann will have to stay, at all events, for the present, and Winnie can go to school."

"O," said the doctor, indifferently, "Winnie will have to go with her, until Unie gets acquainted with the rest of them."

"Yes, I suppose she will have to go," said Mr. Giles.

"Perhaps," said the doctor, "I had better see father to-night: time is precious. If she goes, Hester must stay and fix her off, and perhaps she could take Elevia in her strong arms. I'll see." He went in.

"Now keep quiet, sister," he said. "You mustn't even think. Leave the future in the hands of God; now you have enough to do to get well. Hester, pack her trunk; you know sick folks need a good many things."

"I understand," was the arch reply. Hester found it difficult to keep her patient quiet.

"O, auntie," she said, "death would be preferable to life under such circumstances. I should not be afraid to die. I believe my sins are forgiven, and yet I hardly dare to live. I hope in Christ, but I cannot rejoice. What is the reason? Perhaps I ought to be willing to stay with Mason, and bear it all patiently. If I could know my duty, I would try to do it."

"I remember the dying words of dear Harmony," said Hester, "after receiving her husband's penitent letter. 'One cannot die just when they please, or live either. I have longed to die.' But then she was willing that God's will should be done. She was calmly, serenely hpapy, resting like a weary infant in its mother's bosom. O, it was a blessed privilege to be with her! She was a perfect illustration of the power of faith. I want you, my dear Elevia, to find rest in trusting God. Go home, recover your health, and wait. God, in his providence, will lead you in the path of duty. 'Cast your care upon him, for he careth for you.' I will go out for a walk with Unie. Winnie is having a fine sleep."

"I am glad," said Elevia. "Poor child, she has had a hard experience here! I hope something better will turn up for her."

"I hope so," was the reply; "now you try to sleep, dear." Hester stooped, kissed the pale cheek, held Unie down for a kiss, and left her.

"I wonder what makes Hester know just what people want," thought the invalid, "and just what to say I was feeling worried with baby's noise. Hester is a living epistle, known and read of all men. I never heard the most sceptical doubt her sincerity. Mr. Giles thinks she is a Christian, if there is such a thing." Hester reflected upon Elevia's remarks concerning Winnie's hard experience, and thought sadly of the experience of her whole life.

"Who has a better right to her than I have?" she mused. "Her dying mother confided her to me; and when Elevia is able to take care of the baby, she shall come home, and go to school."

"O, O, O!" cried Envena Wiley, as she ran towards Mr. Giles' — "O, dear!"

"What is the matter?" said Hester, going hastily to overtake her, and prevent her entering the house in such excitement. "What has happened?"

"O, O!" was all Envena could say, 'mid the wildest kind of weeping. Hester hurried on, and overtook her, laid her hand on her shoulder, and said, kindly, —

"What is the matter, dear? Don't go in. Elevia is very sick: tell me what it is."

"Dead, dead," sobbed Envena; "Johnnie is dead: they found him by the jug, dead." Ann was as much terrified and as wild as Envena, when informed.

"I can't bring 'im to," she cried. "What did you come to me for? O Lordy, Lordy! if there is a decent child, it dies, or something."

"You had better go over, Miss Ann," said Hester, "and try to comfort the poor mother. Perhaps he is in a fainting fit, and may be brought to life." Envena caught at that idea, said, "Come," and she herself started for home.

Hester awoke Winnie, left baby in her care, and went to see if she could assist in any way. She found the little one, not quite four years old, still lying on the ground beside the jug, the hot, scorching rays of the sun falling on the cold, dead face; the mowers standing around in silent bewilderment, too much intoxicated to fully realize the meaning of what they saw; the distracted parents weeping bitterly. O, what a sight! Hester understood it all at a glance.

There stood the destroyer, with the sugar, glasses,

and all, on a waiter; and there stood the human accomplices, mute with amazement and consternation. Her first impulse was to raise the dear remains in her arms, and remove it from the beastly, brutalizing scene to a place of security; but it occurred to her that it was customary to hold an inquest in such cases; so she knelt there by the dead, and, holding her apron so as to protect the face, begged one of the men to go to the house for an umbrella. She inquired if the doctor and a justice had been sent for. "No," was the reply.

"Then go for them immediately," she said; "life may not be entirely extinct."

Ah, it might not have been had the proper efforts been made when the child was first discovered. It was deep, deep intoxication then; the hot, scorching sun, falling directly upon him, had finished the work; and now he sleeps in death. The demon of the still has received another victim offered at midday.

"O God of justice!" murmured Hester, as, kneeling on the green, fresh grass, she chafed the little soft baby hand, and removed the flaxen curls from the smooth, white forehead, "will the accursed fire never, never be extinguished, except by the blood and tears of little children? How long, O Lord, how long? When wilt thou arise in thy might to avenge the wrongs of the innocent, and punish the guilty?"

And the answer came back slowly and distinctly to her inner consciousness, —

"When my servants do my bidding, when my soldiers are brave, courageous, and self-sacrificing, then shall my kingdom be established, and the kingdom of Satan, with all its terrible engines of destruction, shall fall with a mighty crash; and I, Jehovah, will reign, and send peace on earth!"

They buried him; and the evening dews fell, like teardrops wrung from Nature, over the untimely dead, slain by her own munificent gift to man, converted by his cupidity and ingenuity into a consuming fire. Let all who oppose the Temperance Reform go look at the little grave! Ay, at thousands of little graves, scattered all around them, made by the accursed influence of intoxicating drinks! Let them look into the homes desecrated and desolated by intemperance. Let them look into the helpless, hopeless face of the drunkard's wife, and her prematurely old children, and oppose the passage of any law that may send relief, if they dare, while God is looking on.

The love of gain, the pleadings of a vitiated appetite, may impel them to oppose any and every effort of the friends of humanity. But there will be a day of reckoning which they cannot evade. God, the Judge, will hold them to a strict account.

Little Johnnie's death caused quite an excitement in the village; all thought the liquor had been drugged. Mr. Stillman was accused of the sin. Mrs. Stillman was distressed beyond measure, while he still persisted that it was a lawful calling.

"I feel very thankful," said Mr. Trueman to his family, "that I have been brought to see the evil of rum-selling, and left it off. I once thought it was right. Did you know, Linnie, that my father used to sell a hogshead per week, out in this store? Why, our minister used to buy ten gallons at a time."

"Is it possible?" was the reply. "Why, people talk as if there was more drunkenness now than ever."

"Yes, I know it," said Mr. Trueman; "they talk so, and sometimes I speak so; but is it true, considering the increase of population? I think a little reflection will show it to be false; at least, as far as the quantity is concerned, I think the quality is poorer and more poisonous. I don't think a clergyman can be found, now, who would use ardent spirits for a beverage. Why, it isn't a great while since the bells were rung in one of our cities, at eleven and four o'clock, for the workmen to take a drink of liquor, while no bells called them to their meals. I admit that there may be more real drunkenness and crime; mind, I say there *may* be; but it is owing to the drugging of liquors. Population is increasing, and people come in contact with each other more frequently. We know more of each other's affairs. Once a man got drunk, beat his wife and children, and went to bed: that was the end of it. Now, if a man beats his wife in a drunken fit, it is known and talked of. Opportunities for crime are greater, the denser the population. At all events, the cause has begun to be agitated; drinkers and rum-sellers are distressed; that is encouraging. Mr. Wiley talked very hard to me the morning before Johnnie died, because I had taken the course I have; threatened to ruin my trade, and make a poor man of me yet."

"He can't — can he?" said Susie.

"I don't know," said Mr. Trueman; "I must leave the result of my actions with our heavenly Father. I have done what I thought was right. If nominally temperance people would come to a knowledge of the truth, all would be well."

"Never fear, husband," said Mrs. Trueman; "I had rather be poor than be made rich at such a sacrifice of principle. We are all well; and, with a clear conscience on that point, we shall never want for the necessaries of life."

Elevia cast a long, lingering glance at the fine new house, with its capacious barn, its neat flower-garden, as she left, and, lying back in Hester's loving arms, thought of the bright hopes that had been blasted, of the sorrow, disappointment, and pain, which came to her, instead of the peace and happiness she had anticipated. All was dark, dark in the future of *this* life. Mr. Giles was very happy and talkative. Dr. Edward rode beside them with Winnie and the baby. To him, to Hester, and to the whole family, this was a more trying event even than Harmony's death. Now they realized the truth of the old saying, "Living trouble is worse than dead trouble."

Several times the little company stopped to rest the invalid, who seemed more feeble than they supposed. The doctor was shocked at the absence of all affection or tender solicitude on the part of Mr. Giles. He was in haste to get back and attend to his hay.

"Come, Elevia," he said, briskly, "hurry up and get rested."

"Tell him to drive on," whispered Elevia; "I can bear it." And so on they went, and deposited the almost fainting daughter in her father's arms — a wreck of her former self.

"She don't look so fresh, and fair, and happy as she did when I gave her to you, Mr. Giles," said Mr. Lovering. "*But*"— and he emphasized the word — "but we will try to bring back the smiles and roses, and see to it that the frost don't kill them a second time — won't we, Mr. Giles?"

"Why, yes, she *has* faded amazingly since she was married. I've noticed it, but I can't understand it: every wish has been gratified. We men don't fade so."

"That depends upon circumstances," said Mr. Lovering, thoughtfully. "But all women do not fade and become sickly as soon as they go to housekeeping. My Mary didn't, the doctor's wife hasn't, and many others I could mention. I think it was not intended that it should be so. Women are sensitive plants; they need kind, tender treatment, Mr. Giles; but it *pays;* I tell you nothing pays better." Mr. Giles stepped just inside the door, where Hester and Mrs. Payson were engaged in reviving Elevia, who had fainted from fatigue and the mental suffering she had endured, and said, in a careless manner, —

"Hurry up, Elevia, and get well; for Ann isn't a very good housekeeper. Good by." Mr. Lovering plunged his hand into his hair, when he was gone, and said, —

"Zounds, Edward, he hasn't the least bit of affection for her. She is the same as a slave; I see that. She shan't trouble *him* in the future."

"She will trouble no one long," said the doctor, sadly, "unless she rallies soon."

CHAPTER XXIII.

THE STRUGGLE AND THE TRIUMPH. — THE COUNCIL. — MR. GILES' VISIT.

"O, IT is hard!" sighed Elevia, as the united efforts of Mrs. Payson and Hester restored her to consciousness again. "I am just a burden to you all; *he* does not care for me; no, no! And I thought I was going so easily; it is hard to come back just to suffer and be a burden to you all."

"Now don't feel so," said the widow, bustling about with her eyes full of tears; "you are just no burden at all to me. Why, I really think I shall be better contented, now that I have you to wait upon; so don't worry."

"But baby will be such a care! She is teething, and you can't think how worrisome she is."

"I guess I know all about that; my youngest child had a hard time getting its teeth; she cried day and night. Don't let that trouble you — don't. Come, the front chamber is all ready; you will be away from the noise. I'll do the best I can for you. It won't be like having mother, I know; but I've been a mother, and I've lost a mother; so I know something how you feel. There, don't try to walk; you haven't come to yet," she said, as Elevia made the attempt, and sank back in an almost helpless condition. "Hester and I can make a chair, school-girl fashion, and carry you. There, now!

isn't the bed soft? I stirred and shook it with all my might, for I knew you would be tired after your ride. Now you stay with her, Hester, — you understand her ways best, — and I will see to the baby."

"Winnie will tell you just how to prepare her food," whispered the invalid.

"O, yes," was the reply; "I will let Winnie fix her food; so rest easy about that. And if you want any namable thing in this house, you can have it, I know, just the same as ever. I hope you will get a nap and feel better soon."

Elevia lay quite still for some time after Mrs. Payson left the room. Hester took a seat by the bedside, and waited; now and then she stroked the soft but somewhat faded hair.

"I think I shall like her," said Elevia, suddenly, "and her quick, bustling way won't trouble me; it will divert my mind."

"You are right, my child," said Hester, relieved from anxiety on that account; "she is the very soul of sincerity and kindness. She and your mother were firm friends, but as different as could be in many respects. Now try to rest, dear."

Another pause. Hester hoped she was sleeping.

"It is hard, O, so hard!" moaned Elevia. "Life was so bright! I thought he loved me; our home was pleasant; we had everything I could wish. That makes the cup more bitter, auntie, and yet I must drink it all."

"Remember, dear," said Hester very softly, for her heart was full, "remember it is a Father's hand that holds the cup. Remember the words of the dear elder Brother, in his untold agony in the garden — 'Not my will, but thine, be done.' Dear Elevia, can you say thus?"

"Not yet, not yet, auntie; my heart is hard. I can't be willing to have all my beautiful dreams of happiness fade out in such terrible darkness. I can't say it. O, I am not a Christian, after all! Pray, auntie, pray; I can't say it; I can't feel it. I am not a Christian — all my beautiful things are laid waste — I am so unhappy! I must die; I feel sure of it; I must die — and after death is the judgment — and I have no Advocate with the Father — no hope! I shall go from misery to misery more awful than tongue can tell, and I deserve it all. When in health and prosperity, I scorned the message of mercy, and now I am dying without repentance, without pardon, without peace."

Hester laid her hand soothingly upon the hot, throbbing head, and begged her to be quiet, while she should commend her case to God.

"O, yes, pray, auntie," she said; "pray that, if it be possible, this cup pass from me."

"If it may not," said Hester, "what then?"

"That I may be willing to drink it, even to the very dregs."

Hester was no stranger at the mercy-seat; the language of prayer was familiar and pleasant to her. Her armor was always bright. Every want, every fear, every desire of the poor suffering one was spread out before the Lord and his Anointed, fervently and effectually. Word by word the sick one followed her, slowly and painfully, as if the words sprang from her own burdened soul; and when Hester said, "Amen," she added reverently, "Not my will, O Lord, not my will, but thine, be done."

All was silent again for a few moments, and then Elevia remarked, —

"That was a terrible struggle, auntie, but it is over for the present, at least, thank God. I thought I loved Jesus before, and that my sins were forgiven for his sake; but while coming here, I realized how entirely my husband was alienated from me, and also that my days were numbered; and my heart rebelled. O, the bitterness of that hour, auntie! may it never, never return!"

"I think it will not, dear; I trust your faith will grow brighter and brighter, until it overcomes the world. Perhaps, if I sing to you some of the beautiful hymns your mother and Harmony loved so well, you will drop asleep."

"Do, auntie, for I am so very tired; take my hand in yours, please."

Hester sang, "My faith looks up to Thee," &c., till the weary sufferer fell into a quiet sleep. She was startled as she noticed the change that had taken place in the last few hours. All their efforts to save her would be in vain, she feared. About her soul she felt quite easy. She had noticed a change in her for some time past. Her great darkness she attributed to bodily weakness, and the mental suffering through which she had just passed.

"If it is God's will to take her," she said to Mr. Lovering, "we must not hold her back. Under the circumstances, we ought to be willing, and more than willing, for only a life of sorrow and bitter disappointment is before her, if she lives. Mason Giles will never change much, I fear. Elevia was right when she said he did not care for her; she is only a slave to him. Some women would have sunk down to the position quietly, uncomplainingly, and died, scarcely knowing what was the matter with them. But Elevia could not; she has struggled ineffectually to keep her true position, simply because she had a cold, calculating, selfish being to deal with. It must be servitude and slavish submission, or open warfare. I think Elevia never fully realized, until yesterday, how utterly hopeless is the task of gaining and retaining her husband's love, and occupying the place of a wife. My feelings were never so outraged in my life as they were by his unfeeling conduct yesterday. I feared she would die in my arms, she was so pale: and yet he never showed the least concern, to say nothing of affection. When I begged him to stop and let her rest, his manner was as brisk as if he were going on a pleasure excursion."

"Yes, I noticed that," said Mr. Lovering; "it pained me severely, and I resolved that she should never return to his house, unless she greatly desired it. For if he had the least bit of affection for her, surely her suffering look yesterday would have called it forth."

"Yes, that is so," said Hester. "I think that was a bitter, bitter disappointment to the poor child. O, how many times the dear girl has said to me in the last few months, 'If he only loved me, I could put up with his faults. I wouldn't mind his locking up everything and doling it out to me as he would to a wasteful, thieving domestic, too mean to be trusted: that might be a foolish whim. I wouldn't mind his fretting, if he fretted at others as well as me,' she says often."

"Hester," said Mr. Lovering, sternly, "do you pretend to say that Mason has treated his wife in that way? What! locked up the provisions, sugar and tea, and all, and doled them out to her in driblets? Zounds! I never heard the beat of that! Why didn't you tell me before?" he said, plunging the right hand into the innocent gray locks.

"Simply because she requested me not to," was the calm reply. "She wished to keep it a secret, hoping that he might see his mistakes, and rectify them."

"Niggardly man!" he groaned; "and at the same time spending so much for outside show. Now I understand why Elevia seemed to fail in cooking, and why she always looked so distressed and vexed when Mason rallied her about the scantiness of her provision for the table." After a short pause he continued, sadly, "Hester, I need Mary at such times as this. I need the tender, mournful glance of her eye, when passion, my old enemy, begins to rise. I was a terribly passionate man once; quick as a flash. I thought I had conquered a peace. You know the reason why I used to pull my own hair," he said, smiling sadly; "it was to keep my tongue still. But lately my tongue runs first, and the pulling comes afterwards, as a punishment. Heigh-ho! I fear I shall get to be as ungovernable as ever, if some loving hand don't hold me in a little."

"Your Christian hope, Mr. Lovering, ought to be as an anchor to you, both sure and steadfast. You have been sadly tried recently."

"That is no excuse," was the quick reply. "I know where to look for strength and help; I'll go there. I am ashamed of myself."

A consultation was held over Elevia's case, soon after she reached her father's house, and nearly all hope of her recovery was relinquished. Hester and Martha went back and forth, like ministering angels. Judith, even, lent a willing hand, and made herself very useful, and won the gratitude of the whole family by her skilful kindness. Hester proposed to take Unie home, saying,—

"Martha and I can take care of her as well as not, and Winnie can stay to sit with you, she is such a quiet little thing."

Elevia found it difficult to express her satisfaction.

"Auntie," she said, "tell me the secret. "How is it that you always know what I want without asking? I can do nothing more for my precious babe; I have given her entirely up. O, it was hard to do it! Her noise disturbs me. I want to be very quiet while I live; and with you and Martha I know baby will be faithfully tended. Yes, I should like that; but," she continued, with a saddened look, "what a labor, what a task for you! Do hire some one to help you."

"Rest easy, dear," said Hester; "I will do so if necessary."

"When I am gone," said the sick one, "father will be her guardian; that is a comfort. And he says, if Mrs. Payson consents, he shall adopt her, and give her my name. And Winnie, dear little Winnie, you will keep her, Hester. Father has promised to pay for educating her out of Unie's property. What a mercy that father was so firm about securing my property to me! I was vexed and annoyed at the time, but now I see the wisdom of it."

Mr. Giles was informed of Elevia's danger, but seemed almost angry.

"I expected it," was his reply. "Ann said she would die if she went there. I'll have her brought home, and see if we can't get her up. Exertion, Mr. Lovering, is what she needs. If she had more energy," he mused, "I think she might get well. She gave up too soon."

Mr. Lovering remained silent till quite composed, and then said, —

"Mr. Giles, I think my daughter will never leave my house while she lives."

"Won't she, though?" said Mr. Giles, thrown off his guard. "We'll see, we'll see. My wife won't do as I say — will she? Who will hinder?"

"*I will*," was the firm reply; "I will, or the strong arm of the law will. She is unable to be moved for any cause now, and you cannot touch her. Come over and look at her; perhaps you will be sorry for treating her so cruelly when you see her."

Mr. Giles started nervously.

"I tell you, Mr. Lovering, I have always treated her well; I have nothing to be sorry for, only that —" He hesitated.

"Only what, Mr. Giles?"

"She always said she was well," he said, evasively. "That is the way a man gets cheated. I wish I never had consented to her going home. How is the child?"

"Better," said Mr. Lovering, holding on to the gray locks firmly — "better."

"Well, I can't say I am glad to hear that. If the mother dies, it would be better if the child could follow her. She would be better off, you see."

He was thinking of money.

"Perhaps so; but I am selfish enough to want it to live. Come over and look at your injured, suffering wife."

"I don't understand you; you speak in riddles," was the sharp reply. "If my wife suffers, it isn't my fault, but her own. I tell you, Mr. Lovering, she has a good stock of the old family pride and stubbornness. A wife shouldn't set up to have her own way, as she has. The Scriptures say, 'Wives, submit yourselves —"

"I must go," said Mr. Lovering, in a low, tremulous voice. "Some other time we will talk about this."

Mr. Giles came over Sabbath eve, and seemed somewhat surprised at the change in his wife, and sobered by her deathly look.

"Mason," said Elevia, holding up her pale, attenuated arm, "you see that I am going. I may have been a poor wife to you, but my heart was yours; and now, as I stand so near the portals of death, I can say that I have always tried to please you. If I have failed, forgive me; it was not intentional."

She turned her large, lustrous eyes full on his face, and waited for a reply. Mr. Giles was not expecting this; he was somewhat softened.

"Perhaps you have," he said, hurriedly; "we all make mistakes. I think you have resisted my will rather too much; but I will forgive you. I hope I have a forgiving spirit. You are willing to be moved home, I dare say; it is more proper for you to die in your own house. Of course you will make me the guardian of our child's property; no one can do better for it than I can, I am sure. Ann and I have been missing her, and you, too, Levie. We want you both at home."

The pale face flushed deeply, and she glanced hurriedly from her father to Mrs. Payson, who started up and stood between Mr. Giles and the bed.

"Why, Mr. Giles," she stammered, "you are — why, I don't know exactly what I am going to say. You see she only just lived to get here — that was all; Hester thought she wouldn't — but she couldn't live to get back, noways at all. She is weaker, a great deal weaker, now. And about the baby — it is real troublesome. Miss Ann would get tired to death of it, it worries so. Why, it takes Hester and Martha half their time to keep it quiet."

"O, as to that," said Mr. Giles, "it is good for children to cry. But, if you please, Mrs. Payson, Levie can speak for herself. What do you say, Levie?" he said, cheerfully. "Shall I come for you the first fair day? Your being here is making a good deal of talk, sister Wiley tells me."

"O, Mason," she said, pleadingly, "look at me, and tell me if you think I am able. I am almost through. Let me die here, please."

Mr. Lovering saw that she was becoming very much distressed, and he could endure it no longer.

"Mr. Giles," he said, striving to speak calmly, "I wish to see you alone." He motioned Mrs. Payson to stay and comfort Elevia.

"You shall do just as you have a mind to, and that child shan't be carried to Miss Ann — never; so rest easy, dear. It was too bad for him to talk in that way. How I wish Hester was here — this blessed moment! She would know just what to say to you, and one of her prayers would make you as quiet as a lamb. There, let me read some of them hymns, or something out of the Bible — shall I?" Elevia made no reply. "If you just want me to keep still, tell me so. O, I know; I'll call your little comforter."

Elevia nodded.

"I won't be gone a second," she said, darting out of

the room, saying to herself, "I wish I was her mother this blessed night, I do. Poor child! I could say some things then that I can't now. If he ever asks me to marry him again, I will, if it's the day after the funeral. I should like to see them get that child then. Why, why! who would a thought it of him! the old brute, he hasn't a mite of feeling. Winnie," she said, "Mr. Giles has worried your aunt's life almost out of her. She's got one of them terrible nervous turns. Run, child, and see if you can quiet her. I can't."

Winnie saw at a glance that silent sympathy was the best medicine. She kissed her tenderly, and passed her small, soft hand gently over the throbbing temples.

"That is nice," whispered the sufferer, closing her eyes wearily; "it rests me." An hour passed, and still sleep came not. Patiently Winnie kept her post. "Can't you sing, Winnie? Perhaps that will stop my thinking; I feel terribly. I can't keep still," she said, tossing her arms.

"Uncle Edward is in the parlor; let me call him," said Winnie. "He will give you something to take."

"Not while Mason stays here," was the reply. "I know what they are talking about, and it distresses me."

Winnie came back in a moment, saying, —

"He is going now, auntie, and uncle is coming to relieve you."

All that passed in the parlor we may not tell; but Mr. Giles threw off all disguise, and said many hard, unfeeling things; declared he had been cheated and deceived about the property. He wouldn't have married her if he had known.

"Didn't you tell me, Mr. Giles," said Mr. Lovering,

"when you asked me for my daughter, that you didn't want the property? that you had enough to support her, and wished she was poor, that you might prove your devotion to her? You can't deny it. Is that a specimen of your sincerity, Mr. Giles?"

"O, well, I didn't care for that paltry thousand or two; if she had been poor it would have been all the same. But then a man wants his just rights — that's all I've had the trouble of her, and it's just that I should have the control of the child, and what little property there is. Who has a better right to control a child than a father, I should like to know? I'll see what the law says about this thing. You've rather got the whip-row of me; but we'll see." And he strode away.

"Unmasked," said Dr. Edward.

Mr. Giles called at Mr. Manlie's to inquire after Unie; was very pleasant and sympathetic; spoke of "poor Elevia" with much apparent feeling, and said nothing of what had been transpiring. Unie was shy of him at first; but he showed her his watch, gave her his knife, &c., until by and by she sat composedly on his knee, when his manner changed.

"Miss Manlie," he said, in a commanding tone, "bring the child's cloak; I am going to give her an airing. And you may as well pick up her clothes generally; she will remain at my house for the present."

The family were astonished; Hester remonstrated; Martha pleaded; but all in vain.

"It will kill the baby," said Hester. "She is a stranger to you, and Ann hates her, and you know it. Come, let us keep her; it won't cost you anything. Elevia will be distressed beyond measure."

"I can't help that," was the cold reply. "I have a right to my child. She has got to die, at any rate; it won't make much difference; and the baby would be better off if it should die too."

"I think so," said Hester; "but I don't want her to cry herself to death. Come to auntie, darling."

The child reached out her arms.

"No, no," said Mr. Giles; "little girl, you must go with me whether they get your things or not." He started for the carriage; baby commenced crying piteously. "O, that won't frighten me," he remarked, looking from one to another; "I've heard that before."

"If you wish to prove to the world that you are a monster, why, take her," said Hester. "Wait, and I will get her things."

By this time all the family were in tears. Little Mary opened her large eyes in utter amazement.

"Ganpa kie, artie kie, Mamie kie," she kept saying.

Little Elida stamped her tiny foot, saying, —

"Naughty man to carry off my little baby-dirl. Gis her to auntie, naughty man."

"God reward you," said Hester, as she fastened the little cloak and unclasped the tiny hands that clung to her.

"God punish you," said the gentle Martha, "for this and the other —" She broke down and wept aloud.

When Elida saw him drive off, she exclaimed, —

"Now, I'll tell God 'bout him;" and she too commenced crying.

Hester hastened to her own room. Grandpa and baby tried to comfort Martha.

"Don't kie, artie, don't kie. Mamie kie."

In a short time Hester appeared all ready for a walk.

"Martha," said she, "I shall follow her. Mind that Elevia don't know anything of this. If she wishes to see baby, why, make some excuse till I bring her back. Don't tell it to anybody. If Mr. Lovering comes, charge him to keep it from Winnie and Elevia. I'll bring her back," she said in a husky voice.

Mrs. Payson was very uneasy after Mr. Giles left.

"Mr. Lovering," said she, "it is my humble opinion that he will go straight to Mr. Manlie's and take the child, and I wish you would take the doctor's horse and head him off. Now, come, do; it will be awful if they get her."

"O, no danger of that," was the reply; "it would be too much trouble. What would he do that for? He can't get the property."

"Perhaps not," was the quick reply; "but couldn't he torment your life out of you? and couldn't he let that child cry its eyes out of its head? What would he care? And if the child worries itself to death, wouldn't the property go to him?"

"It would if steps were not taken to prevent it," was the reply.

"Well, then," said the earnest little woman, "take all the steps that are necessary — do; but don't let him lay his hands on that child. Didn't he say it was good for the blessed little things to cry, and die, too? You heard him."

Mr. Lovering looked thoughtful.

"If he is going to take her to-night, I am too late; his horse is a fast one. I can't get there in season; but I will go over early in the morning, and put them on their guard."

CHAPTER XXIV.

ABOUT THE BABY. — TROUBLE UPON TROUBLE. — THE PROPOSAL.

EARLY the next morning, Mr. Lovering rode up to Mr. Manlie's door. Somehow, his heart misgave him. He dreaded to inquire for baby, who had learned to reach out its little arms, as it had never done to its father.

Martha burst into tears as soon as she saw him.

"What is it?" said he, dropping into the nearest chair. "Where are Hester and baby?"

The old emphatic "Zounds!" sprang to his lips when Martha informed him; but he resolutely held it back, thinking how the word had troubled Mary. He simply said, —

"Heigh-ho! This will be a terrible blow to Elevia. Martha, that man is a villain. I'll ride over and see if I can't bring them back."

"You had better not," said Martha; "Hester will get along best alone. Does Elevia know you were coming here?"

"No, Mrs. Payson knows it. She wanted me to come last night; she thought he would take it; I didn't. I promised her I'd ride over and see."

"Well, don't let Elevia know a word about it; don't tell her you have been here; and if she wants to see her, make one excuse after another, and put her off. Just the moment she gets back with her, we will let you know."

"I'll do as you say about that," said Mr. Lovering; "but I'll see Mr. Leonard to-day, and know what the law says about these things."

He returned home disheartened and anxious.

"Then he has taken her," said Mrs. Payson, as soon as he rode up to the door.

"Yes," was the reply, "and that isn't the worst of it; I don't know how in the world we shall get her again. Hester followed her; what she intends doing I don't know. But Elevia and Winnie must know nothing of this; so you had better not speak of it to any one. If he loved the child, or had almost anybody to take care of her, except Ann, it would be different."

He leaned his head on the table in a desponding mood. Mrs. Payson fluttered about like a wounded bird.

"Now, if I had only married him," she thought, "I should know what to say to comfort him. Well, I won't refuse again if he ever asks me."

Tears came into her eyes; she couldn't bear to see him feel so. She sat down at the other end of the table, leaned her elbow on it, her head on her hand, instead of going to his side, as her heart prompted her.

"You have had trouble upon trouble, Mr. Lovering," said she, "and you bear it as a Christian should. I could not bear it half so well."

"I don't know about that," was the reply. "I am sure your life has been full of self-denying, Christian love ever since I knew you. My esteem for you has been greatly strengthened recently, and my children are learning to respect and love you; so your objections to becoming my wife are growing less and less. Perhaps, when Elevia took your hand and placed it in mine last night, you did not fully understand her meaning. I did. She had expressed a wish to me that you might become my wife, and be a mother to her child before she leaves me. They have gone — one at a time — Mary and Harmony; and Elevia is almost through, poor child," he groaned. "It will be a comfort to her to know that you will help me train her child. You can do so as my housekeeper, but better, much better, as my wife. I know I am asking a great deal of you," he said, sadly; "perhaps I am selfish; but I need you, Mrs. Payson; yes, I need you as much as the baby. I believe I am getting to be a child myself, or I should have waited until it was all over before speaking to you again on this subject."

He bowed his head, and wept.

"No wonder if you are weak and childish," said Mrs. Payson, herself weeping, "after all you have suffered; and then to think how you have been kept awake nights; it is enough to kill you. On some accounts I would rather wait until it is all over; but if it will be any comfort to you or her, why, it is no matter. I have been sorry ever since she came home that I didn't marry you before; and if I could have seen all the trouble that was coming upon you, why, I would in a moment. But I was afraid I wasn't just the one to please the children, and then I shouldn't have been happy. But now, if I can be any help to you, take me; I am a poor creature at best. I hope you won't be sorry, and I feel sure I shan't."

"I thank you a thousand times, Mrs. Payson," he

said, rising and taking her hand. "Come, let us cheer up, and go and tell Levie about it. The dear child is feeling anxious lest the additional care may drive you away from me."

"O, she needn't, poor darling. I shall stay all the sooner. I shouldn't be fit to live if I could leave you with the care of a little, helpless babe. I was only afraid they wouldn't like me — that's all; I am so different from Mary. I never can fill her place. I feel almost afraid now." She hesitated, and turned pale.

"You need not fear, my dear Mrs. Payson."

"Call me 'Lizzie;' William always did," said the widow.

"I know of no one that will please me or my children but yourself," said Mr. Lovering. "We have proved you, and you were Mary's friend, you know. Life has been robbed of its romance; we have learned to live amid its sober realities, to enjoy its blessings and bear its sorrows — have we not, Lizzie?"

"I should think we might have learned," was the reply. "I, at least, am a dull scholar. But we have both seen affliction, and can understand each other, I think. I am not afraid on my own account."

"Then you need not fear," was the prompt reply. "My poor, wounded affections are yours, and you have quite won the hearts of my children. Olive, even, the most obstinate of them all, had no objections. Come, let us make Elevia glad for a moment." He led her in, and with a calm, peaceful look on his face, said, "Bless us, my child; she has consented to take me for better or for worse — little Unie, sick Elevia, and all. Can't you thank her?"

The sick one reached out her pale, thin hand, and said, with a smile, —

"Yes, dear father, I can; and you, too, for coming so soon to tell me. And O, Father in heaven," she said, fervently clasping her hands, "I thank thee, too, for raising up one so kind and worthy to be a comfort to my father and a mother to my babe."

Mrs. Payson was much affected; she stooped over the sick one, saying, —

"Can you love me, dear, and trust me with your child? Are you willing I should occupy your mother's place? Then I am happy. God helping me, I will try to do right by little Unie, and help your father bear the burdens of life."

Sealing her promise with a kiss, she busied herself in making the invalid comfortable.

"What does Winnie say to all this?" said Mr. Lovering. "Do you think you will like to have a new grandmother?"

"Why, I have been saying, 'Bless the Lord, O my soul,' ever since you came in," was the joyful reply. "I had a great deal rather have Mrs. Payson for grandmother than housekeeper, for now she is ours, you see; she belongs to us; she is all our own, and we can have her always, unless —" Winnie's voice faltered — "unless God takes her."

"You precious, darling child," said Mrs. Payson, folding her in her arms, "it won't be very hard to belong to you; that is a fact. I loved you the moment I laid my eyes on your blessed face. And you are such a patient little nurse, it almost kills me to see you so confined. I can't have it so much longer. There, dear, now we are good friends for life I hope; so go and play out in the open air for an hour. I will stay with auntie."

"I should like to read my new book uncle Edward bought me," was the reply, "if you are willing."

"Why, child, haven't you had time to read that yet?" said Mrs. Payson. "Well, I never! You are the patientest little thing I ever saw. Read it? Yes, indeed, only go and find some good, cool, shady place out of doors. And don't stir till it is finished, unless you wish to."

"I thank you," said Winnie. "I wanted to read it very much, but the leaves rattled and made auntie start. Can I bring you anything, auntie," she inquired, "before I go?"

"No, darling," was the reply; "go and enjoy your book now. You are auntie's comforter in every sense of the word."

CHAPTER XXV.

Hester rescues the Baby from its unnatural Father. Dr. Edward's timely Arrival.

It was quite dark when Hester arrived at Mr. Giles'. The nervous sobbing of little Unie smote her ear painfully. She listened a moment.

"W'at did you bring that young un 'ere for, I wonder? I won't touch 'er, more'n I would a snake."

"Come, Ann, don't be so mean; I thought you'd do that much to help me. Undress her; she is most used up. I've conquered her; I don't believe she'll raise the neighbors again to-night, screaming. It's the real Lovering temper — isn't it?"

"Do'no; guess she got some on't t'other side," was the glum retort. "Young uns are a plague, any way. Come 'ere, then."

A quick, sharp cry followed this speech. Hester raised the latch and entered.

"Good evening, Miss Ann," said she. "I thought you would have trouble, and came over to help you take care of her, till she gets acquainted. Poor little thing; she is as timid as can be." Mr. Giles arose, and strode towards the baby; but Hester was before him; she had little Unie folded tightly in her strong arms.

"Mr. Giles," said she, "this child is almost dead. If it should go into a fit and die to-night, it would go hard with you. She was perfectly well when you took her. There! look! see what you have done," as the nervous sobbing ceased, and the little form writhed in strong convulsions; " see!"

"I see!" was the startled reply. "I didn't think of that. Why! I never! What shall I do?"

The little face was black and distorted; the frail form shook and quivered. Hester wiped the froth from the blue lips, and said, —

"Promise me, Mr. Giles, that in two or three days you will carry her back with me, unless she seems perfectly willing to stay, and I will try to save her. Will you promise?" Another struggle.

"Yes, yes, save her, and do what you please with her. Don't let her die on my hands so suddenly." He had never seen any one in a fit before; it was truly appalling. Hester saw that he trembled.

"It is strange," said she; " it acts something like poison. What have you given her, Mr. Giles?"

"O, nothing! nothing! Have I, Ann?"

"Do'no; good nuff for ye; needn't bring 'er 'ere," was the reply. Hester applied herself diligently to relieving the little sufferer; and after a while, the muscles relaxed, the eyes opened.

"Birdie, bird," said Hester, "'tis auntie."

The frightened look passed away, the little stiff hand was raised painfully to Hester's face, a smile parted the yet blue lips.

"She looks very deathly," said Hester.

"Yes," said Mr. Giles; "I never saw anything like it. Do you think she is going to die?"

"I can't tell; you had better leave me alone with her.

If she should have another, as bad as that, right off, I think she would die. It seems to me she must have taken something. Haven't you given her some laudanum, or something, Ann? You had her when I came."

"O, Lordy, no! I hain't gin 'er nothin'. *He* licked 'er; I didn't," she said, as Hester, in removing the child's clothing, pointed at some large red marks. Mr. Giles looked.

"Why, I didn't think I struck so hard," he said.

Baby shrank away from him, and moved her head from side to side.

"Hush!" said Hester; "leave her alone with me, or she will have another fit."

She was obeyed instantly. They were both thoroughly frightened by this time.

"Die, or not die," said Ann, "I ain't done nothin'; ye needn't a' brought 'er 'ere."

Hester slept but little that night. Unie was very restless, starting in her sleep, and crying out every now and then. She was glad when the rays of morning peeped in at the window, for she had passed a dreary, lonesome night, and longed to take baby in her arms and make her escape before the inmates of the house arose, but felt that she must wait.

"Once well done is twice done," was her motto. If Mr. Giles consented to give up the child, that would end the matter.

Three days passed. They were full of trouble and weariness to Hester, full of doubt and anxiety to the friends at home. Little Unie was very sick. The fright, the length of time she had cried, the cruel blows she had received, and change of food, had been too much for her.

Hester really feared that she should never be able to carry her home. Mr. Giles felt mortified and somewhat frightened; Miss Ann, angry.

"Pretty fuss you've got us into — ain't ye?" she said to Hester, when called upon to render some little service.

Hester made no reply, because Ann's voice caused Unie to start, every time she heard it.

"Mr. Giles," said Hester, "I think you had better carry us home; the child will never be any better here. Every time she opens her eyes, it seems as if she would go into fits. It is lucky for you that I came, for I certainly think the child would not have lived through the first night. Had she come out of that fit in your arms, or Ann's, she would have gone into another, and so on till she died. It would have been hard for you to convince people that you were not guilty of a horrid crime. Yes," she said, "I am glad I came, for your sake as well as other reasons."

"It would have been awkward, to be sure," said Mr. Giles, thoughtfully.

"And there are those marks, too," said Hester. "I never saw such a sight on so young a child."

"I had no idea," said Mr. Giles, "that I should leave a mark; but she was a stubborn little thing; she wouldn't stop her screaming till I had whipped her several times."

"For shame!" said Hester; "the little thing wasn't stubborn; she was frightened and grieved, that was all. I never saw her show a bit of temper. Come, Mr. Giles, promise me — yes, promise me in black and white — that you will carry us back, and never take her again without the consent of her guardian, or her own; and I promise that these marks shall never be seen out of the family, and this whole affair shall be hushed up. I promise never to reveal what I heard through the open window."

Mr. Giles started.

"Eavesdropping!" he said, fiercely. "Woman, what did you hear?"

Hester saw the frightened look, and concluded that after all she had not heard the worst.

"O, I heard some things," Mr. Giles, "that had better never have been heard by mortal ear, to say nothing of the ever-present God."

"Eavesdropper! tell me, I say, tell me what you heard." He came close up to her, his whole countenance expressing rage.

"Stand farther off," said Hester, sternly; "you will frighten Unic to death."

"I wish to God she was —" He stopped.

"I know it, Mr. Giles, I know it; but you shall not kill her."

Hester laid her on the bed, and turned towards him with a calm, resolute look. He seemed to be measuring her from head to foot, while every muscle of his face expressed passion, hatred, ay, malignity.

"Devil," he said, hoarsely, "tell me what you heard."

"I shall not," said Hester, resolutely. "Mason Giles, I am not an 'eavesdropper.' I came here that night under peculiar circumstances, as you very well know. I knew you would need me, and you did. I didn't expect to hear what I heard," she said, bending towards him and speaking low, "nor see just what I saw, either. I expected to hear Unic crying, nothing more. I hesitated at the door. Am I to blame for hearing what I heard?

It was lucky for you that it was I who heard it, and not another," she said, impressively. "But I promise in the presence of God, that I will never repeat all I heard, if you will give me the writing I require."

"I'll trust you," said he, the muscles of his face relaxing; "I'll trust you; but if you break your oath, beware. But first give me a writing that I shall never be called upon to pay the child's board, or other expenses, and also that you will forever keep a secret those terrible, thoughtless words you heard. I didn't mean it; I was vexed."

"That I will do," said Hester. "Bring me pen and paper."

The two papers were exchanged, and Hester made a bundle of the few garments belonging to baby, and waited for Mr. Giles.

"I shan't trust 'er, if you do, till she's gin suthin better 'n that; 'er tongue is allers a runnin'," she heard Miss Ann say, as she stepped out to hasten preparations.

A strange feeling came over her as she returned and waited another hour. Unic was in a deep sleep, and everything was still. She felt timid; it was a new feeling to her.

"My nerves are getting weak," she thought; "I haven't slept much for three nights. Mr. Giles," she called, "are you almost ready? Unic is sleeping, and it is getting late. I should like to go now."

"I have concluded not to go till morning, it is so late," was the reply; "and Ann will help you take care of Unic to-night."

"I am sorry," said Hester; "the longer you keep her, the more stir it will make. But Ann can't help me; it would only worry the child, and keep me awake. If you are not going, I will lock the door, and lie down, while baby sleeps. Good night."

Hester knelt in prayer, first of all, and then threw herself wearily on the bed. She could not think she was in danger, and yet she could not feel that she was safe. She knew not what to expect. She arose and looked from the window. The darkness, as it gathered over hill and valley, made her feel more lonely. Unie awoke, and partook more heartily of nourishment than she had done before. When she slept again, all was still in the house and on the street. It was eleven. Hester raised the window which opened on the piazza, put on her shawl and bonnet, took the bundle on her arm, folded baby to her bosom, and stepped forth.

"Only a mile and a half," she thought; "I can walk it.". The night air felt damp. Little Unie lay like a dead weight on her arms. "I am not so strong as I once was," sighed Hester. "Perhaps I had better have staid till morning; but I am getting nervous; that is plain. There is something about that house that is terribly depressing; and I feel as if I must see Elevia. I am afraid this affair will reach her. No, I am glad I started; I am half way home now." She paused in her walk for a moment, and sat upon a stone. The moon was shining brightly. A carriage came slowly up the hill, and Hester watched it eagerly on its winding way. She arose and stepped out into the light. The doctor drew his rein, and looked at the strange apparition, but recognized her in a moment, saying, —

"Aunt Hester, is that you? How came you here?"

"Don't you know?" said she. "I've got the baby,

and, what is more, a writing from the father. Here, help me into the carriage, and drive fast, for I do believe the dear child is either dying or having another fit."

"It is a fit," said the doctor, springing into the carriage. "I shall drive to my own house; it is about as near, and I can attend to her better there."

"I do believe God sent you along just at this critical moment," said Hester. "I can't explain now," she said, in answer to a question from the doctor, as she held the little sufferer so she could feel the air. "This is pretty fast getting along," said Hester; "I am glad we are here, doctor," she continued, as she stepped slowly from the carriage to the ground, "Hester Strong is growing weak, I do believe."

"There is a good reason for it," said the doctor; "worn out in our service. Hester, this must not be any longer; you must rest." The doctor spoke to his wife, and for the first time in her life, Hester found herself unable to render necessary assistance. She was obliged to leave baby in their care and retire. Fortunately, baby did not miss her; she remained in a partial stupor all night. The doctor retired, and his wife was left alone with the care of Unie. While attending to her wants, she made a discovery which agitated her greatly; namely, the large, ugly marks mentioned. They were dark now, and looked worse than ever.

"Edward," she called, quickly, "come here, do."

He was there in a moment.

"Look at that," she said, pointing at the marks; "what is that?" They looked at each other in perplexity.

"Hester has passed through more than we know," said the doctor.

"Yes, and baby too," was the reply. "What can it mean? You don't think Mason did it — do you?"

"Yes; who would, if he didn't? Poor little thing! I should really like to know what this means, and how Hester came on that hill, at that time of night, with an almost dying child. But we must wait."

"Yes," said his wife: "now go to bed again; you need rest. I shouldn't have called you, but I was fairly frightened. I can take care of her. I am to give her this every hour, you say?"

"Yes."

Little Unie seemed better in the morning, but Hester felt quite unwell.

"I shall be better in a day or two," she said to the doctor. "I have been over-anxious and over-worked. I was so afraid Martha would worry herself sick, or that Elevia would hear about it. And there is my little Fossie; I can't bear to leave her. Besides, your father is all broken down. I wish he was nicely married; don't you, doctor?"

"Yes," said the doctor, promptly, "I do. Do you think Mrs. Payson will marry him?"

"Yes, if I understand such matters," said Hester, smiling. "But they must not be kept in suspense any longer. If you are determined to keep us, you must ride over and tell them we are here, safe and sound. But don't tell them how you found me. Tell them baby is sick from crying so long, with fright, and change of food, &c. That is about the truth — isn't it? And you think she will get over it soon — don't you?"

"Yes, I hope she may, with good care; but it will be

some time first. That man ought to suffer; but we must leave him in the hands of God."

"I am willing to," said Hester. "I am glad I haven't got to judge him."

"My father never invested any money so well in his life as he did that which he spent on Hester," said Mr. Lovering, when the doctor showed him the papers which she had procured from Mr. Giles. "She has been the greatest possible blessing to my family. God bless her."

"He will," said Mrs. Payson; "hasn't he blessed her, and doesn't he bless every living soul that she stays with? Only think how she got that baby! There isn't another person that could have done it. Her poor mother is expecting Hester to bring it over to-day. You had better tell her Hester isn't well; that will satisfy her."

Grandpa Maulie and Martha were rejoiced to hear the news.

"Bring them home as soon as it is safe," said Martha. Elida capered about, when told that auntie and Unie were over to uncle Edward's, and coming home soon.

"Dare," said she, "I told God 'bout that naughty man, and he said —" She paused.

"What did he say, pet?" asked the doctor, greatly amused.

"Well, he said 'he'd see 'bout it.' He did — didn't he, auntie?"

CHAPTER XXVI.

MIDNIGHT MUSINGS. — THE DISCOVERY. — CONSCIENCE DISTURBED.

Mason Giles slept but little that night. For the first time in his life he was angry with himself.

"I was a fool to touch the young one, in the first place," he mused — " yes, a d—d fool ! But if Ann had kept still, I shouldn't have whipped her so hard. Of course I didn't mean to kill her." He shuddered. "What if I had ? Hester saved the little creature, I do believe, and my neck, perhaps." He moved restlessly from side to side. "Likely enough I haven't treated Levie just right. I believe she has tried to please me. O, well, women are always fussing about something! She needn't have cared whether I loved her or not. What should *I* care about that if I had a good home? What if I did fret? I had a right to, in my own house. I worked hard ; women don't consider that. They have an easy time sitting round in the house ; and when a man comes in, all tired out, why, it must be, 'My dear,' or 'My love,' like Dr. Lovering.

"Fudge ! that don't get a living, nor pay taxes. A man is a fool to get married. I wish I hadn't locked everything up, though, for I don't think Levie was wasteful. Nonsense ! Whose business is it? Isn't a man's house his castle? I thought all men did so — father did. I wonder if brother Wiley lets his wife manage those things? I'll ask her. Dear me, I wish I could go to sleep! hard work coming to-morrow. Lev did look pitiful when she asked me to forgive her. I wish I could forget it." He moved to the other side of the bed as he thought, "Why, I am lying in her place. She was very pretty when I married her. How the fellows all envied me! And, after all, I can't think of anything very bad that she ever did. I wish she hadn't asked me to forgive her, for I'm the most to blame. But I wouldn't tell her so, to save her. No; I'll be hanged if I do: 'twould please *them* too much. And, after all, wasn't I the head of the family? She should have submitted to me. It is a wife's place to submit. I wish Ann wouldn't make my tea so strong! I shan't sleep a wink to-night. She's as stubborn again as Levie — that's a fact; and not half as good a housekeeper. She is a miserable cook, and it costs more to live, too. I mean to get along alone. I suppose I can't, though, till after harvesting; so I will try to keep still. There is one thing I'm determined to do: I'll get that paper back, or Hester shan't leave. Unie will be big enough to keep house some time, if she lives; then I'll want her. If Ann could have got in there and stolen the writings, why, they wouldn't have got any more — that's certain. If the child should die after Hester has had the care of her three or four days, I'm safe enough. And then, if Lev should happen to die suddenly, I don't believe they'd think to secure the property. I don't know but what things are working well enough. Why in the world can't I go to sleep? Here it is past midnight. O, dear!" He tried to sleep, but his mind was thoroughly waked up. "There now, I think of it," he said aloud, sitting up in bed, "it isn't at all likely that Hester heard me swear I would ' kill the young one, if it didn't stop, and its grandfather, too,' or any of that foolish, passionate talk, for that was before I whipped her the last time. I paid on as if I meant to; she never could have stood that — never; she would have rushed in and pounced upon me, thinking, sure enough, I meant to kill the child. Why, I had no idea of doing it, or of whipping her half so hard as I did. It was provoking to have Ann say, 'Kill 'er, and done with it; you'd better. I shan't bury 'er, nor lie nuther, to save yer neck.' She might have kept still. I could have wrung her neck, I was so angry. I declare I believe I should have killed the baby if Hester hadn't come. But she didn't hear that part, I know. What a fool I was to get so frightened! I'll make her tell what she did hear before I carry her home."

The night wore away at last; breakfast was ready.

"I'll skim the milk while yer eatin'," said Ann, "and slip round when I carry out a panful, an' see if I can't find that are writin'. Good 'nuff for ye, if ye don't get it; ye'd no business to gi'n it to 'er."

"Perhaps not," said Mr. Giles. "That is a bright thought, Ann; get it if you can, for I don't want another fuss with her, and the sooner they're off, why, the better, you know." They called Hester; but there was no answer. They tried the door; it was locked. They called again, but could get no reply.

"Both dead, likely as not," muttered Ann; "a pretty fuss you've got us into." Mr. Giles stood aghast.

"Sure enough," he muttered; "but I should have

carried them off last night only for your interference.
A pretty fuss," he muttered, "sure enough. Come,
let's go round and look in at the window. Gone! as
sure as —," said Mason, " papers and all. Well, that is
better than to have them found dead on my hands.
That old fox was too much for us, Ann."

"Pretty fuss you've got into," was the reply. "Make
a nice talk — won't it? Hey? Gittin' out of the
winder at the dead o' night, sick young un, an' all.
Good 'nuff for ye; ye needn't 'ave got married."

"It was your fault, Ann," was the angry reply; "if
you had minded your own business, I should have carried them off last night, and you know it. Now, there is
no telling what will come."

"Why, she'll say ye insulted 'er, or threatened to
kill 'er, or suthin', pretty likely. I would if ye'd used
me so." Mr. Giles raised his hand as if about to strike;
he dropped it again, and strode off, saying, —

"That woman will be the ruin of me yet."

"Strike an' ye dare," was the mocking reply. "I
ain't 'fraid on ye, if Lev was." He turned in a terrible rage, and shook his fist defiantly at her.

"Ann Thropee, if you were a man," he shouted, "I'd
beat you to death if you didn't stop! Curse you, and
the laws too!" The breakfast was eaten in silence.
Mason scowled at Ann. Ann scowled back. When it
was over, he said, —

"Well, I've got her promise to keep still, and if she
don't, why, she is a liar, like the rest of her sex."

"'Elp yerself if ye can," said Ann. "W'at will ye
do 'bout it, if she tells on't — hey?"

"Ann, hold your tongue — will you? I'll —" He

hurried from the room. Ann laughed mockingly, and screamed after him.

"Git another 'ousekeeper, an' ye will. I shan't stay 'ere."

"Why, Mason," said Mrs. Wiley, on being consulted, "I should have thought you would have known better. What a talk this will make! Hester is on good terms with all the first families in the village. I am sure I don't know why, but she *is*, though she has got her living nursing, and pretty likely sprang from some low family. The Lowells, and Leonards, and Trueman's think everything of her. I am mortified. Envena is just getting acquainted with the Truemans. How could you be so thoughtless?"

"They ain't no better 'n other folks," said Ann, "if you do creep arter um."

"About locking up things," continued Mrs. Wiley, "why, that depends upon circumstances. My husband never thought of such a thing. Why should he? He knows I am capable of taking care of them. About Levie, I ain't sure that you were wrong there. She hadn't much judgment, I suppose; she was brought up at school."

"Mind ye don't bring Veene up in the same way. She don't git a cent o' mine, if ye do. Leve's good as you are, fur 'z I know."

"Don't worry, Ann: Envena isn't going to school always; I mean she shall learn to work by and by. If she makes as good a housekeeper as you are, that will do — won't it? Did you say she got out of the window in the night, and walked home with that sick child in her arms? Don't you suppose she called at Mr. Trueman's on her way home?"

"'Ow do I know 'ow she got there?"

"Mason," said Mrs. Wiley, "I tell you what I would do. I would disinherit that child, and never let her have a cent of my property, unless they would let me manage hers. Why, it is monstrous to treat you so; but I wouldn't lay it to heart. Venie will be a daughter to you — won't you, Venie?"

"Yes, mother," was the reply, as the girl arose, and put her arms around her uncle's neck. "It is too bad, uncle Mason; but I will come and keep house for you, when I am old enough — can't I, mother? And aunt Ann can live with us; then I shall be an heiress — shan't I, uncle?" Mrs. Wiley was chagrined at the last remark.

"I see you are thinking of self, as usual," said Mason, who had been a silent listener. "You are like all the rest of them."

"You mean the Gileses, I s'pose," said Ann, laughing. "It's my 'pinion the Loverings and Gileses are 'bout alike."

"Come, don't, Ann; you know better," said Mrs. Wiley.

"Why, daughter, you shouldn't have said a word about the property," she said, sorrowfully, when they were alone.

"I guess I shan't go for anything else," was the reply, "and Ann is a tedious old thing. If I thought I shouldn't get hers, I'd just leave off trying to please her; that's all."

"O, you will get it, no doubt, if you are only cautious, and uncle's too, unless he marries again. So be wise, my dear."

Mr. Giles didn't feel very comfortable for several

days. He expected every one he met to speak of those events about which he could not help thinking. He started at the sound of every carriage, looked for something unpleasant to take place, wished he could know where Hester was, and what she was saying about him, what she really did hear, and why she left as she did. Was she afraid of foul play?

"Well, I don't wonder at it," he thought, "for I did show off, and no mistake; and Ann is a real old Hottentot. If I could get Elevia back, I'd treat her better; I declare I would. She wasn't so selfish as other women, I do believe. I'd give a dollar to know if she has heard about Unie; but I dare not go there. So men generally don't lock up provisions. I wish I'd known that before. It is all a sham about men being the head of the family, and I might as well come under petticoat government as other men. Elevia could manage as well as sister Wiley. Why not? She knows as much as two of her. Well, I guess I've gone the length of my cord, and got brought up without bettering myself. But if Hester Strong keeps her promise, I'll believe in religion, I declare I will." He concluded to drive over to Mr. Trueman's store, and see how he appeared. "If he has heard anything, why, I shall know it. He is none of your hypocrites, if Wiley does call him so. And Hester would tell him before any one else out of the family, I am sure."

Mr. Trueman appeared just the same as ever; he was entirely ignorant of the unhappy affair. Mr. Giles felt better.

"I hear your wife is failing," he said. "I am sorry. She will never be able to go home again, Mr. Lovering tells me. It is sad."

"I fear not," was the reply, spoken in a subdued manner.

"And your child is very sick, too — did you know it? It was taken sick while on a visit to the doctor's with Hester. She is sick, too."

"Is she? I hadn't heard of it." Mr. Giles was very much agitated. Mr. Trueman noticed it, and remarked, —

"The baby, I hear, is better, and Hester, I hope, will be soon. I don't know what we should, any of us, do without her. I have had great reason to honor and respect her, Mr. Giles, as well as yourself." Mr. Trueman was called another way, much to Mr. Giles' relief. He felt satisfied that Hester had kept her secret so far.

"But it will get out," he mused. "There are those marks. I wish they were in — If the family keep still, why, I'll believe in religion. I want to see Levie; but I won't go there unless she sends for me. If she should send, why, I will tell her I am sorry for some things. But she needn't have felt so bad about it; most women wouldn't.' But Mr. Giles did not know much about women; had not had the best models to study.

CHAPTER XXVII.

Passing Events. — Scenes and Incidents.

"We live among the dying, Jennie," said the doctor, as he seated himself wearily at the breakfast table.

"Who is dead, my dear?" said his wife, as she ceased pouring his coffee, and looked anxiously in his face.

"Mr. Pearsons and Patty Stearns; she died at four this morning."

"Is it possible?" was the reply. "How did she seem in her last moments?"

"Calmly and serenely happy. Poor old lady! she tried to doubt her acceptance with God, feared that her peace was insensibility, &c. 'I am such a sinner,' she said often, 'have been so ungrateful, so fault-finding, that it don't seem right for me to be so calm.' You know she was very familiar with the Scriptures. Well, formerly she delighted to repeat those passages which speak of God as a judge, as offended with the wicked, &c.; but recently she has repeated those which reveal the other side of the Divine nature, his mercy, his pity, and compassion. Her last moments were spent in repeating that beautiful psalm, 'The Lord is my Shepherd, I shall not want,' word for word, slowly and emphatically, as was her custom when in health; particularly when she came to the verse, 'Though I walk through the valley of the shadow of death, I will fear no evil; for thou art with me; thy rod and thy staff they comfort me. Wonderful, wonderful!' were her last words, as she passed from a world of suffering to her rest on high."

After a few moments' silence, Hester, who was still something of an invalid, remarked,—

"Doctor, I am more and more impressed, the longer I live, with the responsibility of training children. Miss Patty's faults were very much the result of early training. It is a fearful responsibility to take in our own strength.'

"O, if parents could realize their unfitness for such a work without religion," said Jennie, "how earnestly they would seek the Lord!"

"Wallace was a great favorite with Miss Patty," said the doctor; "she has willed him fifty dollars."

"Why, has she?" said Hester. "The dear child will be so pleased."

"Yes," said the doctor, smiling, "he talks of going to college with it, and says it is all owing to your Christian talk about the sugar, vinegar, &c. He concluded the poor old lady had received a very large portion of vinegar in her life, and thought he would use sugar profusely, I suppose; for I never saw a little fellow so intent on pleasing another as he was her, and he succeeded, I think. She wanted him near her all the time."

Tears came into Hester's eyes as she remarked,—

"He is a noble, generous child, but rather impulsive. I hope he will get an education and do well; and I believe he will. Your sister's faith will be rewarded. I feel sure of it. Those children will, every one of them, be a blessing and an honor to us."

"I forgot to tell you that Mr. Gray brought his bride home last night," said the doctor. "That is quite a pleasant affair; she was an old acquaintance of many of the neighbors; they had a reception. Mr. Gray was regretting that you couldn't be there, Hester. He says you were a friend in need to him, and he is anxious that you should renew your acquaintance with Mrs. Gray."

"I wasn't much acquainted," said Hester. "I knew her. I am really glad for Mr. Gray and his family. Have you called there since the house was repaired and furnished?"

"No, I have not; I have noticed the improvement outside."

"Well, it is greater inside," was the reply; "and I heartily wish them much joy."

"How are the children pleased?" inquired Jennie. "I should think they would be delighted."

"I should," said Hester; "and they are, all but Hattie. Poor child! she has imbibed that unreasonable prejudice against step-mothers, and insists upon going to the factory again. My creed is just this," said Hester, earnestly—"that if a woman is fit to be a mother, if she is a true, noble woman, she will make a good step-mother; otherwise she will not. It is a difficult place to occupy, one which needs judgment and tact; for if a woman has any faults, they will show off in that position like fireworks in a dark night. It is like putting a black patch on white groundwork."

"Sometimes it is the reverse," said the doctor, laughing; "it is like putting a white patch on a dark background — isn't it so? For instance, when the little widow marries my father, which I see by a notice on the church door will happen before long."

"Is that so?" said both women. "Isn't it queer, when Elevia is so low?"

"I believe it was her wish that it should be so. She wants them married in her room, in the presence of all the children. It is an odd notion, but she must be gratified — that is, if she lives till the time arrives; and I rather think she may linger some time longer: she may not live till then — we can't tell. She is anxious to see you and baby, Hester. I told her I thought she could in a day or two. I fear the change in little Unic will distress her. I am glad there are some more teeth to lay it to; I can't help pitying Mason, after all. I met him to-day; he seemed changed. He avoided me. Hester, I wish you would tell me just what happened while you were there, and why you left in such a way."

"Well, I can't," said Hester; "there isn't much to it any way, only I got sick and nervous, and felt as if I couldn't stay; and I am glad I didn't. What should I have done without some one to help take care of Unic for the last few days?"

"Well, one thing is certain," said Jennie: "he whipped that infant shamefully, for there are the marks."

"I don't deny that," said Hester; "but it was before I arrived there. Men have no judgment about children, and never ought to whip a baby. But I pity Mason, myself. You know his father is the prince of tyrants, and his mother was the queen of martyrs. The children never knew that wives had any rights, only the right to minister to the wants of their families. The sisters were all older, and left home when Mason was young, all except Ann, his half-sister."

"Such boys are to be pitied," said the doctor.

"Such men always get wives when they want them," said Jennie. "I don't understand it."

"Did you ever hear about his striking one of the children with his first wife's coffin lid?" said Hester.

"No," was the reply.

"Well, he did — you needn't look so incredulous. The child remarked to another, 'I'd rather see mother there than to see father abusing her,' just as he entered the room. He seized the lid and struck the child, and would have injured it had not a neighbor come in. He was a man of most ungovernable passion."

"I should think so," was the reply; "and yet he has had three wives. Perhaps Ann is to be pitied, too."

"I suppose she is," said Hester. "How do Charles and Judith like the new arrangement?"

"O, pretty well, I should think. Judith is doing nicely now; she is very kind to Elevia. Charles talks reasonably about it; he has a kind heart; and Winnie can scarcely contain herself, she is so pleased. I have one more item of news for you, and then I must go. Morgan has been to father's and grandfather's."

"Why, you don't say so?" said Jennie. "And what did he want?"

"He was there yesterday, and wanted money. He says father has cheated him out of three thousand dollars, or so."

Hester groaned aloud.

"Don't let it trouble you, aunt Hester."

"I can't help it," was the reply. "I am getting

weak. O, dear, dear! what a mortification he is going to be to the children! He was ragged and dirty, I presume?"

"Yes, and saucy, too. Father got rid of him easily enough; but Martha made a great mistake."

"What did she do?" said Hester, eagerly.

"O, nothing, only hired him to go home; gave him three dollars, and he stumbled into Mr. Trueman's store, and called for rum. Mr. Trueman talked to him faithfully for drinking; and when he found out that he was Winnie's father, he tried to get him to his house, that he might labor with him. He couldn't, of course. He hurried over to Stillman's, and got some, without doubt, in some form or other. That is the last I know of him. That store is a nuisance."

"That is what we get for putting such a man in as agent to sell liquor," said Hester. "Our new law won't amount to much. It is a shame; any toper can get it of him. He likes it so well himself that he won't deny others. Mr. Crafty is the man of his counsel. Edward, now I think of it; how can you consistently give certificates to such men as Crafty and others, when you know they use it as a beverage, and abuse their families?"

"I don't," was the emphatic reply. "I have given but two or three certificates since the law was passed. I have had numerous applications, made so dolefully many times, that I could scarcely help laughing outright. It has been exceedingly awkward, and really I think I shall lose some practice in that way, but not much that is paying. Who started that story? I should like to have Stillman show me one of the certificates with my name on it. I shall look into that matter. My name shan't be used for a cloak in such dirty business."

"I am glad to hear you say so," was the reply. "I have been feeling grieved that you did not stand by Mr. Trueman. He felt it, too."

"Why, I never thought of doing anything else. The law would have passed all the same; but if he felt it his duty to advocate it, and sacrifice custom by doing it, why, I respect him for it. He will be the greatest loser in town for the present; but eventually he will be the gainer. Next year he shall be agent, or I am mistaken. People will see by that time that we want a man we can trust. Wife, patronize him all you can."

Hester bowed her head, and remained silent.

"What did Winnie say to her father?" said Jennie.

"I don't know; but Mrs. Payson said she had a long cry after he left. But Sunshine went into a tempest right off when he called her his little girl.

"'I isn't your 'ittle dirl; I spects I's auntie's Sunshine, I is. Go away, naughty man; I isn't your 'ittle dirl.' He didn't seem to realize that Fostina was his child at all."

"I am thankful for that," said Hester. "I see that I must gird myself for another conflict. I thought, when I brought Unie home, that the last foe had been conquered; but I was mistaken, you see, for I am determined that he shan't torment those children. I must go home to-morrow; perhaps I shall gain faster with the harness on. Martha, the dear girl, did a foolish thing when she gave him money. I shall have to fight all the harder. O, well! 'As thy day, so shall thy strength be.'"

CHAPTER XXVIII.

ABOUT HESTER'S CALL. — WINNIE'S TALK, AND GRANDPA'S WEDDING.

HESTER called to see Elevia on her way home. She had not changed much, and seemed very happy. Providentially, little Unie brightened up during their call.

"She will be better soon," said Hester; "she has two new teeth, the darling!"

"But the care of her is wearing you out, auntie," said the mother. "Can't you get some one to help you? You said you would. Lay her beside mamma. Darling, precious one! mamma's birdie! O, how much your poor father is losing in not loving you better, little one! I want to save him. I wish his eyes could be opened. Hester, I think if I had been a Christian, trusting in Christ, I might have shown him his errors. Won't you try when I am gone? I regret that he cannot have Unie. If Ann were like you, I should want her to go there, but he wouldn't be willing she should have the care of her, if I was. And I, O, I *couldn't* leave the little thing with her, she is so soured! Mason didn't have much to improve him at home — did he, auntie? He has a very low estimate of female character. He respects you, though, and you might do him good." Hester remained quiet, thinking of what had passed during the last week or two, and rejoicing that Elevia was in blissful ignorance of it.

"The Lord helping me, I will try," was the low response.

"The dear Lord and Master reward you, Hester," she said, taking her broad palm in her own, so pale and thin. "The dear Lord reward and bless you for all your kindness to me and those dear to me. Come and see me as often as you can. Only for Unie, I should be selfish, and want you all the time I stay here." Winnie followed her aunt from the room, and, as soon as they were alone, she said, —

"He has been here, auntie; my father has been here. O, it is awful! He don't look as he did. He wanted rum. He asked me to get him some; said he was sick. I can never, never be happy any more!" she cried. "He will come again, some time, I am afraid."

"I guess not, dear," said Hester; "and if he does, will that destroy all your comfort? Won't Jesus remain the same, dear? Can't you rejoice in him?"

"I could, if I didn't rebel so. But when I don't feel willing to have things as they are, and want my own way, I think Jesus is displeased and grieved, for he seems farther off, and I am so unhappy."

"My dear child," said Hester, "ought you to be unhappy all the time because God has taken away one tenth of your earthly good? He has left you nine tenths — ought you not to enjoy that?"

"Yes, auntie, I know I should, and I will try," sobbed the child. "But isn't my father a pretty large tenth, auntie? It seems to me that a little girl with a good, kind father ought to be very happy all the time. Only think! He came with his old, every-day clothes on, and I guess aunt Abigail and grandmother don't mend them, as mother did. And he talked so, right before Mrs. Payson! and he says I am to go to the factory, and earn something for him, instead of working here for nothing. Mrs. Payson told him, 'For shame!' to talk about a frail child like me supporting a great, stout man like him. She told him he ought to work and support his children. He said he was sick, and looked terrible angry. But, auntie, I haven't told you the worst," said Winnie, going close to Hester. "Uncle Charles gave him a glass of bitters, and there is a good lot of rum in them. He used to give him some when mamma was alive, and make her cry. And when she would ask father not to drink, he used to say he was no worse than the parson, and her father and brothers. That always made mamma cry, and she used to say she was sorry they drank, for it was bad to drink ever so little, for fear they might drink more some time; and grandpa don't now."

"Uncle Frank and uncle Edward don't drink a drop," said Hester; "and I hope uncle Charles will leave off soon. It was wrong for him to give it to your father. Winnie, if I were you, I would ask him not to drink it, nor give your poor father any. Tell him what you have just told me about it. Perhaps you can help along the glorious cause of Temperance. You ought to be grateful to God for sending Wallace where he will not be tempted in that direction. He has signed the pledge — did you know it?"

"No, auntie — has he? Can't I sign? I want to. Then I can have a better chance to talk to others."

"Why, yes, dear, you can sign the pledge. But auntie must go now. Don't trouble your little head, darling, about the factory. You are my little girl. I have got you all in black and white now. You are to go to school, if nothing prevents, and prepare yourself to teach, or be useful in some other way."

Mr. Lovering's wedding took place in Elevia's sick room, very quietly. It was a solemn occasion. Brothers and sisters stepped softly, ay, reverently, into the presence of one apparently so near the eternal gate. The ceremony was performed by the aged pastor, whose white locks fell gracefully back from his noble brow. His voice faltered as he said, "What God hath joined together let not man put asunder," for he remembered the past. It had been his privilege to unite both bride and bridegroom in their former marriages. He had also married several members of the family. He thought of Elevia's joyous wedding festival. Only a few short years had passed, and what a change! When it was all over, Mr. Lovering stepped to his daughter's bedside, and said, —

"Are you tired, dear?"

"Not much," was the reply. "May God bless you, my dear parents, and make you a blessing to each other and the world." Mrs. Lovering stooped and kissed the cheek of the sufferer.

"Raise me up, dear mother. I have something which I wish to say to you, while you are all together.

> 'I am going home to heaven above:
> Will you go? — will you go?'"

She said, earnestly, looking from one to the other, "O, *will* you go?" She seemed to be waiting for a reply.

"I will try, I will try," passed from one to the other, until all had promised. She smiled contentedly.

"That promise is registered in the book on high," said the aged pastor. "O, keep it, my dear friends; keep it."

"Yes," said Elevia, "I expect you to keep it, and God expects it. But those of you who are out of Christ, don't wait until death calls you, or until earthly pleasures fade, and life grows dark; but come to Jesus. *Now* is the accepted time. Don't do as I did, — you know it all, — but come while in health and strength. Little Winnie, tell them what Jesus is to you."

"He is precious," said the child, folding her hands, "and very lovely."

"Is he always near you?" said the aged pastor, placing his hand on her head.

"He never leaves *me*," was the reply. "Sometimes I wander away from him, and get lost; but he never leaves me. He has said he wouldn't; don't you remember it? 'I will never leave nor forsake thee.'"

"How do you feel when you get lost, little pilgrim?" said the pastor, patting her tenderly on the head.

"O, sorry and frightened; and I just run back as fast as I can, saying, —

'Jesus, Lover of my soul,
Let me to thy bosom fly.'"

"I trust you are, indeed, a lamb of his flock," was the reply. "Should you like to confess Christ before the world?"

"Yes, sir, I should, when I am good enough. I should like to tell the whole world how good he is, and what he has done for me."

"I think we had better retire," said Mr. Lovering. "I fear Levie is overdoing."

"One thing more, father, and then you may go. I want you all, every one of you, to forgive Mason. He does not know how he has wronged me. Forgive him, and try to bring him to Christ. O, treat him kindly, and teach him the living way. To-morrow, when I am rested, I want to see him. You will not deny me?" she said, as she saw them look from one to another. This was a hard thing to ask of them; but they could deny her nothing. "Thank you," she said, as they promised. 'Blessed are the merciful, for they shall obtain mercy.' If God can forgive us, for Christ's sake, ought we not to forgive each other? I have but one other duty to do, and then I am ready to go, if it be God's will. Pray for me, dear brothers and sisters, that I may prevail, that my faith fail not. Dear pastor, pray for me and him. Good by."

CHAPTER XXIX.

SELF-COMMUNINGS. — THE STILL SMALL VOICE. — LIGHT IN DARKNESS.

"How cheerless and dreary this house has become," sighed Mr. Giles, "since Elevia left it! Why, it seems like a tomb. I wonder that I could ever have complained of her housekeeping. It was perfect, compared with Ann's, and her food delicious — better than sister Wiley's. I never thought of it till lately. If she had only submitted without arguing, as a woman ought, why, we should have been happy. Heigh-ho! I wonder if I have been exacting. Mr. Lovering and the doctor said I had, and that no mortal man, in his senses, ought to expect a woman to put up with such tyranny and miserly meanness. Yes, those were their very words. They said I was a chip of the old block.. How that cut me! For I confess father is a tyrant of the deepest dye to wife, children, and all. Poor Ann was his special aversion. Heigh-ho! I wonder if I haven't copied him, after all? Pshaw! I never struck Elevia. I'm not sure I shouldn't, though, but for fear of the family. I have wanted to; but Elevia always seemed so superior to other women, I mean Lucy, and Jane, and Ann. I know but little about females at large; I never thought them worth much notice."

Thus thought Mason Giles as he walked his room late

at night. His nights had been nearly sleepless since the
one he remembered as "the terrible night." He was
striving to solve a serious problem—he was searching
for the truth. The pale, beautiful face of his wife
haunted him day and night, as she looked when she said,
"I may have been a poor wife to you, Mason; forgive me. I tried to please you." Conscience echoed,
"She *did* try to please you, with a devotion few wives
could command." He seemed struggling to throw off
these unpleasant convictions; but in vain. He trembled
when he thought how nearly he had added the crime of
murder to his other sins. Strangely enough, as he
thought of little Unie, struggling in his arms, shrinking
away, and screaming as if in great pain, his feelings
softened towards her. O, was it fear and grief, and not
stubbornness? as he had thought. "Poor little thing!"
he murmured, walking rapidly up and down the room.
"Such a baby! How could I handle her so roughly!
I was mad with them, and spent my wrath on a helpless
baby—*my* baby—bone of my bone and flesh of my
flesh. Cowardly man! I hate myself for it. O, if I
had killed her! I felt as if I should like to do it. I
thank God I was kept from dashing the little head on the
floor. I fear I should if Hester hadn't rescued her. I
thought she was defying me, resisting my will. For the
first time in my life, I do feel truly thankful to God.
When Elevia spoke in that way, how angry I used to
feel! I thought I was my own keeper; I gloried in my
own strength. 'What had I that I did not get?' I
often inquired of her. 'Mason,' she would say, 'God
gives you the ability, the strength, and the opportunity
to do everything. Without him you could do nothing.'

I think now she was right. O God," he groaned, "what a miserable sinner I am, when I thought I was about right! Self-deceived and ruined for time and eternity! O, I dare not think of meeting God! And yet Elevia is as peaceful as a lamb, and really looks more cheerful than she has for a long time. Strange, strange! I should be in an agony if I thought death was near."

He threw himself heedlessly on the unopened bed, and wept for the first time since a child. Then said he, resolutely, —

"What a fool I am! I am no worse than many others, I suppose. I wonder what there is in the chapter about 'Wives, submit yourselves.' Hester wanted me to read it. She is a Christian, I declare, or she would have told of me. And what else but religion could induce her to spend her life taking care of other people's children — mine, for instance — and for nothing? How that child loves her! How safe she felt in her arms! Why should she follow it, and walk, too? That is the mystery. Yes, I do believe in religion. It is that which sustains Elevia now, that which makes Winnie so different from Envena. Yes, yes," he said, impatiently, "it is that which makes them so different from me, wretch that I am. I might have been happy with my wife but for this hateful disposition of mine. But I have driven my wife and child away from me, if not killed them both; and now my house is a tomb, and my soul a whited sepulchre. I am a 'hissing and a by-word.' O God, have mercy, have mercy! I can't bear this misery; my sins have found me out, and they are enough to sink me down to hell."

He shuddered, and, pressing his open palms close to his face, remained silent a moment. He then opened Elevia's Bible, which he had never looked into before, and read, "To my dear daughter Elevia, on her wedding day."

He then read the chapter named before, and found, to his great mortification, how far short he had come of doing his part in the marriage relation. He read on, turning from place to place, like a weary, discontented child. His eye fell upon the parable of the returning prodigal. "That I can't do," he mused; "I can't go to her. Haven't I said I wouldn't? Haven't I said it? No, I won't go near them; I'll fight it out alone. I have been a wicked, foolish man; but I won't own it to them. If Elevia's mother were alive, I could confess it all to her. She was a saint, if there ever was one this side of heaven. I must sleep. Ann never will learn to make my tea weaker."

Thus this night also wore away; but little sleep came to refresh Mr. Giles. It was the night after the wedding. Never had he known a more cheerless one. He arose looking so pale and haggard that Ann was moved to say, —

"Sick?" as he arose from a scarcely tasted breakfast. "Why don't ye eat suthin', or fret, as ye did to Lev? 'Fraid to — ain't ye? Ye needn't be," she continued; "I'd rather ye'd fret than die."

"Ann, let me alone — won't you? I ain't sick," was his only reply.

"Yes, I'll let ye alone, an' yer work too, an' ye like. I shan't keep 'ouse for a ghost much longer," muttered Ann.

"Well, Ann, you keep still; I'll be all right soon. You make my tea too strong; I can't sleep — that's all." He left the room without further delay. "Miserable man!" he thought, as he tried to busy himself about the place. "I can't set myself to work. Why, I miss *her*. How neat she always looked, and the table, and the house! But I didn't know it. Well, the Scripture is true — 'His house shall be left desolate:' that is something like it, and it is true. I almost wish it was burned down. It reminds me so much of what I might have enjoyed. O God! it is gone, all gone; henceforth there is nothing but sorrow and darkness for me, and I deserve it all — all, and more, too," he groaned. "O, I wish I could see Elevia once more."

That was indeed a prayer, and it was heard and answered almost as soon as it was uttered.

Let us return to grandpa Lovering's, and see what has been transpiring there on this eventful night.

When the company reached the parlor, Mrs. Lovering said, "Mr. Lovejoy, stop and pray for her here. If the dear child could see her husband converted, why, it would almost save her life. I can't bear to see her so distressed about him. That is the only thing which troubles her."

"I will," was the reply; "and as she is wishing to see him to-morrow, I will make it a subject of special pleading that the desire of her heart may be granted."

Earnestly and tenderly the case was presented at the throne of grace, with an importunity which seemed to admit of no denial. Tears came to every eye.

"I hope you will not depend upon my poor prayers," said the pastor; "but pray, as did the Master, all night.

If no answer of peace and promise come, pray till the morning. I feel the inspiration of prayer as I seldom do when no favorable answer is to be given. Lay hold on the mighty arm of God, my friends, wrestle as did Jacob of old, and God will bring it to pass. "The joy of his salvation" might save your daughter. If I see aright, it is hope deferred, or wounded affection that has prostrated her. Am I right? Could she see her husband clothed in Christ's righteousness, a new creature in him, with affections purified and elevated, it would, perhaps, prove an elixir of life more potent than all your efforts to save her; better for her than any remedy prepared by the most skilful practitioner, for 'a wounded spirit who can bear?'"

"She cannot recover," was the united voice of father, brothers, and sisters; but Winnie caught at the idea with the utmost tenacity.

"It won't do her any harm," said Mrs. Lovering; "let us pray — all of us. If the blessed child can only see him converted, she will die easier; that will be a comfort."

Winnie crept away to her little closet, and kneeling, said, tearfully, —

"Dearest Lord, I shall stay here until you tell me what you will do about uncle Mason, unless they call me. Blessed Spirit, help me, for I don't know how to wrestle, nor 'lay hold by faith.' Help me, for I want my uncle Mason converted. I want you to make him sorry, O, so sorry, that he can't help asking to be forgiven, and then, dear God, forgive him. O, do, do, Lord. Please to save him, and make auntie so happy that she will want to live; and then make her well, so that little Unie can have her mother to love, for that is better, O, so much better, than anything. O, make her well, so that she can live in her nice new house, and be happy with uncle and all of us. Dear Lord, I don't know how to tell you what I want, but the blessed Holy Spirit knows all about it. He sees that I want my uncle Mason to come to Jesus and see, as that other blind man did. Auntie said, 'O that he could see!' Make him see, Lord; don't let him go, but make him see and believe in Jesus."

Thus the child prayed on, weeping, and asking over and over again, until, weary, she paused in her prayer, saying, —

"I can't say any more about it now, dear Jesus: won't you see to him?" and dropped asleep.

Mrs. Lovering looked into the child's room, and found her there, still upon her knees — her head resting on the hard stool — her cheek still wet with tears.

"The spirit was willing," she said to Mr. Lovering, "but the flesh was weak. Just you come and see a sight you may never in your life see again."

"The dear child has been wrestling," said grandpa, as he raised her carefully in his arms and laid her on the bed. She roused a little, and murmured, "Dear Jesus, don't let him go."

"What if she has prevailed!" said grandpa, looking at his wife.

"What if she has?" was the reply — "why, we will thank the Lord, to be sure. But it can't be; it seems impossible that he should be converted."

"Nothing is impossible with God; otherwise I should think him given over," said Mr. Lovering. "But that child's zeal for God shames me, Lizzie. She will far outstrip us in the Christian race, if we don't wake up."

"I know it," was the reply; "it is high time we were up and doing. And now, my dear, I want to tell you that I think one stumbling-block is taken out of the way, and we can run the race more swiftly. I mean the banishment of all kinds of spirits as a beverage. Now, I think the blessed Holy Spirit don't want to live in the same place with one of Satan's engines of swift destruction — don't you think so? I think the church ought to arise, and shake herself clear of that sin; and she will have to before the gospel will run and be glorified."

"Yes, I think we have been blind in that regard — wilfully so, I fear. I am determined to clear my skirts of that sin; but I am afraid I have waked up too late to save Charles. He thinks he can't work without it."

"I should think he saw a living epistle of the effects of it when Morgan was here," said Mrs. Lovering; "how he has changed!"

"Yes, he was a noble fellow. It pains me to think how often he has taken a social glass with me," said her husband. "He has fallen low enough, while I am saved. By the blessing of God I am what I am; and by the same power I mean to be more consistent."

"I am glad you feel so," was the reply. "I feel just so, too. But you must go to sleep, or you will be sick, as sure as can be."

"Why, how came I in bed with my clothes on?" thought Winnie. "I must have got up in my sleep, and put them on. I am glad I went to bed again, and didn't get out of the window, or anything. I wonder if grandpa will let me go with him to tell uncle Mason. I almost love him now. I guess it won't be so hard to love him as I thought it would. For *her* sake," she said, " I must love him, and for Christ's sake, forgive him; that is it. Mrs. Payson — O, no! I forgot — grandmother, can I go with grandpa? I want to tell uncle Mason something."

"Yes, dear, I guess so. I'll ask him. You look pale: are you well?"

"O, yes, indeed; I feel nicely: my heart is as light as can be. I guess He is going to save him, — uncle Mason I mean, — and perhaps auntie will live, after all. Do people ever get well when the doctor says they can't, grandma? I shall speak to you pretty often, now I can call you that," she said, smiling brightly.

"Do; I like to have you. I never had a grandchild of my own."

"Well, you have got some own children, and grandchildren too, now — haven't you, grandmother?"

"Well, I hope they will own me. And I am pretty sure folks get well, sometimes, when the doctors say they can't, and die, too, when they say they won't. O, I know that too well," she said, sadly. "They said my Lizzie was in no danger, and my Lydia might get well; but they died, both of them. And there was my Samuel; he lay in a dying condition three days, with the fever; but he got well, and is married, you know: so we can't tell."

Winnie was allowed to accompany her grandfather, and found her uncle just as he had uttered the wish that was a prayer wrung from an awakened heart.

"Uncle Mason," she said, running eagerly to his side, "come; auntie wants you. Grandpa and I have come for you. He was married last night; and we are all going to love you now: auntie made us promise. She said you didn't mean to make her sick; you didn't know how she felt. O, you are feeling badly; well — I am glad — no, I mean I hope you will be better."

He had stood half bewildered while Winnie was talking.

"She wants me — she wants them to forgive me," he mused. A little while since, and he would have been angry; but now he is humbled. "Winnie," he said, as he sat upon a log, "I do feel badly. I am a wretched man. Your aunt is going to die," — he shuddered, — "and I know, now, that I killed her; yes, killed her slowly. You know how hard and unfeeling I was; and when she felt badly, I thought she was foolish, and I was angry. I believe I was possessed. What do I care for that pile of fine buildings, now, child?" he said, fiercely. "They *were* my gods. I thought your aunt ought to be happy in such a place. Now I have learned their value. I live here, but I am not happy, and never can be again."

He covered his face and groaned. Winnie felt frightened.

"O, I didn't want him to feel so dreadfully," she thought. "Dear Lord, help him to see the other side. O, do!". Tears came into her eyes. "I wish aunt Hester was here," she said. "She would tell you about the goodness of God, and how you must go to him and confess your sins, and he would forgive you for Christ's sake. I asked him, and he forgave my sins."

"You, Winnie," he said, "*you* have sins? What were they? It wasn't much to forgive your sins; they were nothing compared with mine."

"O, well, that don't make a bit of difference; we

can't go to heaven without a new heart, and God can forgive a great sinner just as well as he can a little one. But I was a dreadful sinner, uncle. I didn't love God, and I didn't want to stay where he put me. O, I was as bad as you. But my verse says, 'Though your sins be as scarlet, they shall be as white as snow.' I repented, and he forgave me all. He gave me peace when I believed on his Son Jesus Christ; and now I feel happy, almost always."

Mr. Giles had raised his head and listened.

"Winnie," he said, "do you think that I could be happy — even if my sins were forgiven — after I had killed my wife, and done so wickedly? No, never! You hadn't much to forgive," he said, almost savagely. "I tell you my sins can't be blotted out in a lifetime, no, nor through all eternity. Lost! lost!" he cried, bitterly; "sold unto sin."

Winnie went close up to the unhappy man, her fear all gone, and laying her hand on his, she said, —

"Dear uncle Mason, 'whosoever believeth on the Lord Jesus Christ shall be saved.' Why can't you believe on him, when he is so very lovely, and he loves you so? I will say that pretty hymn, —

> 'Just as I am, without one plea,
> Save that thy blood was shed for me,
> And that thou bidd'st me come to thee,
> O Lamb of God! I come! I come!'

Can't you say that, uncle Mason? O, it is so easy! I want you to come to Jesus first, and then go to auntie. Perhaps she will live when she knows you love her; and if you love Jesus, you will love everybody."

"Where is he, child?" said the distressed man; "where is he? I can't find him. He isn't for such as I."

"He is here," said Winnie, reverently. "He is here. Do you want him? Come, say it after me — in your heart, —

> 'Just as I am, without one plea,
> Dear Lord, I give myself to thee. Amen.'

Now, if you have said that truly, he will take you, and give you a new heart. But grandpa will think I am gone too long. Will you go to auntie now? — she wants you."

"I will come soon. Did you say she might live, if I loved her? Tell her I am not fit to love her, but I do. O, if she can only be spared, I will love the Lord as long as I live, and trust him even until death."

"Well," said Winnie, "I knew he would take you if you went to him. You are almost a Christian, so soon; only you must love the Lord, and let him do just as he pleases. Aunt Hester says he knows what is best for us. The Psalm says, 'Though he slay me, yet will I trust in him.' Mother used to say that when she was sick. He did slay her, for it was best," sobbed Winnie; "but she is in heaven, and don't want to come back. Now try, uncle Mason — say the hymn, all of it — and pray and wrestle, just as the minister told us to for you, last night. And we did. The Holy Spirit will tell you what to ask for, and perhaps before you go to auntie you can come to Christ."

Grandpa, as he sat in his carriage, heard enough of the conversation to satisfy him that the Spirit had begun its work. He prayed mentally that it might be perfected. When Winnie returned, he asked no questions.

"He is coming pretty soon," she said; "but I do hope he will go to Jesus first, for he is feeling dreadfully, and he looks sick, too. Grandpa, I think he will be a Christian."

"Then they were praying for me last night," mused Mr. Giles. "That is religion — is it? Well, it is a good thing. I wish I was a Christian — I do, I do. 'Just as I am' — O, that is vile enough; but there is all the more need of my going. 'Just as I am' — well, that is all the way I can go. I can't forgive myself, nor cleanse my soul from guilt. 'Just as I am' — O, I want to go, and I *will*, so help me God.

> 'I can but perish if I go;
> I am resolved to try;
> For if I stay away, I know
> I must forever die.'

Yes, —

> 'I'll go to Jesus, though my sins
> Have like a mountain rose;
> I know his courts, I'll enter in
> Whatever may oppose.'"

He sang almost unconsciously as he entered the house to change his dress. Ann looked up in amazement, but said nothing. He had sometimes sung in the choir, but never before in the house; and a psalm tune, too! what could it mean?

> "Prostrate I'll lie before his throne,
> And there my guilt confess;
> I'll tell him I'm a wretch undone,
> Without his sovereign grace."

"Crazy, I s'pose," said Ann. "Where are you goin'?"

"No," said he, "I guess not; I have been all my life.

Ann, I am going to be different. I want you to forgive me all my unkindness to you. Elevia has sent for me. Don't look for me back till you see me."

"Dyin'—ain't she? Is that w'at makes ye look so 'appy all to once?"

"No, she isn't dying, and I have a hope that she is going to live; and if she does, why, I am a happy man; for if she dies, I have killed her," he said, in a low, solemn voice. "You know it, Ann, just as my father killed another good woman—I mean your mother and mine, Ann. And that isn't the worst thing that he did, for she was a Christian, and has gone to heaven; but, Ann, I see it now; he killed all the tenderness out of your soul,—or soured it,—and made a petty tyrant of me. You know it, Ann; you were abused, but you fought it out and lived—you wouldn't bend. But, after all, if he had been your husband, it would have been harder—wouldn't it?"

Ann sat down as if overcome with sudden faintness.

"Don't bring it all up agin," she said, with a little quiver in her voice, "don't;" and she reached out her hand as if to put far away some dread object. "I know it; he killed 'er; an' I swore I would never forgive 'im, an' I 'oped God wouldn't. I never loved anything agin, an' I won't."

"That is it, Ann; I see it now. I have been seeing it more and more, ever since that terrible night. Why, it seems to me I have been blind all my life. What a mercy that I didn't kill that child!"

"I thought ye'd do it," was the reply; "but she'd been better off. I wish 'at somebody'd killed me when I was born—I do. I hain't seen nothin' but trouble, nor done nothin' but grow wuss and wuss — an' shan't. Don't say nothin' to me 'bout forgiveness — I shan't ask for it. I shan't forgive yer father; an' I shan't ask for nothin' I won't give," she said, as Mason spoke of the goodness of God, and his willingness to forgive sins. He looked at her pityingly, as he said, —

"I don't wonder you can't forgive him. I ought to have known better, and taken her part. She was a kind mother — wasn't she, Ann? I can't forgive myself for not treating her more respectfully. I was young when she died — wasn't I? But I must go; Elevia will be looking for me. Get Envena to come and stay with you, if I don't get home. I want to watch with Elevia if they will let me."

CHAPTER XXX.

BITTER MEMORIES. — WELCOME NEWS. — LOVE REWARDED. — ELEVIA SAVED.

ANN looked after Mason, in blank amazement, as he rode away, shading her eyes with her hand, and peering around the corner of the house, to make sure that he was really going to Mr. Lovering's. "Sunthin's got into 'im," she muttered; "goin' to die, likely as not. He was a pooty little feller, and mother sot 'er eyes by 'im. O, Lordy, Lordy! I never meant to think on 'er agin — never." She swayed her body back and forth like a reed shaken in the wind, and moaned aloud, "O Lordy, she wanted me to promise to meet 'er in 'eaven! Well, I didn't; I was cryin': she thought I couldn't speak. I ain't cried since, 'ardly, an' never meant to agin. There, I'm a fool!" she said, brushing a tear from her eye, spitefully. "Ketch me cryin' agin; 'twon't bring 'er back, nor make me young an' 'appy agin, nor take away this millstone out o' my 'eart. I 'ate 'im, an' I mean to 'ate him — so there!" She arose and busied herself about the house, struggling to overcome the feelings which Mason's words and his altered manner had aroused; "I've fit it out so fur," she thought; "I'll fight it all out. I never knuckled, an' I won't, to — to — " She was about to say "to God nor man;" but the impious thought startled her. She cowered and trembled before the unseen awful presence for a moment, and then continued, "I'll 'ave to knuckle before 'im, any 'ow; but I'll wait till I 'ave to."

"What has come over me?" said Mason Giles, as he rode along. "I feel easy and calm. My sins don't feel so heavy. Did I really go to Christ — did I? And did he receive me — *me*, such an incorrigible sinner, so hateful in my own eyes and in the eyes of God and man? Why, it can't be possible! Why, I only waited a moment at the door of mercy. I *did* go, I believe, with all my heart, and I cried one long, bitter cry, for I thought I should die. My sins seemed weighing me down, down to despair. Can it be that I had only to go to him and be healed? Then blessed, thrice blessed, be the name of the Lord. I will praise him while I live, and trust him when I die. I didn't deserve it — no, no; it is all of grace — all of grace. Hester must know this, for she saved me from an awful crime. Dear little Unie, those cruel blows I gave you in my madness sank into my soul! The image of Elevia, stretching out her little pale arms to me, saying, 'Forgive me, Mason!' I tremble to think how hardened I was. It is nothing but grace, free grace, that has removed the burden of guilt." He put the reins over his arm, took out his pocket-book, and removed the writing Hester had given him, and read it over and over again. "It was Mason Giles that extorted that writing — was it? I am ashamed and humiliated. What was I thinking of? Why, how much that sounds like a miserly heathen, as I was! O God, break once and forever this chain of selfish avarice, which has bound me, hand and foot!"

"There is Mason Giles driving up to the door," said

Martha, as she caught up the cradle in which little Unie was sleeping, and bustled into grandpa's room, and locked the door.

"What can he want?" said Hester to little Fostina — "what can he want, darling? You and auntie will go and see — won't we, darling?"

"Um," said the little one, smiling. "Artie Fossie, go see." Hester did not wait for him to knock at the door, but met him at the gate. She was calm externally; but her heart beat, and her limbs trembled. She nodded; but he reached out his hand cordially. Hester looked into his face, and felt more puzzled than ever as she reached out her reluctant hand. "You feel suspicious of me," he said, in a broken voice. "I should blame you if you did not. You ought not to trust me. How is little Unie? I won't ask to see her. But, Hester, I called to thank you for saving me from the crime of murder, and snatching my child from death. Here is that shameful paper I extorted from you. I don't ask for the one I gave you. If you ever see the time when you can forgive and trust me, why, give it to me — not till then." Hester sank down on a large stone by the gate, greatly agitated. As she did so, Martha, who was looking from the window, exclaimed, —

"What now, father? What do you suppose he is saying? Hester is all overcome. I wonder if Elevia is dead. Mason looks changed. I wish I knew what it all means."

"Wait, child," was his reply as he tottled to see for himself. Hester sat there, still bewildered.

"I can't understand it," said she. "Mason, am I dreaming? What is it? What does all this mean?"

"It means that the Lord has been dealing with me; it just seemed as if the Almighty hand had been placed firmly upon me: I could not shake it off. O, Hester, it was a terrible conflict; no one but God will ever know how awful!"

"What gave you relief?" said Hester, as she arose and went close up to him. "What changed you so, Mason?"

"Grace, free grace," was the joyful reply. "Little Winnie came with Mr. Lovering to tell me Elevia wished to see me. She found me distressed beyond measure, and insisted upon my going to Christ. I can't tell you what I felt or suffered in the few moments she was there. It seemed a long time to me. I know not how long it was. She seemed to compel me to go to the door of mercy just as I was. 'Lord, have mercy on me!' I cried — 'on *me*, who am worse than the chief of sinners.' He heard me, I hope, and saved me from despair. But I must go to Elevia. Forgive me, if you can. I don't ask you to trust me." He held out his hand. Hester took it, and said, "Truly, goodness and mercy shall follow me all the days of my life, for mine eyes have seen the salvation of one who was lost. Welcome to my Father's house — welcome. No longer feed on husks which the swine do eat, but feed on the bread of life. Mason, I have prayed for this, because I promised *her* I would; but my prayers were faithless. I could not feel that they reached the throne. But God is good; give all the glory to him. Break the news carefully to Elevia: great joy might kill her."

"Is that so, Hester? How ignorant I am! What shall I do?" He looked thoughtful and perplexed.

"I don't know how you will manage," was the reply. "You must ask God to guide you: that you will have to do in all things."

"I will ask him," was the reverent reply. "I will trust him. Pray for me while I am gone. I feel as if she were going to be spared."

"Poor man!" sighed Hester; "he will be disappointed in that. This has come too late to save her life. Poor man!"

"Is Saul also among the prophets?" said Martha, when Hester had relieved her mind by telling her what the reader already knows.

"Yes," said Hester, with tears of gratitude in her eyes, "and the scales have fallen from the eyes of Saul the persecutor. Martha, I thank God that Paul left his experience for our encouragement. It helps me to believe in Mason's conversion. I feel rebuked for my want of faith. Why, I didn't believe the grace of God. even, could change that man so! I want you to see him, he looks so different. O, it is wonderful! I have faith in his conversion. God grant he may not be deceived, and deceiving us!"

"Well, if Mason is really a Christian, and holds out to the end, I will never be so faithless again," said Martha. "I thought he, at least, was given over. I never could pray for his conversion."

"Child," said grandpa, "hasn't he promised to save all that come unto him, even to the uttermost? Don't be so faithless, Martha. Nothing is too hard for God." When Winnie, in her simple, child-like way, had told her grandmother all she knew about uncle Mason, the little woman was all astir with expectation.

"Why," said she, "I don't believe it—no, I don't mean that, Winnie; but it doesn't seem possible! What will Elevia say? Dear child, she isn't expecting it—is she? Won't it kill her if it comes all at once? What shall I do? I wish Hester was here."

"God is here, and Jesus is here," said Winnie, timidly. "Why don't you ask him, grandma?"

"I will, this blessed moment. If his coming to life should kill her, it would be sad enough. You say he prayed that she might live?"

"Yes, I called it a prayer. He didn't kneel or say 'Amen;' but he folded his hands tight, so, and said, 'O, if God will only spare her, I will love him as long as I live, and trust him when I die!' He said it like an earnest prayer, grandma."

"Well, child, I think it was; for prayer is desire, spoken or unexpressed." Mrs. Lovering came back soon, saying, "Why, child, he told me what to do almost before I asked him. Run, child—no, don't run; but go quietly, and tell her he is feeling badly about his sins, and says he is going to do better. Tell it a little at a time, dear; be careful."

"Yes, I will," said Winnie, as she went with her little heart fluttering like a caged bird. "Grandpa and I have been for uncle Mason, auntie," said she; "he is coming pretty soon."

"Is he?" said the sick one, languidly. "Winnie, did you know I had given him all up? The distress is all gone. I heard you pray last night, dear, in your little closet, right at my head. O, so earnestly! My heart went out with every word I could hear at first. Then came a strange, sweet peace, as if your prayer was really answered."

"Did you hear me, auntie? Why, I did not think you could. Have you always heard? I thought no one but God heard me in there." Winnie seemed disconcerted.

"It was all right, dear. I thank you for that prayer, although I could not hear it all. I knew that you were praying for poor Mason, and it lifted the burden from my soul." Winnie remained silent a while, and then said, —

"Uncle is sorry he has been so wicked. He loves you, auntie, and wants you to get well. I think he is seeking Christ." Elevia had raised her head from the pillow as if fearful that she should not hear every word.

"Say it again, little comforter, say it again."

"I think he is seeking Christ, and will find him. But you must lie down and be very quiet, or you can't see uncle when he comes."

"Seeking Christ," said Elevia — "wants me to live. Winnie, don't deceive me. I know you don't mean to; but if it is true, can I — can I — bear to die?" She pressed her hands tightly over her face. "O Lord, could I say it, then? Could I say, 'Thy will be done'?"

"Yes, auntie," said Winnie, hurriedly, "I think you could. He could help you say it, if he wanted you to go; but perhaps he will let you live. Grandma says she has known people to get well when every one thought they were going to die."

"Well," said Elevia, "I will try to trust him. He doeth all things well. All is well. I will lie here and wait, and see what the Lord will do for me and mine. And, Winnie, couldn't you just pray here, a little prayer, that I might endure to the end? O, do! Pray that I may have peace and strength." Winnie prayed; the words were few and broken, but they brought rest to the excited invalid. "I can bear it now," said she, looking up with a smile.

"Shall I go out when uncle comes?" said Winnie.

"Yes, dear, I think you had better. But don't go farther than your closet, Winnie. If I want you, I will speak." Mrs. Lovering fluttered about like a bird in a plum tree, when Mr. Giles drove up to the door. She looked through the blinds, and tried to read his face. It was sad, very, and pale, and his step, she thought, faltered. She pitied him.

"He must be thinking of all those wicked actions," she thought, as she met him at the door, and held out her hand. He shook it cordially, but seemed agitated.

"I will show you right up to Elevia's room," she said, "if you can be calm. I guess you can. You won't have to say much, for Winnie has prepared her for it all. Mr. Giles, I am so glad you feel different! it will be such a comfort! We are all glad. Go in, and if she wants me, speak right at the head of the stairs."

"Will she bear it?" said he, speaking low and fast.

"O, yes, I think so; only be calm." They looked into each other's faces for a moment, when Elevia, again reaching out her arms, exclaimed, —

"Dear Mason, I am so glad, so glad!" He took the pale, cold hands in his, as he whispered, —

"Elevia, my wife, my poor, poor wife, forgive me. Can you forgive me? I have seen my sin and folly." He folded his arms about her, and wept. "I shall kill you, after all," he said, raising his head, and looking at her, wondering that she was so very, very still.

"No, Mason; I am happy — too happy to speak. Can it be, can it be, that you love me? I thought I should be willing to die if you would only love me; but now it would be sweet to live," she said, clasping her arms about his neck. "O God, help me to still say, 'Thy will be done!'"

"Hush! you are not to die. God will spare you. I feel it; I have felt it ever since I cried for mercy and was heard. You will live to let me atone for the past, to win back the confidence I have forfeited. You will live to help me conquer the evil demon that has possessed me, to bless your father, and take care of *our* baby." He used to call it *hers*. She looked up into his face tearfully, and said, "Mason, I fear this cannot be. See how emaciated I am — see."

"Yes, I see," said he, taking the thin hand in his. "Elevia, I think these little emaciated arms helped to convict me, when you reached them out to me, and said, 'Mason, forgive me.' Ah, Elevia, I was lost! but I trust, by the grace of God, I am found! I shall nurse you day and night; you shall have everything that money can buy — *anything*. For, since I really believed I must lose you, I have felt that life is nothing without you."

"But, Mason," she said, "I shall be nothing but a baby, worse than ever, for a long time; it will wear you all out."

"I think not, Elevia. I know I shall be clumsy and awkward; but I feel as if I just wanted you to be a baby, and let me tend you. I used to want to when we were first married; but I thought it would be weak and foolish. That was the way I felt about Unie; but I thought it would be silly and womanish to love her, and I stifled it all, Levie. I stifled it all until I really thought I disliked her, and you, too. O, but for your sickness I should have gone on from bad to worse! But I am talking too much."

"No, no," she said; "go on. It makes me feel stronger to see you. Can't you just take me in your arms a moment? Call mother." Mr. Giles started.

"Why, you don't call her that — do you?"

"Yes, I call her mother. She likes to have me, and I like to. It pleases father. He has been a good father to me. Mason, can't you love him for my sake? If you would only call him father, it would help to unite you."

"I will," was the reply. Mrs. Lovering came at the first call. She looked eagerly at the sick one. She was no worse — that was plain; and something in her face made her think, 'She is saved.' Together they raised the invalid, and placed her in the arms of the husband. She lay there contentedly, as a weary child in its mother's bosom. Winnie slept that night — grandpa, grandma, aunt Judith — *all* slept, leaving the sick one with the repentant husband, who, if awkward, was very tender, and quite acceptable to the invalid.

CHAPTER XXXI.

THE DAY OF MIRACLES, OR MR. GILES AND MR. LOVERING MADE FRIENDS.

NOT "Herod and Pilate," but Mr. Lovering and Mr. Giles, "were made friends that day," as Mr. Giles confessed his faults, and told him of his new hopes, and of his determination to lead a different life.

"I shall stumble often," he said, humbly; "but with Christ for my Saviour, and Levie for my helper, I think I shall be able to overcome at last. Father, — if you will let me call you so, — I have enjoyed more in these few days, which have been spent in my wife's sick room, than ever before in my life. But I have some terribly stubborn enemies to overcome — I mean selfishness and avarice. These are a part of myself. Other sins have sprung from these false, deceitful roots. Shall I ever overcome them?" he said, sadly.

"The grace of God is sufficient for all our necessities, my son," said Mr. Lovering, taking him warmly by the hand. "I thank my God that you are hoping in his mercy, and, as I hope and believe, are a regenerated, changed man. But regeneration is not sanctification. You have a conflict before you, a race to run, a victory to obtain. Look to Jesus, my son. He is the Author and Finisher of our faith. Look to Jesus, and go forward; seek, and you shall obtain help in every time of trouble.

But there is one thing I wish to caution you against. Don't spend your time in vain regrets for the past. Improve and enjoy the present; so shall you be prepared for the future in this life and that which is to come. God bless you, and help us both to be wiser and better men. I scarcely realize that Elevia, the dear child, is to be given back to us. Let us not be too sanguine; it may not be, after all."

"Why," said Mr. Giles, "brother Edward (it was the first time he had called him 'brother') thinks she may. Don't you see, she is stronger, takes more nourishment, and sleeps better?"

"That is favorable," said the father — "all favorable. But consumption is so deceptive, and I have so entirely given her up!"

"That is it," said Mr. Giles, earnestly; "you saw how low she was, and gave her up, long before I thought she was much sick; that makes the difference. To be sure, she does look poorer and paler for a day or two; but Edward says that is not bad. Come, you must not be as loath to believe her better as I was to believe her sick. How you must have despised me!"

"And you must not so constantly refer to the past," said Mr. Lovering. "Forget it as much as possible. I believe you have seen your mistakes, and are trying to rectify them; so don't dwell upon them."

"That is what Elevia tells me," was the reply. "But you must let me look into the old volume a little, until I am confirmed in the faith, and established in the new life." Mrs. Lovering smiled as Mr. Giles returned from a foraging expedition, with raisins, figs, dates, and wine, and dolefully exclaimed, —

"The very things I wanted most for her are not to be had — grapes and peaches. I told Mr. Trueman to get them for her at any price. Edward says there is nothing so good for her. It is too bad!"

"O, well," was the reply, "he will get them for her in a day or two. But why don't you ride over to T——, and get some of my son? He has a hot-house. He wrote me some time ago that he should have grapes from then until Christmas; and as likely as not he has early peaches."

"Why, I never thought of it! I'll ride over; I can get back before night." He went into the sick room, noisily, to be sure; he was not used to it; but he went lovingly, and it was no matter. His step was like music to the sick one, and his love was the very elixir needed to send the life-blood coursing through the veins, slowly, at first, but surely, until the wasted energies were restored sufficiently to take a firmer stand.

"I make you a sight of trouble," she said, as he took leave of her; "but I shall be better by and by. I think the grapes will help me."

"Don't think of the trouble," he said; "if I can get you well, it is enough;" and he kissed her good by. "I wonder if I am really the same man," he thought as he rode along, mind and heart full of gratitude. "I wonder if I am Mason Giles, who always thought these little attentions and affectionate ways foolish and childish, especially to wives. O, father, would that I could show you your sin and folly! But I cannot; nothing but the power of God can show you how much you are losing, how much suffering you are bringing upon others, how much injury you are doing. I can pray for you;

that is all; for I verily believe you would knock me down, or throw the first thing you could lay your hand on at me, if I should speak to you about it ever so kindly. Well, I wouldn't go back to the old life for the whole world; for I have never been happy in it, and I think that very unhappiness, that dissatisfied feeling, which I have always had, has caused most of my fretting at Elevia. Dear child, I wonder she can confide in me so soon. How I have made her suffer! I can't help thinking it over, unpleasant as it is. I suppose these sad reflections are the legitimate fruits of my sin, just as much as peace and joy are the fruits of righteousness. How the old burden comes back again! Father Lovering is right. I must 'pray without ceasing.' But I suppose I had better not look back too much, but 'press forward.'"

"Is this the day of miracles?" said Hester, as she called to see for herself, "or am I dreaming? Elevia is certainly better — a little better. How satisfied she looks!"

"Yes," said Mrs. Lovering, "I see it. I think she will live. But she will be months getting up, blessed lamb! But that don't puzzle me half so much as the change in Mason. Just you look here now. See all these figs, and raisins, and things. What shall I do with them?"

"That is just like a man not used to sickness," said Hester, laughing. "And then we poor mortals always go from one extreme to the other. We swing back and forth like a pendulum when you strike it a smart rap, until, after a while, it swings about right. But I don't know what to think." She was silent a short time.

"Lizzie, love is a powerful agent. It *kills* sometimes," she said, with a strange smile; "it *kills*. And now we see that it makes alive; that is, if Elevia lives, it will. Nothing else could have saved her. O, what a wonderful gift it is, but dangerous, if used carelessly or thoughtlessly. Lizzie, you remember Horace." She waited for no reply, but went on. "If I could have known of Mehitable Sharp's perfidy in season —" She buried her face in her hands for a moment, while her whole frame shook with emotion. Mrs. Lovering sat motionless, wondering if Hester's affection had been so strong as to outlive all these years. "Why, I supposed she had got over it, she is always so cheerful," she thought. Hester raised her head soon, saying, with another of those strange, sad smiles, —

"Lizzie, if I had known, I might have saved him. Religion saved me. There, don't speak of this. I came to rejoice with you all, and not to weep for myself; that is the best medicine for a wounded spirit. I must not stop to weep or repine, but do with my might what my hands find to do, that I may be all ready when the Master calls."

"That woman deserves to be hung," said Mrs. Lovering, impulsively, "to make you suffer all this time! Why, I — well, I know I am not as good as you are, I couldn't forgive her, nor do as you have done."

"By the grace of God, I am what I am," was the low reply. "I do not hate her; but as, day by day, I draw nearer to eternity, nearer to God and Horace, I pity her. May God have mercy on her. How can she dare to meet the judgment, with her sins like a millstone about her neck?" Winnie was delighted to see aunt

Hester, she was *so* happy! Uncle Mason and aunt Elevia were saved; she felt sure of it. "And now," she said, "there is but one great burden left — *my father*," she whispered. "But I don't try to carry it alone; it is too heavy. I have given it to Jesus, and he carries it most all the time now."

"That is right, dear," said Hester; "I am glad for you. But you are looking pale, and must come home and play and romp with the children, or you will get sick."

"But, auntie," was the quick reply, "do Christians play? I am a Christian, I hope."

"I hope so, dear; but you are a child also. Play, amusement, recreation of the right kind, is not sinful. Children should play, and run, and rejoice in their youth. You know there is a time for all things, Winnie, and whatsoever we do we should do for the glory of God."

"How can I glorify him playing?" said the child, with a puzzled look.

"O, you can strengthen your body, which is his, preserve your health, and make those about you happy. The little lambs and kittens play, and praise God in that way as well as they can. Do you understand?"

"Yes, I think I do; but I don't feel much like playing now. I had rather praise him by praying."

"Well, dear, pray till you feel like playing, then." Hester saw that the child was suffering from her confinement to the sick room, and was sadly needing rest. She was becoming morbidly sensitive. Her childhood had been crushed, cruelly crushed. "I must find some way to take her home," she said to Martha, "or she will be sick."

"I know it," said Martha, thoughtfully. "Suppose I go over and stay to help them, and let Winnie come home a while. Playing with the children will be just the thing for her."

"That will do," said Hester; "but we must let her stay a day or two longer, until Elevia takes a fair start in the way to health. It will be a long road, poor child!"

"How funny it seems to have you feeding me!" said Elevia, as she looked up in her husband's face with a smile. "Those grapes are very nice, but it does seem to me they taste better from *your* hand. It is so strange and pleasant! O, how glad I am I can live some longer! How happy we shall be, now that we know how to live!" A tear came into the husband's eye as he looked into the pale, thin, but happy face, and thought of the past.

"I hope you will not be sorry that I live," said Elevia, as she saw the sad expression.

"Don't speak in that way — don't, if you love me. What would life be without you? I was thinking of the change in you since I took you from your home, so full of life and joy, and how I brought you back broken-hearted, suffering, almost dying, and left you so coldly, without dreaming I —"

"O, Mason," was the tearful reply, as she laid her hand pleadingly over his mouth, "dear Mason, don't look back — look forward. It is all over now. You didn't understand me — how could you? I was to blame, too."

"I don't know how or when you were to blame — though I blamed you then. But this subject pains you;

we will drop it. Take another grape, while I say, once for all time, I thank you, Elevia, for not submitting to my unreasonableness. I should have been as great a tyrant as father, if you had. I should never have been happy, nor let my family be happy. Under God you have saved me. I shudder to think of the yoke I have escaped; so let us thank God and take courage. But don't expect me to be perfect — will you? I am so different from you and your family! That was why I didn't like them — did you know it? They were a standing rebuke to me; but now they shall be my example."

"Let Christ be our Example, our Leader, the Captain of our salvation, my dear husband," was the fervent reply. "I long to be well and strong again, so that I can realize the dream of my girlhood, in my own house, with my own dear husband. I long to show you what a good little wife I shall be, now that I have you to love and lean upon. How happy we shall be with little Unie! O, you will love her so, now that you don't shut your heart against her! You will have a family altar — won't you, Mason? How pleasant our home will be! Our friends will love to visit us. Won't it be delightful?"

"It will," was the abstracted reply. He was wondering how such a sinner as he had been should ever erect an altar of praise in his house. What would father say? What would brother Wiley and Ann say? His heart failed him. There was a cross. Should he be able to take it up? He noticed the sad eyes of his wife upon him, and told her of what he had been thinking.

"It will be a cross," was the reply; "but Hester says we must never go round a cross, or step over it, but stoop to take it up, and we shall find it easy, blessed work to carry it. So cheer up."

He thought a moment, and then said, hesitatingly, —

"There will be a cross for you, Levie, when you get home. Can you bear it, think?"

"Perhaps so: what is it? I can't bear much now. I see every little thing depresses me, even a sober look on your face. I am so childish, I wonder you all bear with me so patiently."

"I wonder," said Mason, "that you are not more childish. About the cross: I have been thinking over Ann's past life, and I pity her. She was only a little thing when she came to father's. What a place for a fatherless child to come to! She was looked upon as an intruder. I was taught to think so. No one loved her but mother; and she loved mother with a passion you would not think her capable of feeling. I remember how she wept and sobbed when mother died. Father sternly sent her from the room, saying, she was 'enough to raise the dead.' I shall never forget her look as she turned and said, 'Only that you would abuse her so, I would cry until I did wake her up.' He sprang after her with his hand upraised. She darted like a bewildered spirit from the room, exclaiming, 'I'm glad, I'm glad she is dead — now you can't beat her any more.' Father muttered a low curse, and left the room."

"It was a terrible scene over the dead," said Elevia — "wasn't it? Why didn't she leave the family?"

"Strangely enough," was the reply, "all the property belonging to her own father was entirely in my father's hands during his life. How it came so I never knew. He would never come to any settlement, nor give her anything. Said she might stay there as she had done, if she would *behave*, which meant that she must be a slave."

"Poor Ann!" murmured Elevia; "what a life to lead."

"Yes; you may well say that. From that day a warfare has been waging between them. Both have fought with a zeal worthy of a better cause; neither is conquered. Father can't send her off empty, and she won't go without what belongs to her. And now, as I remember my mother's dying words to me, boy that I was, I want to do something for her, if you consent."

"What were they?" said Elevia, eagerly.

"'Mason, take care of Ann when you are old enough. You will see how it is,' she whispered; 'take care of her. You are all she will have left, and she loves you. She is a good girl.' My father entered; I heard her saying something to him about Ann and the property. He grew angry, and I left the room. Yes, Elevia, I left the room, bewildered, to be sure, for I loved my mother, but, strangely enough, with the feeling that she had said something wrong to father; for I thought no one ought to gainsay or withstand him, and this my poor mother had taught me. But I shall tire you all out. I will tell you the rest some other time."

"No, no; tell me all now. What can you do for Ann? I can't rest till I know."

"Why, I want her to have rooms in our house, and live in peace the rest of her life, if you consent. I know how unpleasant it will be for you, and you must count the cost."

"Mason, Mason," was the quick, nervous call, "do you know what you ask of me? Could we be happy with her there? Wouldn't Unie be like her? O, I wish I knew!"

"There, there," said Mr. Giles, alarmed at the excitement he had caused; "be quiet, Elevia. You shan't have her around unless you are willing. I ought not to have spoken of it now."

"Willing? O, I am willing that you should do right. I am; yes, I hope I am. Poor Ann! poor Mason! I am so selfish!" She wept hysterically. "O, Mason, you must do right — don't mind me."

"O, dear," thought Mr. Giles, "I have made a foolish blunder now. I wonder if I can ever understand women and children, and sick folks. Elevia," he whispered close to her ear, "Elevia, don't cry; you shall have it all your own way. I am sorry I —"

"Well, you needn't be," was the gentle reply; "you ought to speak about it. I am sorry I am so selfish. I shall get over it; and when I am stronger, I shan't give way to my feelings so. I promise you that, if you will put up with it till then." She looked inquiringly into his face. "Will you?"

He stooped and kissed her, saying, —

"Yes, indeed; and when you are stronger, perhaps you will stoop to take the cross, and find it lighter than you think. If not, I shall put it out of your way."

"No, you shan't," she said, smiling through her tears; "that won't do. If God don't remove it, I shall take it up. Ann shall stay if he wills it so. But I am wasting precious strength. Kiss me again, and then soothe my head so that I can sleep. I am very tired."

Mrs. Lovering's predictions proved true about Elevia's recovery. She had relapses and break-downs; but health at last rewarded those who had so carefully watched over her. Mr. Giles, in his turn, went back and forth, spening all the time he could with his wife. Ann muttered, sighed, and scolded in turn.

"Ye'll go to the poor 'ouse, all on ye, yet, likely's not. I can't 'elp it. I work 'ard 'nuff."

"O, no, we shan't, Ann," said Mr. Giles. "I am pretty well off yet; and Elevia is getting well. She'll be home by and by, and then we want you to keep house in the west room. You'll be company for us, and can come and go when you please."

"Do'no 'bout that; w'ere's the money comin' from?"

"O, it shan't cost you anything for rent, or wood, or milk, or vegetables; and I'll fix things so that father will pay you so much yearly; at least I think I can. He ought to, and shall, if —" He stopped, for Ann was looking at him in astonishment.

"Be ye crazy, Mason?" she said, at length. "Lordy, Lordy! 'ow much ye look like *'er.* O, Lordy!" Ann covered her wrinkled face. "'Ow it all comes back! I wish ye'd fret and fuss as ye used to; I can stan' that, but I can't stan' this 'ere; I ain't used to 't. Nobody but *'er* ever spoke a kind word to me after, after —" Ann broke down.

"You mean after your father died and mother married again. I know it, Ann; it was a shame. I am going to be a different man from my father. But the Lord knows I came near killing my wife, as he did our mother. I remember it all now, and see it all. You won't go back there — will you? It is bad for you both."

"Do'no; Leve won't want me when she gets well. Nobody wants me when they can 'elp it."

"Yes, she will; you see if she don't. She is a good

girl — Elevia is, Ann. She loves me, with all my faults. You will be the best of friends yet."

"She's good 'nuff, I s'pose. W'en is she comin'?"

"Pretty soon, if nothing happens. Ann, do you remember how father pulled off mother's flowers, — red and yellow, great and small, — and put them in a gorgeous wreath, round her poor dead face?" No answer. "Ann, I think you pulled them out and threw them to the hogs — didn't you? I am glad you did it. I didn't understand it then. What did he do it for?"

"O, Lordy! I do'no ; 'e said she liked such trash, an' 'e wanted the ground."

After a little silence Mr. Giles said, "Ann, I think mother was a Christian."

"Course she was ; w'ere'll ye find one if she warn't?" was the gruff reply.

"O, I think she was, and I hope I am one. She told me to take care of you when I was a man. I haven't done it — you have taken care of me. I am going to do better. I shall pay you for keeping house ; and I hope you will be a Christian some time."

She looked up at him bitterly as she said, —

"I tell ye I won't forgive 'im; an' I won't be mean 'nuff to ask arter w'at I won't give." She left the room. "O, Lordy!" she mused ; "w'ats come over 'im? I can't stan' it — I can't — I'd rather he'd beat me."

She wrung her hard, toil-worn hands, as if to wring out the bitter thoughts that came creeping in at the door of her heart, so long closed to human sympathy, which, as she thought, had been rudely pried open by the voice of Christian love.

"No, no ; I won't forgive 'im," she muttered. "I won't ; I can't. Didn't he kill 'er — didn't he? If I ever do forgive 'im, it'll be w'en I can't 'elp it — there now. God may forgive 'im, but I can't; no, no, I can't. She don't want me to — I know it — O, I know it."

"I can't let you carry your wife home till Thanksgiving," was Mr. Lovering's reply to the importunities of Mr. Giles. "She will be stronger then. No; I want to kill the fatted calf, and have the whole family together. What do you say to that?"

"Why, I shall have to submit," was the reply. "But when I do get her, I shan't give her up again so easily," he said, laughing. "But I can never thank you enough for what you have done for us. I insist upon paying our board since I have been here."

"Well, I shan't refuse to take a moderate sum. You will feel better; and besides, I am not as rich as I might be, and Harmony's children must be looked after."

"I know it," said Mr. Giles, "and I want you to carry out Elevia's wishes, and pay for Winnie's schooling out of her portion. I have engaged the best girl I could find to help Elevia, and think we shall be very happy after this."

"If Ann troubles her, and renders her life miserable, I shall expect you to make different arrangements," was the reply. "You see I talk to you now just as I do to my own boys. I have always been an old patriarch among them," he said, laughing. "Frank and Edward consult me about as much as Charles, and then they all do as they please. That is about it, I believe. So you won't mind my taking liberties," he said, as Mr. Giles changed color.

"No, I won't mind — or I will try not to. I have been out of the way, and I don't wonder you can't trust me."

"Yes, I do trust you; I only speak about these things. I believe you mean to do right, and I think you will."

Perhaps my readers will think me a great while telling my story. Please be patient while I tell you what became of the children who had been the objects of so much tender, unselfish love; so unfortunate, and yet so richly blessed. The little, pale, sallow baby we introduced to you at the beginning has been maturing into a lovely, thoughtful child. The circumstances of her little life have prepared her to begin the work of self-denial, for which she seems to have been rescued from an untimely death. She had one of those confiding natures which steal into all hearts not barred against them by selfishness. That seems to be the mission of all babies. They are the golden keys that the All-Father sends to unlock the deepest fountains of human affection, and draw out the hidden sympathies of the soul, which lie buried beneath the dust and ashes of selfishness and corroding cares. Theirs is a glorious mission. Rusty and crusty must that soul be, which resists the holy influence of the baby, and refuses to take in these little ones, who come to us like sweet odors from the source of love — like bright, sparkling drops from the great Fountain of all good. But *our* baby had a wonderful smile, wonderful eyes, and a wonderful faculty for creeping into the snuggest, warmest corner of all hearts. Perhaps, as she was to be left a helpless infant, worse than fatherless, she came more richly freighted from the Infinite Source of love. Perhaps, as she had a dangerous, difficult road to travel, a mission to accomplish, she came armed for the conflict. We shall see.

CHAPTER XXXII.

Fostina's Mission.

"Where is my father?" said a little girl of seven summers. "Where is he?" she repeated, fixing her large, dark, beautiful eyes searchingly upon the yet fair, pleasant face of our old friend, Hester Strong.

"Fossie, darling, why do you wish to know? Are you not happy here with us? Get your dollie, dear, and I will try to help you dress it."

"No, no," was the impatient reply; "I want to see my father — I must. You say my sweet mamma loved him, and I must see him. Tell me where he is; please, auntie, do. Now grandpa Maulie has gone to Heaven, I want my father — I want him." She laid the little pale face wearily against the broad, loving bosom which had sheltered her so tenderly all those years.

"You grieve me, darling," said Hester, putting her arm about the child, and stroking the rich, dark hair; "darling, you grieve me. If I thought it would make you happy, I would carry you to see your father; but —"

"But *what*, auntie — what is it? What has he done? Is he blind, or lame, or crazy, like poor Mr. Davis? I must know. The children at school whisper about him, and ask me where he is, and laugh because I don't know. And I must know. I am seven years old.'

now," she said, disengaging herself from those loving arms; and, brushing the tears nervously away, she raised herself to her utmost height, saying, "Don't you see how tall I am? Such a big girl, and don't know my father!"

"Yes, I see," said Hester, smiling at the attitude the child had taken; "but you always loved to have grandpa call you '*Little Mary*;' '*My Mary*'—didn't you?"

"Yes, I did; but he is dead now, and I want to see my father: you said I might when I was old enough."

"Well, dear," said Hester, thoughtfully, "if you think you know what is best for you, I will tell you all about your father; but I think you had better wait."

"Auntie, I don't know what is best; but I am very, very unhappy." She threw herself into those ever-open arms, and wept passionately.

"Better tell her all about it now," said Martha Manlie; "she can't feel much worse."

"Darling," said Hester, softly,—"darling, do you remember the large, ragged man that used to come here when grandpa was alive, and how grandpa used to call you into his room, and tell you stories while he staid?"

"Yes, auntie; who was it? He had an old hat, and walked crooked all round. And Elida used to scold at him, and call him 'naughty.' Who was it? I used to look out of the window when he went off, and breathe just *so*,"—taking a long breath,—"and grandpa used to put his hand on my head, and say, 'Thank God!— thank God!' What made him? *He* isn't—" She raised herself, and started back so that she could fix those strange, beautiful eyes on Hester's face, and waited almost breathlessly — "*he* isn't —" she repeated.

"If he were your father, could you love him, and should you still want to go and see him?" was the reply. The child looked at one, then at the other, and then her eye rested on a little picture of her mother. She seemed bewildered and perplexed. At length, bursting into fresh tears, she exclaimed, vehemently, —

"I think you are naughty to talk that way. What would *she* say? She wouldn't love that man, auntie — never!" After she became more quiet, Hester told her all about her father, and the circumstances of her mother's happy death, and her father's rapid fall into drunkenness and ruin.

"Do they ever get better?" said the child, stifling her grief — "do they, auntie?"

"Yes, dear, sometimes."

"Who cures them? God?"

"Yes; he sometimes blesses the efforts of good people, who labor for the temperance cause; and drunkards sign the pledge, leave off drinking, and become good again."

"What is the pledge? Do any but drunkards sign it?"

"Yes, dear; Martha and I have signed it, Winnie and Wallace have, and a great many others."

"Then why don't you get my father to sign it?" she said, reprovingly. "I want to sign the pledge, and then I shall get him to sign it, and he won't wear those ragged clothes any more. He shall walk like uncle Edward, and I will buy him a new hat, and then he shall come to the school-house, and they shall see that I have a father as well as they — can't I, auntie?" she inquired, eagerly.

"Why, yes, dear; you can sign the pledge, and labor, and pray, and be a nice little temperance girl," said Hester, cheerfully. "Now that is settled, get your dollie, and we will see what we can do for that."

"O, but I want to sign it now, auntie. What if he should die? I must begin right off." Hester wrote what she called a pledge, and guided the little fingers to sign it. A sigh of relief escaped when it was accomplished.

"There," said Hester, "you must ask God to lead you now, and wait till he opens the way."

"You pray about it, auntie. I shouldn't know anything but 'Our Father,' and 'Now I lay me,' and such prayers." Hester prayed, and then called the child's attention to her dollie again.

"But, auntie, I shall want a prayer like that."

"Well," said Hester, "after you have said, 'Our Father,' you can say, 'Dear Lord, please to help me reform my father; please to save him from the power of sin, for Jesus' sake;' and then you must wait till he opens the way."

Elida Lentell was a general favorite in school. No one attempted to tease her. They couldn't; or, if they attempted it, they were obliged to escape ignobly from her keen, sharp wit. One boy, who knew something of her history, maliciously inquired, —

"Do you remember when you lived in the swamp?" alluding to 'the small house near the swamp,' where we first found Elida.

"Why, no," was the prompt reply. "What was I

then? — a fish or a frog? I don't remember a thing
about it. You came there to drink — didn't you, after
chasing a squirrel? I am glad dogs don't catch frogs
nor fishes." This was said in her own inimitable manner, and caused a roar of laughter, which greatly dis-
comfited the enemy, and caused the boys and girls to
gather more closely around her. She was the same funny, joyous child that she had been seven years before —
the 'Sunshine' of the school-house and the play-ground,
as well as the home circle. Cheerfulness was her gift;
but underneath it was a firm, persistent will, which it
had caused Hester much pain and effort to control.

"She is the hardest one among them to manage," she
used to say; "for sometimes her wilfulness is so covered
up with apparent good nature, that I find it difficult to
get along."

Wallace was a fine scholar, the pride of the family.
Howard Trueman had entered college, was half through,
and Wallace had day-dreams of college life and a pro-
fession. Albert Gray is attending school with Wallace;
they are firm friends. Lottie and Winnie are bosom
companions.

Mr. Stillman is keeping store yet. Seven years have
changed him, but not for the better. He curses in his
heart the Temperance Reform, and attributes his want
of success in business to the Maine Law and Mr. Trueman, who is now the liquor agent, and is complained of
bitterly for "corking up the bottles so tight," and refusing to sell a drop without a manifest reason for it.

Mrs. Stillman is leading a quiet, consistent life.
Jack's term at the Reform School has expired; but he
is not reformed. He is still a wanderer, they know not

where; and the mother sighs as she thinks how different it might have been. Clara, now a fine-looking girl, is in the factory, boarding and intimately associating with Regena Steele, who has also been forced to earn her own finery and gewgaws by "that miserable liquor law," as she calls it.

Hattie Gray has, at last, become convinced that stepmothers are not necessarily monsters. She is at home, enjoying life; and rumor whispers that, somewhere in the future, she is looking for a happy home which shall be all her own. Elida, the sly rogue, enjoys inquiring after her *brother Henry*, often, and wonders if he is as bashful as ever.

"It would be funny if he should take a fancy to me when I am old enough — wouldn't it, Hattie? How should you like me for a sister? Let's see: you like *'im* (as Ann would say) better than you did — don't you? How funny it sounds to hear her say, '*I 'ate 'im*' (old Mr. Giles). Rather tough eating, I imagine. It had the effect of making her cross. Why, how handsome you look when your cheeks are red!"

"You are a perfect little tease," said Hattie one day; "but nobody can get angry with you. But if I should act so, folks wouldn't bear it."

"Well, I know it; I was born so, and you weren't — that makes the difference. You shall come and live with Henry and me. Now, don't tell auntie I am talking about such things: she will look so" (drawing down her face). "I had rather she would whip me," she said, as Hester stepped in at the door to call her to finish some work she had left half done. "O, I am going to do it! I will have it done in a moment, auntie, darling.

You know *Sunshine* is always dancing around — don't you?"

"Yes," said Hester, "and that is what makes so many shadows and clouds." Thus the merry girl moved on without the many cares and sorrows which constantly harassed Winnie and Mary F.

There is a little Mason at Mr. Giles'. Unie is father's girl now, and Master Mason belongs to aunt Ann, while little speck of baby sleeps in mamma's bosom. Mr. Lovering patted Elevia on the cheek, as he peeped in at the wee thing, saying, —

"My daughter, I think the second crop of smiles and roses which came back to you, after we gave you up, look quite as pretty and interesting as the earlier crop. Mr. Giles, you haven't allowed the frost to nip them — have you?"

"I have tried to preserve them," was the reply; "but Elevia has a good deal to put up with now. Old habits stick to me, and always will."

"I haven't complained — have I?" said Elevia, taking his brown hand tenderly in hers, and smiling up into his face.

"No, you haven't; but you have had reason to, often."

"I didn't know it," was the reply. "I wish no one had more reason to complain than I."

"O, you are doing well," said grandpa. "What shall you call this little lump here?"

"We call her Annie T. Isn't it a pretty name?" said Elevia.

"Why, yes, I suppose it is; but how did you know I shouldn't want to name her after my Lizzie here?" said grandpa, laughing.

"Why, bless you, my dear," said the happy little woman, "I shouldn't want you to name her that. I won't have a rival, no ways at all, you see. But how does Ann like her namesake?" she inquired.

"O, she is evidently pleased," said Elevia; "but no one is equal to little Mason."

"But, my dear," said grandma, "don't begin to call him 'little Mason.' Everybody in town will be calling him 'little Mason,' and then there will be 'big Mason,' you see?"

"I suppose they will, mother. How shall we manage?"

"Call him by his middle name, or Mason Edward. If I were you, I should call him Eddie. O, here is Miss Ann."

"You needn't 'Miss' me," said Ann, with a dry laugh. "I'm 'ere, you see."

"Yes, I see; you have a pretty little namesake here, too; I am almost jealous of you."

"Needn't be; do'n'o w'at they named 'er that for; 'omely name 'nuff: I didn't ask um to."

"It's a pretty name," said Mrs. Lovering, decidedly. "Ann, you shan't slander the baby so. Did you have a good visit in — ?"

"I s'pose so; I missed this youngster," said Ann, hugging him to her bosom.

"Yes," said Elevia, "and he missed her so I didn't know what to do." Ann gave the little fellow another hug.

"Did ye miss 'er, ducky — did ye? Well, aunt Ann shan't go agin, I promise ye, ducky."

"Mason get the horse, and take aunt Ann to ride," said the boy. "Mason drive."

"That's a man," said Ann.

"Did you see old Mrs. Lentell while there?" inquired Mrs. Lovering.

"Yes, she's broke 'er leg; good 'nuff for her, I s'pose."

"Broken her leg!" said Elevia; "why, you didn't tell me of it."

"Didn't mean to, nuther. I s'posed ye'd want to go an' nuss 'er, or suthin', the whole on ye."

"Well, we must love our enemies, Ann; the Bible says so," said Elevia, "and forgive them as we hope to be forgiven. But I don't think I am good enough to want to go and take care of her. How did it happen?"

"She was goin' acrost to git some fillin' for a web she's weavin' for 'Errick's folks, an' fell a-crossin' the brook. Pity 'twarn't her neck, though! She kep 'er old 'ead out o' water, an' 'ollered an' 'ollered; but nobody 'card 'er but 'Errick's wife."

"How far was it from Mr. Herrick's?" said Elevia.

"Quarter 'v a mile, or so, I s'pose. She better put 'er 'ead under, an' done with it. I 'ate 'er, if the rest on ye don't." After she left the room, Mrs. Lovering inquired, —

"Don't you feel afraid Eddie will imitate Ann's speech and character?"

"Yes," said Elevia, "I do. I shall try to guard against it. So far I have had no trouble. But I can see that the child is doing her good. Poor Ann, I never supposed she would ever love or be loved. She is very much changed. You see she uses three words where she formerly used one. Truly, kindnesss is a powerful instrument for good. But Ann's affections were so chilled and blighted when young, and her heart so sealed up, as it were, by cruel, unkind treatment, that she will never get over it. It seemed as if she grudged every word, and was afraid the old crust would be broken up. Last night I was affected to tears when Mason Eddie (you see I profit by your suggestion) went to her, and said, —

"'Hear Mason pray, aunt Ann.' She don't allow him to say auntie.

"'O Lordy!' said she, 'I guess I can't. There, little Mason mustn't say Lordy; it's a bad word. Aunt Ann must be whipped if she says it again. Kneel down an' say it, little man. He knows — don't he?' He folded his baby hands, and said it very reverently. Ann listened, and sighed deeply when it was over. 'She learned me to say that, too,' she almost whispered, bending over the child.

"'Did she?' said he; 'it is a nice little prayer — isn't it, aunt Ann?' Who was she?

"'O! (the *Lordy* didn't come that time), — 'O, it was my mother — my mother, ducky! I 'ad a mother like you, once, little man, an' I loved 'er, as you do.'

"'I am sorry,' said the child, supposing, by Ann's manner, it was a great trouble that she was talking about, — 'I'm sorry; don't feel bad, aunt Ann; you shan't have another mother next time. My mother shall be your mother, aunt Ann; and I am your little boy — ain't I?'

"'Yes — yes; there now, run in, an' kiss 'er, as I used to. I wish them days was back agin — I do. I warn't such an old hackmatack, then.'

"'Hatch–ma–tatch!' said the child — 'what is that? Hatch–ma–tatch — how funny!' Ann laughed, and waited for him to kiss me good night. She didn't know I overheard her. 'A little child shall lead them,' you see. I hope Ann will be benefited, without injuring the child. Mr. Wiley's folks were not at all pleased with the idea of Ann's making her home with us. They lay it to mercenary motives. They give us a great deal of trouble; but there, we must have trouble of some kind; and it is so much better to have it out of the house than in it — out of the heart than in it."

"Yes, you may well say that," was the reply. "Isn't it pleasant to think that God understands our motives, if our fellow-men do not?"

"Yes, it is a comfort; yet how much of sin and imperfection he sees in these hearts of ours!" said Elevia. "I am glad," she continued, "that Winnie has finished going to school. Envena has been a constant trial to her."

"I know it," said grandma. "Isn't it strange that she will let her tease and fret her so? Why don't she cut her acquaintance, and have nothing to say to her?"

"I don't know, I am sure. Strange to say, she loves her still, and thinks she doesn't mean anything. And yet that naughty girl has told every boy and girl in the village about her father's actions, and insinuated some things which were not true. She is the most deceitful child I ever saw, and yet she is the most innocent, sincere-appearing one in the world. For some reason, best known to herself, she admires, caresses, and flatters Winnie in her presence, and slanders her behind her back. She slights her shamefully in company, and then, by skilful management, convinces the child that she didn't mean to — never thought of such a thing — is grieved that Winnie should think so. I am vexed with her. She humors Ann, and thinks just as she does when in her sight, and makes all manner of fun of her at other times. I think she hates my children; and yet she makes a great deal of Mason Eddie, to please Ann. I don't know what will become of her. She brings various stories to Ann about Winnie. I was pleased to hear Ann tell her the other day that 'Win was as good as she was, an' 'nuff sight better.' I have thought her envious of Winnie on account of her position in Mr. Trueman's family. I hope Winnie will succeed well in teaching."

"I do hope she will," said Mrs. Lovering; "she will be faithful, I know. I am glad her prospects are so bright; she deserves it, I am sure. And there isn't a person living who would make a more suitable companion for her than Howard Trueman. Why, she is one of a thousand. No one can help seeing how superior she is to Envena. Isn't that what makes her torment Winnie so, think you?"

"Perhaps it is," said Elevia, with a troubled look. "She is very intimate at Mr. Trueman's. They received her at first as Winnie's friend; but they think a great deal of her now. She is there oftener than Winnie. I never thought of it before; but I do believe she is in some way supplanting her. She is capable of doing almost anything which can be accomplished by intrigue and deception, and she not twenty. Why, when she is here, I can't help believing her truthful, she seems so tender and affectionate, her voice is so low and pleasant; and yet I have good reason to think her very deceptive.

She is a dangerous girl — I never knew how dangerous
until I watched her intercourse with Winnie. She has
tried to prejudice Mason and me against her, but in such
a way that I never could tell any one just how."

"Well, I should think she was artful and envious,"
said Mrs. Lovering. "I hope she won't cause Winnie
any serious trouble. Why should she aim her venomous
shafts at her? What has she done?"

"I think it is partly owing to Winnie's superiority, as
you suggested," said Elevia; "and then, before Winnie
came here, Envena had the whole ground — was quite a
pet. I came to see that she was expecting favors from
Mason as well as Ann; and now Mason and Ann think
there is no one quite equal to Winnie. She knows we
have helped to educate her; and Ann actually bought her
a white muslin dress and blue sash for examination-day.
I was astonished. Winnie cried when she thrust it into
her lap, saying, —

"'Take it, an' wear it 'zamination-day, an' ye will. I
didn't 'ave no sich day, nor dress, nuther. I wish I 'ad,
though.'

"Winnie looked up into the hard, cold face, with the
kindness creeping out of the eyes in spite of Ann's
efforts to conceal it, bowed her head over the package,
and burst into tears. 'Don't want it — do ye?' said
Ann, trying to speak in her usual dry, cold manner.
'Well, Vene would tell as many lies as ye've got fingers
to git it; but Ann ain't a fool, if she does act like one.
So wipe up, an' make yer dress, an' wear it. It's well
'nuff for folks that's true an' honest to wear w'ite once
in a w'ile.' Ann brushed out of the room, and slammed
the door, before Winnie could control her feelings sufficiently to speak.

"'She isn't angry—is she?' said Winnie. 'I am sorry I cried; but it was so unexpected! and then it came over me how hard Ann's life had been compared with mine; and I have had trials. Poor Ann! I must try to be patient with her. O, auntie, why has my life been so full of privileges and blessings more than I deserve?' There, I have told you quite a story. Mason and father are coming in, and I guess I have talked enough for once."

"Why, so you have, child. I ought to have known better. Well, there, it is just like me."

"O, no harm done, I think. I shall soon rest. Isn't it pleasant to see how much Mason and father think of each other?"

CHAPTER XXXIII.

Sunshine and Shadows. — Deception unveiled.

Several years later. Winnie has succeeded, as a teacher, beyond the expectations of her most sanguine friends. Her engagement with Howard Trueman is supposed to be a settled fact. She is established as teacher in the village high school, with a generous salary.

"I have only two *real* causes for anxiety," she says to Hester. "Wallace is in good hands, and is doing well; and Mary F. is a darling bird, only a mite too sad for a child. But there is father — no better of his terrible habit. They say he leaves no means untried to get rum, selling the very clothes I give him for it; getting it most of the time now, when it is so difficult to be obtained, and drinking cider when he cannot get rum. This is discouraging; it is hard, but it don't wear me as it did — I actually forget it sometimes. But Elida's determination to work in that city mill worries me more and more. It is so needless! She is so young, and thoughtless, and pretty! — just the one to be tempted. I have no faith in Clara or Regena; they are giddy, vain, and frivolous. It is strange she can like them for companions."

"I know it, Winnie," said Hester. "I would like to have it otherwise; but she was so desirous of going, I thought it best to permit it. I hoped it wouldn't last long. But I think you need not feel anxious. She is a girl of sterling principle, and as firm as a rock, though not a Christian. And I can trust her to buffet the waves of temptation which will meet her in the city; for I mean to keep fast hold of the overruling hand, by prayer seasoned with faith."

"But, auntie, isn't she trusting in herself? and are we ever safe when we do that? If she were trusting in God, she would be secure. But since you have so much faith, I suppose I ought to."

"Who was it that said there were two sorts of things he never allowed to trouble him — those things which he *could* help, and those he could *not* help? Let that be your motto, Winnie. You can't prevent your father's drinking, nor Elida's going to the mill."

"Perhaps not, auntie," was the reply; "but recently, I feel as if I might have helped to save my father, if I had been more self-denying."

"How could you, Winnie?" said Martha; "I should about as soon expect to raise the dead."

"Well," said Winnie, warmly, "that almost seems to be done, sometimes. Think of aunt Elevia; you said it was like raising one from the dead then."

"I know I said so; and it was. But how would you begin to reform your father? You couldn't get near him," said Martha.

"Aunt Martha, have you forgotten how often grandpa used to say, 'You must have more faith, child: nothing is too hard for God'"?

"Yes, I remember it, Winnie. I know I fail there; but we must have just a little of something to hang our faith on, or pin it to — mustn't we? before we expect to accomplish any great thing."

"Yes," said Winnie, reverently; "our Saviour says, 'Whatsoever ye shall ask in my name, believing, ye shall receive.' Now I have prayed enough to save father. O, yes! I have literally wet my couch with my tears for him; but that wasn't enough in this case. If father should cry to God for help, as I have cried for him, God would reach out his hand and pluck him as a brand from the burning. But I had something more to do. My faith and works should have gone hand in hand. I should have braved all, and gone to him, and led him back to God and virtue. In his strength we can do all things. How I have longed to go! But the fear of aunt Abigail and grandmother has clung to me, even now that my childhood is gone. If I were at liberty again, I would go; but I have entered upon the work which I think God has given me, and since my kind friends have prepared me for it, I feel that it would be ungrateful to leave it. I hope I shall do good where I am; but I sometimes query — 'Am I doing right? Have I done right?' I wish I could know. Besides," she continued, "I have let that opportunity slip. I could have done more for him as a child — he loved children."

Mary F. had listened attentively to this conversation. Her color came and went.

"What is it, dear?" said Hester. "Winnie, we must be careful not to introduce this topic often: you see my wise little girl thinks too much now."

Ah! they little knew how much she thought. One great, earnest, pervading thought was wearing out the life of the lovely child, and making her prematurely old.

"Let us change the subject," said Hester. "You are going to Commencement of course."

"I don't know, auntie. Howard wrote me to come by all means; but I feel some hesitation about it. If he should fail in speaking, — and the best do sometimes on those occasions, — I should feel badly. Envena told Lucy she would not fail of being there for the world, it would be such a rich treat to hear Howard's graduating piece. Of course, she said, it would be splendid. And I presume it will. I know he is capable of writing an oration. I wish she wouldn't compliment Howard so much; it discomposes me strangely — when she does it, no doubt, to please me."

Hester had dropped her work, and was looking over her glasses into Winnie's face, with a mournful, tender look.

"Did you say Envena was going to Commencement? How is she going?"

"She said Lucy told her that if I didn't go, they would carry her. But what makes you look at me so, auntie?" said Winnie, blushing. "I'm not jealous — indeed I am not. I don't wonder that they like Envena best. She is so much more agreeable, and can express her thoughts and feelings so beautifully! I don't blame them — honestly I don't; and as long as Howard is true, I can get along."

"Child, you don't think of giving up your chance to her — do you? when the invitation is a year old or more, and it has been renewed so often, to my knowledge, that it is not outlawed. You are going; so don't say a word against it. What a disappointment it would be to Howard if you were not there!"

"But, auntie," was the tearful reply, "would you like to go when you knew they would prefer another?"

"Winnie," said Hester, "I don't believe they would. I don't believe it. They would feel hurt if you shouldn't go. Just you tell them frankly what she says, and see what they will say."

"O, auntie, I couldn't, it would be so rude."

"It was rude in her to tell you," said Hester, "and I hope that is all. But, child, I don't believe they said so. How can you think so much of that girl, when she has wounded your feelings so terribly, and slighted you so often?"

"Why, auntie, you know she always explains everything so, and I find that I have been too sensitive, or credulous, or something. I don't mean to tell you of her next time. You don't love her, and I am the cause of it."

Hester sighed, and worked on busily for half an hour; and then putting on her things, she said, —

"I am going to make some calls, Winnie. Help aunt Martha about tea; I shan't be at home."

Hester walked with a firm, resolute step, as usual when on important business. She found Mrs. Trueman alone. Lucy and Envena were taking a walk, she said.

"I have come to speak to you about her," said Hester, rather abruptly. "Do you think she is a fit companion for Lucy? How do *you* like her?"

Mrs. Trueman looked up with surprise.

"Why," said she, "what do you mean, Hester? I thought you admired her. She is always telling something you have said in her praise, or praising you, and Winnie is very fond of her."

"That is the trouble," said Hester. "Winnie is perfectly infatuated with her. She slanders her, slights her, and wounds her continually, and yet the poor child can't see that she is a snake in the grass. She will sting her to death, I fear, and then make the dear child think it was a mercy, an act of condescension. And Winnie is not alone in her infatuation."

"Why, you astonish me!" said Mrs. Trueman. "If any one else were talking in that way, I should call it base slander. I know you have reasons for what you say. Will you tell me some of them?"

"Yes," was the emphatic reply.

She then told her what Envena had said concerning Commencement, and how Winnie was feeling; how she had gained Winnie's confidence, and then divulged her secrets, maliciously informing the school children of all the circumstances of Winnie's childhood, coloring and exaggerating shamefully, when the truth was bad enough.

"You astonish me," said Mrs. Trueman, thoughtfully. "She told us confidentially that some one, she knew not who, had told these stories all around. And really, Hester, she did seem sorry and grieved about it. She said it was injuring Winnie very much — it was shameful, &c. I told her Winnie was to be pitied for this, but not blamed."

"There," said Hester, "that accounts for one story. She told some one that you made a great deal of Winnie out of pity, that was all. I tell you her sympathy was put on — a mask, and nothing more. *She* reported those stories; I have traced them all to her. I have had my eye on her these two years, closely. As for saying anything in her favor, I wish I could; but I can't. I have been in the family, you know. She is artful naturally, and her training — all she gets — is in one direction. I couldn't bear it a moment longer. Just look at it! What an adept! Tell the stories with additions and variations, and then come with a lamentation in her mouth, and all to prepare the way for making an impression favorable to herself. Is that all? I am prepared for anything now. She has gone beyond my expectations. How about Commencement? Did you really prefer her company to Winnie's?"

"You must let me collect my scattered senses," was the reply. "What I have learned shocks me. Only that I know you to be above such meanness, I could not believe you. I remember her expressing astonishment that Winnie did not care to go, &c., and that she was not more interested in Howard's success. But," she added, "Winnie is a dear good girl. I suppose she is so absorbed in her school that she can't think of anything else; and, perhaps," she added, lowering her voice almost to a whisper, "she is too much absorbed in something else."

"What do you mean?" said Lucy, sharply.

"O, nothing! I presume it isn't anything. You know stories will fly. I didn't mean to speak of it."

"Of course it isn't anything," said I; "but of what are you thinking?"

"Why, the new minister. I don't think there is anything in it. I have heard it spoken of."

"I believe she is the first and only one that ever spoke of it," said Hester, quite indignantly. "He is school committee. Go on; what next?"

"I guess I have told you enough," was the smiling reply. "You have given me a key that will unlock a good many mysteries. I thank you very much. Then

Winnie thinks we don't love her, and that accounts for her shyness lately. She don't blame us, you say, dear child! I should blame myself if I did not, for she is truly lovely, and every way worthy. Now I think of it, I fear Envena has succeeded in partially alienating Lucy from her. But Lucy is very sincere; and when I unlock that dark chamber, and let her look into Envena's heart, she will be cured. O, there is one thing I do not understand! She said she heard there were some terrible mysteries about Winnie's birth. I never could think to ask you."

"There is nothing mysterious about the child or her birth which you did not know. You know her as well as I do, and I know her better than she knows herself. She is good enough for a king," said Hester, with unusual asperity. "And so she reported that Mr. Lentell was in jail for killing his wife, or some other terrible crime."

"Well, I have heard enough," said Mrs. Trueman. "What shall I do, Hester? Can you tell me?"

"Yes," said Hester, recovering her equanimity; "I want Envena to go to Commencement. Let her ride with you."

"No; I can't do that. Winnie must ride with us. Why, I shouldn't dare to see Howard without her. I really think the disappointment would cause him to fail. I can't hear to that."

"Well, hear me out," said Hester. "It is half a century since I attended those meetings. You know why I went then," she said. "It don't seem so long, and yet it does seem longer. Well, no matter for me, now. I want to see Howard graduate, and I shall go, and carry Winnie. We shall have to spend the night; but no matter. I would do more than that to make Winnie and Howard happy, and I don't mean that the sharpest and most skilful actor shall separate those children. Haven't I known them both ever since they were born? I ought to; I dressed them both in their first suits. I tell you they were made for each other, and nothing but God shall separate them in my day, if I can help it. Well, I was going to say, she shall ride over with me, and Envena can ride with you. Howard must drive Winnie home, and you must give me a seat in your carriage. Will you do this, and promise not to tell any one that we are going?"

"Yes, I see no objection to it. I should like to have you there, and Howard would, and he will be delighted with your arrangements generally."

"Very well. Now keep your eyes open," said Hester, as she kissed Mrs. Trueman good by; "and keep your own counsel."

"Winnie is not going with us," said Mrs. Trueman, when the girls returned from their walk.

"Why not? Then you can go, Envena," said Lucy, without waiting for a reply to her question.

"Thank you — thank you ever so much. I thought Winnie didn't care to go. Isn't it strange? She is afraid he will fail, and she will be mortified. Why, I shouldn't think of such a thing." Lucy bit her lip.

"I'll risk him," she said. "I guess he knows as much as Mr. Elwood. I don't like to hear him preach as well as I did; he isn't much." Mrs. Trueman was not troubled with any more questions about Winnie; but she thought sadly of the injuries the sweet girl had received from one she loved and trusted. She saw plainly that, as far as Lucy was concerned, the poison had taken effect. She felt thankful for Hester's timely interference, and doubted not that she should be able to set Lucy all right when the time came. Envena looked very sweet, sitting on the back seat between Lucy and Susy. She was "sorry, very sorry, Winnie wouldn't go." She was "afraid she would regret it. I should think she would, at least. I tried to persuade her to go."

"What reason did she give for not going?" said Mrs. Trueman.

"O, perhaps I had better not tell; she wouldn't want me to. But I think it was mostly fear that he wouldn't succeed as well as some."

"She needn't worry," said Lucy, with unusual spite.

"Lucy don't understand it," said Mr. Trueman, smiling. "It was the intensity of Winnie's affection that made her feel so. She is so anxious he should excel that she fears for him. I feel so myself; it destroys half of my pleasure. And this is a beautiful day; the horses are in good trim, and everything just right, except I would like to see Winnie's sweet, intelligent face peeping modestly out of the carriage once in a while. Linnie, why didn't you persuade her to go? Howard could return home in the cars as usual. I did not think of it. What reasons did she give for not going with us?"

"O, several," was the reply, as she gave her husband a sign to be silent upon the subject. When they put up to rest their horses, she enlightened him concerning Hester's plan, saying, "I can't stop to explain now. I should have told you last night, only you were out late."

"I am glad she will be there," he said. "I don't like that girl. She is too smooth to suit me; she would flatter any one to death." Mrs. Trueman smiled, as she thought how easy it was for short-sighted persons to see, when their glasses were properly adjusted. She whispered Hester's secret into Howard's ear at the earliest possible moment. He smiled, and said, —

"All right, mother; I am glad aunt Hester can be here. Isn't she good for planning? I have been disgusted with that girl for a long time, she assumes so much interest in me. But you say I don't know her?"

"Yes, I am sure I didn't till very recently. But don't repel her to-day. Let her have all the liberty she wants."

"I will try to be polite," was the reply. "I hope Winnie will sit where I can look in her face; and you, too, mother. I need all I can have to give me courage."

"O, never fear!" was the cheerful reply; "it will soon be over. I shall be glad to have you succeed to your heart's content; but if you should not, it wouldn't alter our opinion. We know the talent is there, and will come out some time."

"Thank you."

"Just run down to Mr. M's. Hester will stop there, and speak with Winnie a moment. It will do you both good."

"Thank you again, mother mine," he said, as he darted off. Envena put on her most fascinating look, her most easy, affable manners, and talked more softly, as she leaned confidingly on Howard's arm to the church, and up the steps. Howard paused at the door; she seemed in no haste to let go.

"Howard," said Mr. Trueman, "I want to speak with you a moment." He turned.

"We won't wait for them," said Mrs. Trueman; "the sexton will give us seats. Howard will go upon the platform."

"I really thank you, father," said Howard; "you have relieved me from a dilemma."

"Winnie is here," said Mr. Trueman, nervously.

"I know it," was the reply. "I have seen her."

"O, all right! I did not know."

Envena's flattering encomiums pleased Lucy and Susie. "Elegant," "Splendid," "I envy you," "How proud I should be!" &c. But Mr. and Mrs. Trueman heard them with pain. Their son did himself credit. His address was modest and sensible, well written, and well delivered; not brilliant nor eloquent. They were satisfied; nay, more than that, gratified. Winnie's eyes filled with tears several times — honest tears of gratitude. Howard saw that she, too, was satisfied, and he was content. Envena exerted herself to the utmost to keep him by her side during the intermission, but in vain. He pleaded an engagement, and left her. When they met for evening services, Howard came in with Winnie on his arm, looking very, very happy.

"The deceitful thing!" said Envena, thrown off her guard. "How came she here?"

"Honestly enough," said Mrs. Trueman. "Winnie never told any one she was not coming. I knew she was to be here. I said she was not to ride with us. You and Lucy took it for granted she was to stay at home. I chose to let you remain in ignorance of her coming, for good reasons, I think. So, you see, I have cleared Winnie from the charge of deception, I hope," she said, smiling. Envena's vivacity forsook her for a time; but she recovered herself, and appeared more charming than ever.

"I am much obliged to aunt Hester for this treat, Winnie," said Howard, looking tenderly into her face. "She knows instinctively what is right and proper."

"You mean, what is *agreeable* — don't you?" said Winnie. "I am sure I enjoy it. But for her, Howard, I shouldn't have been here."

"You wouldn't. Why not? I should have been sadly disappointed, and made a worse failure than I did now."

"You didn't fail," said Winnie; "you did well."

"Then why do you look so sad every now and then, when not speaking, Winnie? Is anything wrong?"

"There has been, Howard," she said, looking trustingly in his face; "but I hope you will set things all right."

"What is it, dear? Tell me. Has your father been troubling you again?"

"No; it isn't wholly that. But, Howard, something has been coming between me and your family, especially between Lucy and me. Howard, it has been dark — we loved each other so; and I don't understand it. Won't you find the rock of offence, and roll it away? It would be a sad drawback to happiness if I thought your family didn't approve your choice."

"But they do, dearest. Don't I know? I learned to love you through them. Why, you are like a daughter and sister to them now."

"I hoped I was," she said; "but what if it should be

pity — only pity — and not esteem? That wouldn't satisfy me."

"Who said that, Winnie? Tell me. I must know. Who said they pitied you?"

"Envena heard so, and told me."

"She did! Well, Winnie, I pity her, poor, foolish girl! She has reason to be mortified. That girl has been like a dark shadow in your path this long time. She meant to supplant you in my humble affections. *She couldn't.* Nothing but death can sever my affections from you. They have been maturing all these years. If you bade me go, I should, but not to love another. Are you satisfied? And father, if he were a young man, I should be jealous. Mother is all right; she has been enlightened. Lucy will see soon, and then, darling, the sun will shine again; for I am determined to roll away the rock of offence from the door of your happiness. And, Winnie, if you love me, you will treat her with politeness — nothing more." He told her many things which she did not know, and said, "Are you willing to have the rock rolled out of the way, Winnie? Don't weep. She deserves it. You and Lucy will be friends again."

"I pity her," said Winnie. "So she thought I was at home? Well, she did come near keeping me there. Howard, my heart aches for her. I have been seeing her duplicity; but I loved her, and could not bear to give her up. But what you tell me convinces me I ought to; our future happiness depends upon it. Aunt Hester told me many things I did not suspect of her as we rode along. O, Howard, what if she had succeeded in separating us, as Hester and uncle Horace were separated!"

"She couldn't have done it, dear, especially while our good angel is round to guard us. Let us forget her, and enjoy this pleasant ride. What a happiness, Winnie, to have you at my side!"

Envena was truly mortified when her father handed her a letter from Mrs. Trueman, stating, in very concise but lady-like terms, that she thought the happiness and peace of her family required that their acquaintance with her should cease. "For," said she, "I cannot allow my children to be influenced by one guilty of such hollow-hearted deception as I know you to have been. I beg of you, as you value your own happiness and reputation, to desist from your hypocrisy. Learn to be truthful and sincere, like our darling Winnie; so shall you make and retain valuable friends. Your friend, L. C. TRUEMAN."

CHAPTER XXXIV.

SCENE IN A FACTORY BOARDING-HOUSE. — THE TEMPTER FOILED.

"BEFORE I would be tied to an old maid's apron-strings, Elida Lentell, I'd run away, or sell myself cheap," cried Regena Steele.

"I suppose *you* would," was the indignant reply. "Pray who among your numerous acquaintances is occupying that very unpleasant situation?"

"Why, you. You are tied, hand and foot, to Hester Strong's checked apron," she added, contemptuously. "Catch me being led round, either, as Martha Manlie leads you! I mean to enjoy life." Elida blushed deeply, and was about to give a scathing retort; but the text Hester had taught her to repeat, when her quick temper was aroused, flashed into her mind. "He that ruleth his spirit is better than he that taketh a city." So she held the reins of her temper very firmly, and, with an effort of her strong will, dashed away the portentous cloud, saying, merrily, as she rose to her feet, —

"Me tied, — did you say? Where, and how? Girls, do look. Am I tied? I didn't know it." She looked this way and that, whirled round with gravity, as if searching for some hidden string. "I declare I can't find the string. Do any of you see it? Cut it, do, if you see it. 'Heigh-ho!' as my grandpa says, I don't believe I am tied, after all. I test the question." And the merry girl commenced dancing and capering around the room, upsetting work-baskets, piles of work, &c., until the laugh was turned against Regena Steele, who, at length, exclaimed, —

"Well, you ought to be tied, if you are not."

"That may be true," said Elida; "that isn't the question. Am I tied, or am I not? If any one thinks I am not tied, let them manifest it by the usual sign. It is a vote that Elida Lentell is not tied to an old maid's apron-strings, nor the button-hole of a dandy," she said, in a whisper.

"Do keep still," said Regena. "I never shall finish my dress."

"O, I'll keep as still as I can," was the meek reply, "if you will only exonerate me from the awful charge brought against me. Come, am I tied? Will you promise not to think I am, if I will sit down and help you tuck that skirt?"

"Yes, yes, I'll promise anything, if you will only help me about this contemptible skirt. It has plagued my life out."

"Which way did it go? I'm good for catching things," said Elida, darting around in her own peculiar serio-comical manner. "Here it is; I have found it," she said, seizing a box of flowers and ribbons, Regena's ball-room treasures. "There! now I'll sit down and help you. Poor thing! I do pity you. You see I don't have my life worried out in that way. My wardrobe is sensible and sober, if I am not. To be sure, I do lose a good deal," she continued, demurely. "I can't be out nights, and come home early in the morning. I'm getting along in years, you see," drawing down her face — "have got to be sixteen and 'up'ards,' as aunt Patty used to say, and haven't had a spark to my elbow. That's bad; but 'w'at 's to be done?' as Ann would say. Girls, how do you go to work to catch 'em? Come, just enlighten my ignorance. I feel anxious: time is passing. Sweet sixteen is the turning p'int now: so I am just on the verge of maidenhood. It is funny — isn't it? — that some intelligent man don't pick me, when I blossomed out so harndsome?"

"You are a funny thing," said Clara Stillman. "I wish you would be serious once in your life, and tell us why you won't go to dancing school. You don't think it is wrong to dance, for you learn the steps of us, and dance like a top. You are as graceful as a kitten. You would make a splendid figure in the ball-room. What objections have you to going with Mr. Kendall? He is dying to have you. It is only to dancing school, you see a select company, different from a ball. It would make you graceful and easy in company."

"O, you say I am as graceful as a kitten; now nothing can beat that. I dance like a top, &c. If I should learn any more, I should go up like a balloon. I couldn't stay down at all. It would be awful to go capering about on air, expecting every moment to come down on somebody. O, I shouldn't dare to go; and if Mr. Kendall is in a dying condition, it wouldn't be pleasant, you know."

"I do wish you would stop your bantering for once, and answer me one question," said Regena.

"I am at your service, Miss Steele."

"Well, is it wrong to dance?"

"I think not. You see I dance beautifully. I shouldn't if it was wrong."

"Come, be serious — do. Why won't you go with Mr. Kendall? He is a splendid fellow. Adolphus has always known him; and he thinks everything of you."

"I am sorry he does. I don't want any one to think evil of me. I don't, truly."

"It isn't any use to try to talk with you," said Regena, tossing her head in disgust.

"Well," said Elida, apologetically, "I wish I wasn't so giddy; but it was 'born into me,' as Artemus says, and I can't help it:"

"I shouldn't want to help it," said several of the girls. "I wish I had your fund of humor." Elida was very thoughtful for a few moments, and then said, in a serious manner, —

"I have no objection to telling you the reasons why I will not attend dancing school, I am sure, or some of them, at least. My mother died, as you all know, when I was quite young. She was a Christian; and when dying, she solemnly commended us to God, and died charging aunt Hester to train us up for his service. She has been faithful, and as kind and self-denying as a mother. I wish I had improved under her teachings as Winnie has. She is a Christian, and I mean to be. I wish I was now. Well, you see sixteen years isn't very old, after all. I am only a child. I know my mother wouldn't approve of my going. My dear aunts wouldn't, and grandfather's folks would all be pained if I went; and sister Winnie would be more anxious than ever; so I shan't go. Besides, I am old enough to know that I am better off at home, — just as happy in my way as you are in yours, and not in half so much danger," she added, solemnly.

"Just hear her! I should like to know what danger there is in going to dancing school or a ball once in a while. Come, go on with your lecture."

"Danger of getting cold, for one thing," said Elida, as Clara coughed ominously. "Secondly, danger of falling in love, getting into a trap or a snare. O, there is danger enough to keep me at home; so let us dismiss the subject. Mr. Kendall, poor fellow, must die or get over it, for Elida Lentell will never attend dancing school, nor a public ball; for, young as I am, I can see that it don't improve one mentally or morally, or make one really any happier. I wish you would give up going, girls, and attend Sabbath school — won't you? We can't live here always, and you yourselves have told me of girls who were led into sin in the ball-room — of terrible cases of wounded affection. Falsehood and deception abound there, you say. Why will you go?"

"Do hear Parson Lentell talk!" said Regena. "If anybody is so weak-minded that they can't resist temptation, they had better not live in the city."

"I don't think I shall leave the city to-night," was the smiling reply; "neither do I mean to test my powers of resistance by going into unnecessary danger. I am well and happy as need be. Besides, if *I* can resist, my example might lead others into temptation which they could not or would not resist, and I should cause my weaker sister to offend."

"There, there," said Clara, with another of those deep, hollow coughs, "I should think Hester Strong had come. 'If meat cause my brother to offend, I will eat no meat while the world standeth,' is her favorite motto. 'Do as you would be done by,' is another. She is so full of the Bible that she runs over."

"It is something worth being filled with — isn't it?" said Elida. "It is the word of God — the way of life. How much better to be filled with it than with beaux and balls, laces and flowers! They must have an end; but the word of God standeth sure. I tremble when I think that I must one day meet him," she said, in a low, solemn voice. "Aunt Hester says we need not tremble nor be dismayed if Jesus is our Friend, our Advocate. There," she continued, drawing a long breath, "give me credit for being serious once — will you? You see I am not so thoughtless as I seem to be." Just then a letter was handed to Elida. "From home!" she exclaimed, joyfully; "now for a treat." In a few minutes she was absorbed in reading.

"Old maids write interesting letters," said Regena. "What pleases you so? Has Hester or Martha had a call to be married? Whom is your letter from?"

"It is from aunt Hester." She made no reply to the ill-natured remarks, but commenced reading items of news. "Howard has graduated. Aunt Hester and Winnie went to Commencement. Envena went in Mr. Trueman's carriage." Clara and Regena looked at each other.

"Then she has made out! I wish her much joy, and hope Winnie will be consoled by the idea that he has got terribly taken in. Envena Wiley will make a sorry parson's wife."

"What do you mean?" said Elida, looking from one to the other. "What are you talking about?"

"Why, you little goose!" exclaimed both girls, in a breath, "didn't you know Envena had been setting her cap for Howard Trueman this two years? Playing pious or anything to get him. Isn't she cute, though?" said Regena, laughing.

"I should suppose you thought something very funny had happened," said Elida, running her eye along over the letter. She read, "'Howard and Winnie rode home together. Winnie is spending a week at Mr. Trueman's, having a delightful time. Fortunately, this is her vacation. They will visit all the friends, and probably ride over to see you. You must have your photograph ready for her. Howard has given her a beautiful album. Hattie Gray and Henry Herbert are to be married soon. Winnie and Howard will stand up with them.' Things don't look very dubious — do they?" said Elida, looking up archly. "So Envena hasn't been so very 'cute,' after all — has she?" The two girls looked at each other again.

"It seems not; but there is time enough in three years. Now don't go to telling Hester and Winnie what we have said. We were only in fun."

"Queer kind of fun — wasn't it?" and Elida looked into the girls' faces with an earnest, puzzled look. "You were not in fun," she said at length, "but in earnest. You mean something. I shall write to aunt Hester, and tell her just what you said. She will unriddle it all, and straighten things out. You know she was served in that way once, and is as sharp as a needle."

"Now don't be such a tell-tale," said both girls. "We didn't mean anything."

"I am sorry you say what you don't mean, and sorry to disoblige you; but I must. I had rather get 'stove in' with love, or 'smashed up,' as your Adolphus says he has, or be brought into a 'dying state,' like poor Mr. Kendall; for such folks are easily brought to life, and get over it nicely. Their feelings aren't quite skin-deep. But Winnie — O, I couldn't bear it if anything should separate her and Howard! for I know they love each other truly, and not after the 'dying rate' that some of our city beaux talk about. But there, I don't mean to worry. Howard and Winnie are all right. I don't like Envena; but Winnie does. They shall have my picture; and besides, I shall go home with them, and look after their interests as a good sister should; for I am beginning to think city life is not so very elevating and instructive. I will try to be satisfied with the country in the future, for if in some respects there are more advantages here, there are also more temptations for the inexperienced. I am afraid I shall catch the contagion, and get perfectly 'fascinated,' or 'bewitched,' or something, if I stay here. I am starving for the truth and sincerity of home friends."

"I am sure I don't care how soon you go, if you are going to lecture us, and set yourself up for a saint."

"I haven't done either," was the quick retort. "I was only rendering a reason, and you importuned me to do it. You see I have run a whole tuck while I have been running my other rig. Good night — my aged head feels the need of sleep."

"I won't let her off so easy," whispered Regena. "I'll contrive some way to get her for him. Adolphus has told him I would, and I will. If he can only get her to go with him once, he is sure of her — the little witch. Hester will have to pray more than once to keep her in the narrow way, I'm thinking — the old fool! Just as if we young folks didn't want to enjoy life a little, before settling down to singing psalms. That is how she came to be an old maid, I expect."

Clara coughed, and turned restlessly.

"Why don't you ask Augustus to get you something to take? Your eyes are getting red, coughing; and besides, you keep me awake. I hate to lie awake, it makes me look so old."

"Does it?" said Clara. "I will sleep with Elida, then; I think she will be willing. It would be a pity to injure your queenly beauty. It might spoil your market," she added, bitterly.

"There, don't act so foolishly," said Regena. "You know I am willing you should cough. But you ought to take something. You won't be able to go to the dance Wednesday night, if you don't — that's all. Lie down; I want you to help me trap that child."

"Well, I shan't," was the reply. "You have trapped me, and led me to the edge of irretrievable ruin. I tremble to think how near. I expect my life will pay the forfeit of my dissipation and folly. I think there are worse evils to avoid than being an old maid, which you seem to dread so much. O, I wish I were as good and happy as Hester Strong is. Elida's lecture, as you called it, has opened my eyes. Better *never* marry — a thousand times better — than to wed unhappily, or lose one's moral integrity by flirting and evil associates," she murmured. "O, mother, mother, my poor, tried mother! What would you say if you knew the danger I have been in? How near to absolute ruin!"

"What do you mean?" said Regena, hoarsely. "You don't mean to say—" She had raised herself on her elbow, and was looking down into the pale face fiercely; "you don't mean to say that you are better than I?"

"I do," was the reply, "if you can plan and execute such a fiendish deed as you propose."

"What do you mean, Clara Stillman? Isn't Mr. Kendall fine looking? Doesn't he dress like a gentleman? How do I know what his intentions are? He thinks her extremely pretty — is delighted with her brilliant, spicy manner — says she is nearly as fascinating as I am."

"He did!" said Clara, mockingly; "then you allow all men to flatter you; and you think he might deign to marry her, since you are otherwise engaged. Regena, I am confounded. You promised Hester that you would take care of Elida. We were the means of her coming here. I have felt guilty every time I have tried to induce her to attend dancing school, knowing how her friends feel about such things."

"Well, I haven't. I think young folks want to enjoy life a little, before settling down to praying and singing psalms. I intend to, at least, and I mean that Elida shall. She will make a sensation yet; and you might if it wasn't for your squeamishness. What is the harm of flirting a little? There is Mr. A., I bewitched him, but 'he has got over it,' as Elida says. They do survive such terrible spasms, and get over them amazingly quick; and I enjoy such things. Life would be intolerably dull without a little romance. I pity the poor fools that always begin to prepare to die as soon as they are old enough to enjoy life. I never was so happy as now. To be sure, I didn't mean to carry the joke quite so far with Mr. P., for I like his wife, and he don't get over his infatuation. When I am married I shall look out for handsome, fascinating girls. I shan't ask them to ride or walk with my husband, I assure you. It is strange how blind some folks are. Just as if we can help such things! We are made just as we are. If married women can't—"

"Stop, Regena Steele! you astonish me more and more," said Clara. "Is it possible that you mean what you say? Is it possible that I understand you? Dare you say that you are not a free moral agent, and accountable to God? O, I didn't think it. I am, indeed, in danger. The sentiments you have uttered are blasphemous and sensual. I know I have been vain and frivolous; spent precious time in childish amusements, and exposed myself to evil, pernicious influences. I tremble when I look back upon the past. O, there have been moments when my feet have well nigh slipped. I stood there thoughtlessly, defiantly. What if I had fallen!" She covered her face, and cowered as if peering over into the awful depths of some slippery chasm. "What if I had fallen!" Her voice was deep and hollow; she shuddered. "I might; others no more thoughtless and giddy than I have fallen to rise no more."

"Come, Clara, you are getting nervous," said Regena. "You needn't feel so; you haven't fallen, and there is no danger of it. You and I are strong enough to stand looking over the most stupendous precipice that was ever gotten up by flirtation, and be in no danger of falling into the yawning abyss. Why, haven't I done it time after time? Just keep a cool, steady head, and you can stand upon the very edge of the bottomless pit, and be saved. I am speaking figuratively; of course there is no such place. God never made us to curse and torment us forever; so let us go to sleep. You are sick; that is all."

"You may sleep — I cannot. I am terribly awake to a sense of my sins. O, I believe the Bible. It is full of threatenings against the workers of iniquity — those that forget God. That I have done. God has not been in all my thoughts."

"Do keep still," was the impatient reply. "I want to go to sleep."

"I can't keep still until I warn you to escape for your life. Forsake the evil companions you have chosen; associate with the good and virtuous, — and there are many even in this boarding-house, — for I tell you you are in danger of ruin, irretrievable ruin. I see it, if you don't. You are playing a dangerous game. You are sowing the wind, and will reap the whirlwind, the storm, ay, the tempest. I tremble for you if you have cast off the fear of God."

"Well, you needn't; I know what I am about. I shall come off with flying colors yet. Adolphus is as rich as a Jew. But don't quote Scripture to me, it don't take effect. Better quote Shakespeare, or somebody we know something about. I expected you would make a draft on Hester Strong."

"O, Regena, Regena! do you disbelieve the Bible? Then I shall talk in vain. I was not aware that I had treasured up so many passages. All that I learned at Sabbath school come back to me to-night, with great force and power. Those were contented, happy days, compared with my most successful days of folly, or what you would call my most brilliant conquests. I thank God I cannot boast of many, and there are no married men among the number. I never dreamed of such a thing. The thought is extremely revolting to me. You say you enjoy it and are happy. You are deceiving yourself; for certainly you appear unhappy, dissatisfied, and irritable. You are growing more and more restless, when not in hot pursuit of some phantom you call pleasure. But I must leave you. We have been companions in sin, — I hope we may yet walk together in the path of peace. I think my mother's prayers have kept me from the commission of any act of immorality, and I mean to pray that your eyes may be opened before it is too late."

"Better pray for the removal of that cough. It is very annoying to me, at least."

Poor Clara lay quite still for some time, wondering if Regena had changed so very much, or whether she had been blinded to her faults. How unprincipled and unfeeling she was! and she had manifested so much affection for her, especially in company. She was imperious and exacting at times, it was true, but she was beautiful and brilliant — could flatter, caress, and cajole in turn. They had been friends from childhood. Regena went to the city several years previous to Clara's going, and was far advanced in dissipation before Clara joined her. Thus far they had gone hand in hand outwardly. Regena, like a skilful general, led her victim along successfully, until sickness, caused by exposure, startled her from her false, delusive dream. She resolved to go home immediately, and persuade Elida to go, if possible. She became so distressed in body and mind, that she could bear it no longer. She arose, dressed herself, and was preparing to leave the room, when Regena said, derisively, —

"Go and expose me if you dare. I have an influence in this house — have been here longer than you. I despise the praying old fool that keeps it; but she don't know it. I looked out for that."

"Regena, I shan't report what you have told me in confidence. I am still your friend, and would save you if I could, but feel that I have enough to do to settle my own accounts. That child's words, 'We can't live here always,' are ringing like a death-knell in my ears. We must one day meet *Him*. O, Regena, Regena! I believe I am worse than you now! I have been to meeting and Sabbath school a great deal more, and my mother has been a Christian for years. What shall I do? — what shall I do?" Regena was alarmed at her distress. She saw that she was very pale.

"I will go call Mrs. D.," she said; "you lie down."

"I can't lie down; but call her — do: I am afraid to die."

"You won't die. Here, smell of my cologne." Mrs. D. soon comprehended the state of the case. She took the poor girl to her own room, and did what she could to make her comfortable.

"What arrested your attention to your sins?" inquired Mrs. D.

"I hardly know. We were urging Elida to attend dancing school, and some things which she said affected me, and I couldn't shake off the feeling. I sneered at religion, and it seemed as if a strong hand was laid on my arm, holding me just in sight of my sins."

"My dear, I am glad you are standing there. Don't turn away your face, but look at them, search for them, till you hate them, and feel that they are such a terrible

burden that you are glad to lay them at the foot of
the cross. I am glad that your false security is disturbed. Don't think me unfeeling. I want you to become thoroughly sick of sin; for I know of a Physician
that will heal you when you feel your need of him.
'Ask, and you shall receive;' knock, and the door of
mercy shall fly open. Shall I pray with you, my dear?"

"Yes, do; for I dare not. O, I dare not pray!"
Thus the hours wore away. Neither Clara nor Mrs. D.
slept much that night. Regena also was disturbed and
sleepless. She regretted having revealed her scepticism
and other secrets to Clara, especially now she was so
unwell. Far down in her soul she feared the Bible
might be true. What if it was? She tried to silence
the still small voice — bade the Spirit depart for this
time, thinking, —

"When I have been married a while, and am tired of
this life and its pleasures, I will consider these things;
but not now. I am getting tired of this folly, and especially of flirting. I think I shall hold on to Adolphus.
He is handsome, and there is a *golden* charm about him.
I led him captive, and now he is at my will and pleasure.
I'll keep him there. I don't care what comes, I'll marry
him, just as soon as his fortune is secure. He says he
must move cautiously, or his aristocratic father will put
him on short rations." And so the deluded girl went
on, weaving web after web of bright, beautiful tissues,
which were to prove as vain as vanity itself, and as false
as the life she was now leading.

"Clara is very sick, Regena," said Mrs. D. in the
morning. "You will have to come out and take care
of her, I think."

"Me? Why me? I can't. I am making excellent wages." Mrs. D. was puzzled.

"I thought you were such good friends," she said, "that you would wish to take care of her. Of course she must have some one. My duties are such that I cannot take care of her. Poor child! I wish she was at home with her mother."

"I wish so, too," was the impatient reply. "Get Elida to stay with her, or send for her mother." She saw that she was falling in the estimation of the boarding mistress, losing all she had gained by flattery and deception for her own selfish purposes. She must make a bold attempt to maintain her standing. "Mrs. D.," she said, "I have good reasons for being disgusted with that girl. If you knew the cause of her sickness, as I do, you would send her off."

"Not while she is suffering so severely, both physically and mentally, I assure you. But what has happened? You recommended her highly."

"I know it; I am sorry I did. But really, Mrs. D., I didn't know her. I have been here a long time, and she was a good, virtuous girl when I left home. Don't blame me — will you? Get Elida to stay with her, and write to her mother. Stay; I will write to her. She will be here in a day or two. But don't lisp a word of what I intimated. She hasn't done anything that will come out and injure you. I am sorry I brought her here." Mrs. D. was sorely perplexed. Regena had succeeded in ingratiating herself into her favor. She admired her self-reliant disposition, and thought her a girl of good moral principle. She regretted that she was so taken up with the world, hoped she would become a

Christian, and Clara, as her friend, had been favored. Her confidence in Clara was shaken, and it was hard for her to speak kindly to the suffering girl. "She must have done something terribly amiss," she thought, "to estrange Regena so much. No wonder she is concerned for her sins." And so there was a coldness in her manner which the sick girl felt keenly. But Elida was a gentle, tender nurse.

"I *must* stay out," she said to her overseer's objections; "I must, even if I lose my place. She has no friends here." She was thinking of the meanness of Regena's conduct.

"Well, if you must, you must," was the reply; "but come back as soon as you can."

"There," she said, coming into the sick room, "I have weathered the cape, and am here safe and sound. And now I shall devote my splendid abilities to this homesick patient. You see, I sprang from a long line of successful doctors, and nurses, and invalids, too; so cheer up, Clara; for I, the renowned Miss Lentell, am at your service just as long as it is necessary." Clara smiled so sadly, that Elida ceased her bantering tone, and inquired, —

"What is it, Clara? You are heartsick, too — aren't you? Don't be discouraged; you will be better soon. I will put some mustard on your side, or hot water; which shall I?"

"Mustard, I guess; the pain is severe. But, Elida, what you said last night is sounding like a death-knell in my ears. 'We can't stay here always.' I feel that. I cannot stay here long, and I fear to die. O, my sins! my sins!"

"Forsake them," said Mrs. D., coming into the room — "forsake them, or they will destroy you. If you are truly sorry for them, and not suffering from fear of exposure, why, God can and will forgive them, though they are many and heinous. I don't know what your peculiar guilt is; but you do, and God knows."

"I don't know," said the sick one, much agitated, "that I have any *peculiar* sins. I have transgressed the holy and righteous law of God all my life. I have been vain and thoughtless."

"Is that *all?*" said Mrs. D., looking her steadily in the face. She was painfully embarrassed, and did not reply. Mrs. D. left her with the impression that she was a deceiver — that her sins had found her out. Elida and Clara saw the change in Mrs. D.'s appearance, but could not account for it.

"I thought she was a Christian," mused Elida. "I wish — O, how I wish — aunt Hester or Winnie was here! But I know you are not a very great sinner, Clara; and, if you were, it would be all the same. Why, if God can forgive one sin, he can a million — of course he can. If Jesus could forgive that vile thief on the cross, he can forgive you; and he will, now that you feel so sorry. I shouldn't wonder if you were forgiven. I wish I could repent, as you do; I should certainly expect forgiveness. I long to be a Christian, like Winnie; and aunt Hester always rejoices when any one is under conviction, almost as much as she does when they are converted. 'It is the Lord's doings,' she says; 'it is marvellous in our eyes.' She says we must always walk softly at such times, and we will. I will stay with you day and night; no one else need come in: I won't let them. I will ask the doctor to tell them not to. I will read the words of Jesus to you; and who knows but he will say, 'Peace,' to you, as he did to his disciples that stormy night?"

"I can't think what has come over Mrs. D.," said Clara. "She seemed so kind and motherly last night! She talked beautifully and prayed with me. It pains me."

"Well," said Elida, "you turn over so that I can apply this poultice. I never made one before; but I have seen scores of them made. There, now, don't think of Mrs. D. again to-day. Perhaps something in the house troubles her. Aunt Hester says Satan is always getting up a fuss about something when folks are serious." Clara grew calm under Elida's affectionate treatment, and finally fell asleep, saying, —

"I thank you, Elida. I shall always remember this hour."

CHAPTER XXXV.

Hester's Faith rewarded. — A Leap in the Dark. — Deceived and deserted.

"Elida, what is it that weighs so heavily on Miss Stillman's mind," said Mrs. D., with a searching look, which called a blush to her face.

"Why," said Elida, "she is under conviction, they call it. I thought Christians knew about those things. I have heard aunt Hester say that the most innocent are very guilty in God's sight. She says when the Spirit searches out our sins, and sets them in order before the very best of us, the sight is overwhelming; because enmity against God and the rejection of Christ are the most heinous of sins, and the only sins that will close the door of heaven against us at last."

Elida blushed again beneath the earnest, inquiring gaze of the boarding mistress.

"I don't know these things by experience," she said: "I wish I did. I have heard so much about repentance and faith, regeneration, and all those things at home, that I ought to be better than I am. But my heart is hard. I wish I was awakened as Clara is; I would arise and go to my Father's house at once."

"Elida," said Mrs. D., "I didn't know you could stop to think a serious thought. I am glad you can. Much good seed has fallen into good ground, as I perceive. I hope it may yet bear fruit to the glory of God."

"I hope so," was the reply. "I have had line upon line, precept upon precept."

"Did you use to see Clara often at home?"

"Yes, we were near neighbors."

"What was her reputation in the village?"

"Good — very. She always went to meeting and Sabbath school there. Her mother belongs to the church. Aunt Hester said she should not be willing for me to come if she were not here."

"Did she? I fear she did not know her," was the mysterious reply.

"You surprise me," said Elida. "Aunt Hester knows everybody in the village. Folks come to her with their troubles and trials, their joys and sorrows, and their sins, too, often."

"Well, what is the cause of her sickness?" said Mrs. D., with an incredulous look.

"A bad cold, or rather several bad colds, taken foolishly, of course. But is it more sinful to be out late, if you happen to get cold, and make a little trouble? Is it?" she said, with some warmth. "If I were a Christian, I wouldn't allow my boarders to have night keys, and be out late. Perhaps it is all right, but my aunt Hester wouldn't think it was."

She retreated hastily, leaving Mrs. D., in her turn, somewhat confounded.

"There," thought Elida, "I didn't rule my spirit that time. I have made a bad matter worse. But it is provoking. I thought Christians were all living for Christ, and not for self. O, yes, they can be out ever so late, in all kinds of company, at all times, provided they don't take cold and get sick. *That* is decidedly immoral; it mustn't be allowed. Poor Clara! She might have kept you in. It is against the rules of the corporation for the girls to be out after ten. But that Regena will wheedle anybody into anything, almost. I wish Mrs. Stillman would come. I don't know, I am sure, why I have not fallen in with some of her numerous plans for my advancement in life. I have felt amazingly inclined to. Mrs. D. needn't be alarmed. I shall take care of Clara till her mother comes: and I shall ask the doctor if she can't be moved into my bedroom. She shan't trouble any of them. There! now I feel better," she said, as she arose from the top stair where she had been sitting, to " smooth her ruffled feathers," as she would have said if there had been any one to speak to.

"Elida," said Regena, who had put her head in at the door to inquire after the sufferer, " Elida, I want to speak with you."

" At your service for three minutes ; my cares are numerous, you see."

"Yes, I see," she said, when the door was closed. "It is too bad. She ought to have been more careful."

" It will be your turn next," said Elida ; "sickness is no respecter of persons. I, even I, venerable and staid as I am, have taken several very successful colds in my day."

" Well, never mind, you little hector, I want you to attend a select party to-morrow evening, at the agent's splendid new house. Adolphus got the invitation for you, and you will ride with us. He says you will grace any society, and I think so. I want to have the honor of introducing you."

Elida was considering. She would like to attend a

select party, and see the inside of the beautiful new house and the imported furniture. Regena saw it, and took courage.

"You could wear your blue cashmere, and I will lend you my white sash, gloves, &c. It needn't cost you a cent. Hester wouldn't object. Why, it is no worse than a donation party. You will go — won't you?"

Elida hesitated.

"What will they do for entertainment?"

"O, there will be music, and pictures, &c., &c."

"What kind of a thing may the '&c.'s' be? Dancing, and whist? or euchre, or what?"

"How can I tell? Mr. —— attends church constantly; of course there will be nothing improper. Come, say you will go, that is a dear good girl."

Elida bowed her head on her hand for a moment, but raised it suddenly.

"No, I can't go; I am 'out a nussin','" she said, in her peculiar, droll way.

"O, nonsense! some of the girls will watch with Clara. She can think you are sleeping, and you need to be."

"Yes," said Elida, "and that is reason number two why I shan't go. I do need all the sleep I can get; but I shall not leave Clara for an hour till her mother comes. I thank you all the same, but I can't go."

"You are a perfect little gosling," was the impatient reply. "I shan't try to bring you out."

"Goslings always come out themselves," was the laughing response, "when they have staid in long enough. Perhaps I shall, for you say I am perfect. Better be a perfect gosling than an imperfect goose — hadn't I? There's hope of me."

"Nonsense! it isn't any use to try to reason with you. You were born and brought up an old maid."

"Pity me, then!" was the doleful reply. "O, pity me, and don't tempt me out of my safe retreat, for I might get terribly 'smashed up' by that wicked, mischievous fellow, whom lovers and poets call Cupid. And there would be nary a beau to pick up the pieces, or a tinker to repair the awful damages. O, I'm better off at home;" and she darted out of sight.

Dr. W. was very inquisitive that day, the girls thought. His examination was thorough, and rather embarrassing. He decided that the case was lung fever, attended with unfavorable symptoms; so he told the boarding mistress.

"Nothing worse than that?" was the reply.

"No, but that is bad enough. I don't like the sound of her cough. She will get up, I think, but not well. She has been neglected."

"I fear she has," was the sad reply. "She has coughed terribly for some time, but she would go out evenings. Perhaps I ought to have let her mother know it, or insisted upon her doing something. I have too many cares."

"Yes, you have," said the doctor, musingly. "You say you have had dark insinuations. Well, I see nothing wrong. Who insinuated?"

"A friend of hers — Regena Steele."

"Why," said the doctor, starting back, "does *she* board here? I have seen her," — he looked at Mrs. D. significantly, — "and heard of her too. A friend of mine, a pure-minded, lovely, unsuspecting woman is suffering severely through her means."

"Why, what do you mean, doctor?" said Mrs D.,

sinking into a seat. "What can you mean? She has boarded here four years. It must be another person."

"I guess not." He described her.

"Yes, that was she. Well, what of her? What has she done?"

"O, nothing new, that I know of. She is an unprincipled flirt — perhaps nothing more; but my faith in her is small. You had better look after her."

"I will, but I can't believe it is she. I am astounded."

"Do you remember Mr. P., that used to visit her two years ago?" inquired the doctor. "At least, I suppose he must have come here. He escorted her to concerts, — I have seen them there, — and to balls I am told. I know they rode together all day one Fourth of July."

"Yes, I remember him; he is overseer in one of the rooms. He calls now, once in a while. What is the matter with him?"

"O, nothing, perhaps. He is the husband of one of the best women I ever knew, and Regena Steele knows it. His wife was an old friend of hers. She betrayed her confidence, and stole her foolish husband's affections, such as they were, and left her sad and broken-hearted. And now Regena is keeping company with a real blackleg, an imp of Satan. I have it from pretty good authority that his business in this city of spindles is — what do you think? I blush to speak it; and I blush, too, that when appearances are so much against him, still he is received into what is called good society."

"Well, what is his business? You haven't told."

"It is — to decoy young men and maidens to destruction. I may as well speak plainly. I cannot say that Miss Regena is his accomplice; but she will be, or fall a victim in her unscrupulous race for conquest. He passes for a Southern planter's son, but his movements are singular, and the city officers are watching him closely."

"I am utterly confounded," said Mrs. D. "What can we put confidence in, since we cannot trust our own observation? I can't, I can't believe I am so deceived, I must have proof, positive proof, that we are both thinking of the same persons. What is the name of that man you spoke of?"

"Adolphus De Wert."

"Then I must give up the contest; he comes here. He is a fine-looking fellow. Is it possible! is it possible! What shall I do?"

"Keep a good lookout that no one in your house is led out of it by her. A trap is set which will be sprung soon. It is my opinion the sick girl is more sinned against than sinning. So take good care of her."

"I will," was the reply. "I cannot be thankful enough that the veil has been raised."

Elida and Clara were surprised again by her frequent calls, and the kindly interest manifested.

"She may be innocent," thought Mrs. D.; "but what firm friends they have been! Perhaps — well, I don't know, I can't know; only Elida says her reputation has been good at home. And besides, whatever her character *has* been, she is suffering and penitent now. I will do all I can for her."

"Well," said Elida, "she has come to her senses at last; I am glad of it. These boarding-houses, with thirty or forty inmates, must cause a vast amount of perplexing care. That accounts for her treatment of you — so don't worry. I am going to get you well enough to go home when I go. Won't it be pleasant to feel safe once more? to know who is who, and what is what?"

"O, I do hope you will go with me!" said Clara, with unusual emotion. "I feel easier now." Elida looked at her thoughtfully, but made no inquiries.

"I want to put an onion poultice over your lungs, my dear," said Mrs. D. "It is one of the best remedies I know of. I ought to have done it before. But you girls can have no idea of the care and perplexity I meet in one way and another. There, I am pretty sure that will relieve you. How are you feeling in your mind?"

"More calm," was the reply. "Elida has read many precious passages which I am sure were penned for me. They have comforted me, and yet I cannot think I am a Christian. I mean to seek until I am."

"I am glad to hear it. You will not wish to attend balls and assemblies when you get better."

"O, no, indeed! I have never enjoyed them as Regena does. I went, in the first place, to please her. But," she added, sadly, "henceforth our paths diverge, unless she will go with me. I went with her until I could go no farther. O that I could make her see the danger, and turn back! but I can't. O, Mrs. D., couldn't you save her?" she said, imploringly. "I warned her; but she laughed at my fears, and despised me for my weakness."

"You had better not distress yourself, dear," said the kind hearted woman, as she began to comprehend the reason of Regena's alienation. "You have done your duty, and now you must try to get well. A life consecrated to God is worth preserving. Can't you breathe a little easier?"

"I believe I can. I thank you for thinking of me."

"O, you are welcome! I will stay with you a part of the night, and let Elida sleep."

"I get considerable sleep," said Elida. "I would rather take care of her than not, till her mother comes. I thank you just the same; but you need your rest, I am sure."

"Where are you going to-night?" said Mrs. D. to Regena.

"O, to a very select party at Mr.———'s. Don't speak of it to the boarders; they are envious. Very few of the mill girls are to be present, Adolphus says. How do I look? I miss Clara about dressing. Her taste is perfect. She ought to have been more careful. Adolphus always sees to wrapping me up."

"Regena, what if Adolphus should be an impostor, after all — a deceiver, and not a planter's son? which isn't much better, in most cases."

Regena turned pale for a moment; and then the color came, and the dark eye flashed, as she said, in a hoarse whisper, —

"I would kill him; that is all. Why do you suppose such an impossibility?" she said, fiercely.

"O, I have good reasons. I warn you to beware what you do. I have done wrong in allowing you so much liberty. After to-night, there will be no night-key. Those who are out when the house is closed must stay out."

"Very well," was the reply; "I can find a home where I can keep the keys in my own possession. You can believe all that Judas Stillman tells you, and welcome. I am provided for."

"Clara Stillman, I suppose you mean, has not spoken a word against you; but you did mislead me, and she has suffered for it. I have neglected her. We fear she will die. Have you nothing to reflect upon? I have."

"No, I have not. She is a free moral agent, she says; of course she did as she pleased. But I wish people would look after their own affairs, and not meddle with mine. There is the carriage now. I am in a pretty plight."

"I couldn't prevail on her to go, Adolphus," she whispered; "really I couldn't. Is Mr. Kendall in the carriage?"

"Yes; he will be greatly disappointed."

"I am sorry," said Regena; "but I will prevail yet."

Adolphus handed her into the carriage, said a few low, indistinct words to the driver, and, springing in after her, closed the door.

"Why, we are alone," she said.

"Mr. Kendall has turned driver for the fun of the thing," was the reply, "and we thought Elida could be managed better in that way."

"Aren't we almost there?" said Regena, faintly, as they rode rapidly on, leaving the city behind them. She thought of Mrs. D.'s warning. "Could it be possible? No, no, it couldn't be."

"Dearest," he said, putting his arm about her tenderly, "I am taking you away from that miserable boarding-house. My father's agent has come on. I wouldn't have him know where I found you for the world."

"Where are you taking me to, Adolphus?" she said, hoarsely, "and without my consent? I think at least you should have told me. I could have gone prepared. How shall I get my trunks?"

"O, I will manage that. My love, I am taking you to a beautiful city home, about thirty miles from here, where you can have everything. I meant to have taken Elida. The giddy little thing could have been easily pacified, you know. She would have been company for you in my absence, until I can take you to your own home in the sunny South. Kendall is so terribly in love with her, that I thought I'd put her where she'd be obliged to listen to him."

Time will not permit us to follow the travellers. Enough to say, that, before they reached their destination, Regena was reassured, and her confidence in Adolphus restored. At length, she found herself on the steps of an elegant tenement, on a fashionable street in the city. Servants were in waiting. It was just as he had said; they were looking for her. How stylish the hall was! It would be better than working in the noisy, dirty mill.

"I shan't have to start up at the sound of the bell, half refreshed after being out late. They are never to know I worked there. I must be guarded. I am glad I am here; but, after all, I should not have consented to come, if he had consulted me about it, especially after what Mrs. D. said. What could have possessed her? Clara must have been tattling. How envious they will all feel when my marriage is published in the Northern papers! De Wert is a lovely name, and the marriage ceremony is to be imposing and grand. I shall feel better to have them think I was born and brought up a lady; of course I shall. Adolphus is right there;

they do look down upon labor with so much contempt, negroes and all. Mr. Kendall admires me so much, I wonder Adolphus don't get jealous. He appears to like to have him attentive to me. I wouldn't allow him the same privilege. I told him so. I will write mother in a few weeks, telling her I am well and happy, but not where I am. I'm glad Adolphus don't know our real poverty. He knows girls of some wealth and standing, in our New England, do work in the mill. He thinks I am such. Curse that liquor law! It destroyed father's trade."

Language would fail me to portray the anger and mortification of the deceived, disappointed girl, when she found herself in an elegant house, but she not its mistress. Her door was locked, but another kept the key. She was a prisoner without hope, filled with rage and chagrin. She remembered the words of Clara, "You are sowing the wind; you will reap the whirlwind, the storm, ay, the tempest."

"I am caught in my own trap," she thought, bitterly. "I have taken a leap in the dark, and fallen — fallen. I am not the mistress of a Southern plantation, but a slave. If I could reach the wretch who deceived me, he should bite the dust. Well, I am in the pit at last; but it isn't bottomless. O God, I wish it was. But I will reign a queen even here. I have been bitten. I will bite back. I can yet make conquests." Thus the misguided girl consoled herself. She found her trunks, nicely packed, in her room one morning. How they came there she knew not. "I will let them think I am at the South," she mused. "They shall never know how fallen I am." Mrs. D. was not much surprised that she did not return that night. "She has found another boarding-place," she thought. The next day an expressman called at the door, and handed her a note from Regena, as she supposed, saying, —

"Mrs. D.: Please pick up my things; pack my trunks, and send them to me by the bearer of this note. He will settle any accounts you may have against me, and take a receipt. I thought it best not to annoy you with my late hours. I took cold last night, and am indisposed to-day, or I would not put you to so much trouble.   Regena Steele."

Scarcely had the expressman departed when the officer of justice came to inquire for Mr. Adolphus De Wert, alias Bill Jones, alias somebody else, and Mr. Morris Kendall, alias Morris Fox, who, report said, visited the house often in his company. Elida fainted when the facts in this tragedy were brought to light. There was no select party — nothing but a plot to secure her person. She told Mrs. D. of all she knew, and how nearly she had been tempted to accompany Regena in her perilous expedition. She wept, and gave thanks in turn. Clara was shocked at the sudden departure of her early friend, but knew not that the deceiver had been so fatally deceived.

When the real character of the pretended Mr. De Wert was made public, the friends of the deluded girl felt painfully certain that she was with her "whose house inclineth unto death, and her paths to the dead. Ay, her house is the way to hell."

"Girls," said Mrs. D., impressively, as they were seated at the dinner table, "take warning by this sad, heart-sickening event. It is a fearful thing to trifle away one's life! We cannot take coals of fire in our bosom, and not be burned."

"O, my daughter! my daughter!" said Mrs. Stillman, who had just arrived, folding her arms around Clara; "thank God that you and Elida escaped their well-laid snares. O, death were a thousand times better than such a fate as Regena's. I cannot thank God enough."

"To him give all the praise, mother," said Clara. "But I must go home. I would die there. I never prized it as I do now."

"And I, too, must go," said Elida. "Providence did not send me here, and I dare not stay."

"There are thousands of good, pious girls in the mills," said Clara. "One needs only to be a consistent Christian to live here in safety."

"I know it — I know it," said Elida; "but only think how near I came to ruin. I can't get over the shock I have received. I must go home."

"I am sorry to lose you and Clara," said Mrs. D.; "but I can't say a word against it. If such things can be done in my own house without my knowledge, you will be safer at home. After this I shall hardly dare to trust my senses. I shall draw the reins tighter than ever. There will be no more night-keys for favorites, especially if they are pleasure-seekers."

"O, Regena!" said Hester Strong, "beautiful and gifted by nature — misguided, deceived, betrayed Regena! farewell! Let the veil of night and mystery fall around thee to hide thy shame, while we weep thy fall. God scathe the wretch that lured thee from virtue to vice — loathsome, hideous vice! Let all such be scorned and treated with the most withering contempt by the friends of God and virtue. Then our daughters and sisters will be safe. The curse of God will follow and consume the seducer, the libertine, the human fiend! We will not stand among that thoughtless, guilty number who smile upon and caress those murderers of innocent loveliness. No, no! we loathe and despise them when we know them, and we pray, 'God help us to discern the truth, that our brother's or our sister's blood be not found upon our skirts.'"

"How true it is that the innocent have to suffer with the guilty!" said Mrs. Stillman. "I am glad that this is not our home; our rest remaineth."

Clara Stillman was but a shadow of her former self, physically, when she reached her home in the village — a pale, weary, emaciated invalid; but her soul was stayed on God; she had found peace in Christ.

"I am happier," she used to say to those who came to sympathize with her, "than I was when standing on the giddy heights of folly and dissipation. Perhaps you cannot believe it; but it is true. To me, at least, the ball-room, the card-table, the theatre were all unsatisfying. They left a sting behind. I enjoyed them by anticipation, and often at the time; then came regret, and often disgust."

Elida fell upon aunt Hester's neck when she reached home, and wept uncontrollably for a time.

"I have come back as good as I went, auntie; but no thanks to myself, for I wanted to join the giddy dance. Why, dancing was born in me, I do believe. If I had been a finished dancer, I should have been overcome by the temptation to attend balls; and the game, once begun, might have ended where poor Regena has gone."

"Well, I am glad to have my Sunshine back again," said Hester. "We have been partially under a cloud since you left home. You are a little wiser, I think, too," she said, looking tenderly into the beautiful face. "Now you will believe Martha and me when we tell you that it is better and safer to dwell in the house of the Lord than to enjoy the pleasures of sin for a season. O, I want my children to enjoy life in a reasonable, rational, substantial way, so that when sickness, or trouble, or old age shall overtake them, their peace shall flow on like a river. I want it to last forever and ever in the kingdom of God."

CHAPTER XXXVI.

FORT SUMTER IS FALLEN. — THE CALL TO ARMS. — WEEPING AT THE VILLAGE DEPOT.

PATIENT reader, you have not forgotten April 14, 1861. O, no! you will never forget it. You remember how the hot blood mounted to brow and cheek, how the breath came slow and hard, and mind and heart seemed crouching, as it were, beneath the mightiest, the newest, the strongest emotions you had ever felt, when it was said, —

"Fort Sumter has surrendered!"

Our flag, that was dearer to us than life, because the most significant flag that ever floated in the air of evening, or fluttered among the storm clouds on the seas, had been disgraced, fired upon by the most cowardly and malicious traitors that ever cursed a nation. The Infinite alone can measure the height, the depth, the length, and breadth of that gigantic deed, which was but opening the door of the most stupendous rebellion the world ever saw. Reader, you know it all. The scenes of that day, and those which followed it, have been written upon your souls, as it were, with a pen of iron, and the ink was blood — the blood of fathers, of husbands, of brothers, and friends! O, how many of those terribly truthful passages are underlined, underscored, by the suffering ones in our land. How many loved ones that *were*, *are* not! Their dust has mingled with the dust of traitors; their bones, whitening on the sin-cursed soil of slavery, have made it free! ay, free! And out of the shadow of the greatest grief which ever crushed the heart of a mighty nation, the beautiful, the sublime pyramid of human freedom has been reared. Founded on eternal truth, built with the solid granite of eternal justice, cemented by the blood and dust of a nation's heroes, of the good, the true, and the beautiful, and fashioned by the almighty hand of Him who ruleth in heaven and on earth, — it shall stand secure. So "let the heathen rage, and the people imagine a vain thing."

You remember that the nation sat thus but one little moment, looking inward and upward. Then she arose, breathed a long, deep breath, which sent the life-blood coursing through every vein, causing the almost palsied heart to leap with a mighty bound. She arose like a giant aroused from a dream of peace and safety to see her flag trailing in the dust amid the smoke of battle and the noise of war; and the cry of "Treason! treason!" flew like lightning over land and sea.

"To arms! to arms! The foe is upon us! God give us victory or death," was the low, deep utterance of every manly heart.

"God give us victory, or give us death," murmured every true, noble-hearted woman, as she pressed her hand over the fluttering heart, and bowed her head in silent prayer to the God of nations and the God of war. "If it had been an enemy that had done this, we could have borne it." The nation arose, shook itself like the newly-awakened lion, girded on the armor, and the conflict, the awful conflict, began. Tyranny and oppression on one side, freedom and human brotherhood on the other. There was terrible earnestness on either side; on one side bitter hate, malicious cruelty, wanton wickedness, such as a demon would shame before, methinks. Such was the wily foe that our dear ones went forth to meet. But we knew that God was with them, and they must prevail.

"God bless and keep you," were the parting words of Hester Strong, as she stood on the platform of the village depot. "God bless and keep you, Wallace, and Albert, and George. Don't forget to read your Bibles. You will find them near the top, on the right hand side. Carry them near your hearts. God bless and keep you in the day of battle, and in the hour of temptation shield you. Be strong. Good by. Dear Mr. Elwood," she continued, turning to the young pastor of the village church, who was going out as chaplain, "God bless you also, and keep you, as you look after the spiritual interests of our loved ones, and those engaged in a common cause."

Mr. Elwood looked pale and thoughtful. He had just come from a sad, sad parting with one who was very dear to him — our old friend Lottie Gray. O, there was weeping in the village depot, weeping in hundreds of little depots, as that early train went on its way; weeping in the country and the city, on the land and on the sea; a nation weeping, as she sent forth her noblest and best to perish, it might be, by the hand of treason; and that, a base-born brother's hand. For this was the second call, and we knew that the conflict must be long, that blood must flow like a river. There was a crowd at the village depot; fathers, and mothers, and sisters, wives and lovers. Little children were there, trying to comprehend the mysteries of war — wondering why so many wept, and smiled when weeping. Winnie was there, leaning heavily on the arm of Howard; thanking God, in her heart, that he was not accepted; chiding herself for the selfish joy, weak from the great struggle it had cost her to say, "Thy will be done," when she thought that brother, lover, and friends were to go together, fight, and perchance fall. Elida was clinging to the arm of Albert Gray in a paroxysm of grief.

"O, Wallace, take care of him. Albert, watch over my brother, my only brother. Good by, good by," unclasping the unwilling arms, turning the weary steps homeward, to wait, and watch, and labor for the absent ones. Hattie Herbert, the bride of a day, was there, silent and pale. No word escaped her lips; a smile sadder than tears, a kiss, and the clasped hands open nervously, and the train passes on. How near those friends, left standing there, drew together in that hour of parting! How their hearts beat in unison, as they tried to fill the great void, made by that parting hour, with hopes of victory and success! How they tried to hide their fears, their doubts, their griefs!

"You are doubly my daughter now," said Mrs. Gray, folding Hattie's shrinking form to her bosom. "We will wait, and weep, and pray, till the tempest is over, dear, and our Henry restored again."

"What if he should never, never come?"

"We will hope and trust till the blow falls, darling; and if come it must, God, *our God*, will help us. Let us be cheerful. This is no time to sit idly down. Poor Lottie! it will go hard with her. The great hope of her life may never be realized; the new and beautiful joy which has sprung up in her heart may go out on the field of blood. And Elida: how strange it seems to see her bright face veiled in sadness! O, we must be strong, and try to strengthen them. How inexpressibly sad Mr. Frank Lovering's folks looked!"

"Why, has George gone?"

"Yes. How brave the boys were! how they tried to be cheerful! none more so than George. 'I shan't come back,' he said, 'without a laurel wreath, or an epaulet — see if I do.' I suppose he and Lucy are engaged. How very calm she appeared! How noble, yes, I may say beautiful, the boys all looked! for Henry is a boy to me, if he is married. Hattie, how little I thought, when you received us so coldly, perhaps suspiciously, that we should ever be drawn so very near to each other, and by such a tender cord!"

"O, mother, never speak of that again, I beg of you. I am ashamed of it, heartily ashamed of it. I saw my mistake very soon, but was too proud to own it. I regretted leaving home very much, when the time came. I longed to have you or father urge me to give up going, and stay at home; for I found, soon after you came here, that it was my home still — a pleasant, comfortable home, such as I had not known for a long time. It was hard to work in the mill after that, I assure you. The motive was gone, the stern necessity removed. It didn't seem pleasant to go day after day, rain or shine, sick or almost sick. It was such a confinement I could scarcely endure it; but I thought you were displeased with me for going, and I resolved to stay it out."

"Obstinate little thing," said Mrs. Gray; "I don't know who suffered the most, you, or I, or your father.

How long should you have held out but for that sickness, think you?"

"I don't know, I am sure. How long did you take care of me before I realized it was you?"

"A week, I think. I found out your secret when you little thought of letting me know it, and resolved to take you home with me as soon as you were able to be moved. You came; I have never been sorry: have you?"

"I should think not, judging by the way I have nestled down here, grudging every day spent away from home. Mother, there is just a little drop of comfort in the cup of sorrow the war has brought me. I shall stay in my home a little longer. I shrink from going into a strange place."

How short the days seemed to the busy village folks! New cares and new interests had sprung up in the families of the absent ones. Home duties were interspersed with labors of love for the soldier boys; letters written, with bits of news, kind messages, loving words, warnings, and words of cheer; letters received — sad letters, hopeful letters, full of love and bright with anticipation. How they passed from one to the other in the families of the soldier boys! How they rejoiced together, or wept together, as the case might be! And in those awful pauses, when man was arrayed against man in the deadly conflict, and there was no voice to whisper at nightfall the fate of the absent, as the days lengthened, and the hours moved slowly on, how hard it was to wait, how difficult to hope and pray! Then it was pleasant to see the noble self-forgetfulness of those who suffered most, and see them smile into each other's faces, as if they would cheat themselves, and rob sorrow of half its sting.

"What a blessing work is!" Hester used to say. "Our girls seem almost to forget their pain, in their eagerness to encourage their soldiers and make them comfortable."

Reader, you know all this: why need I tell you? The village in our story was much like other villages, and the human hearts in it like other human hearts, that beat on and on in spite of anguish. Grief kills — but slowly; and hope is strong. Justice and truth go hand in hand in the march of years. Let us leave our noble Lincoln, our Abraham, chosen of God and the people to lead our nation through the storm and the tempest, our generals to lead our soldiers in the battle, and God over all, to the end, and see what is the destined life work of our little Fostina, or, as she is now called, Mary F. Lentell. These are trying days to her. Hers is just the nature to suffer and endure, and suffer on — bend even to the dust, and let the waves pass over; to lie shivering, bruised, and bleeding for a time; then, arising to wipe away the blood, and dust, and tears, patiently gathering the mantle of hope about her yet cold and shrinking limbs; walking steadily on and on to meet and breast another wave; struggling to outlive the last one, beating no retreat. Such ones are heroes — God's heroes, man's blessings.

CHAPTER XXXVII.

FOSTINA'S LIFE WORK BEGINS. — HESTER'S STORY OF HER OWN CHILDHOOD.

"WILL my poor father be drafted?" Fostina inquired often. "Would it cure him of drinking if he went to the war, auntie?"

"Dear child," said Hester one day, "how very, very much you think of your father! Is that what makes you so pale and thin?" Fossie leaned her head on that broad, loving bosom, closed her eyes wearily, and sobbed, —

"Auntie, I can't help it. My darling mamma loved him, and I am his little girl. I have heard you say that a little child shall lead them. You found it in God's book. I am growing older and bigger every day, and then I shall have to say, as Winnie did, ' I have lost that opportunity.' " She buried her face in Hester's bosom, and wept passionately, as she had often done because of her father's inebriety. "Rum-maker and rum-seller," mused Hester, "what do you think God, the Judge, will do with this child's tears, and thousands of other children's tears? wives' tears, and sisters'? Ay, husbands, and brothers, and fathers are sometimes called to weep over the sin and shame you cause. What if God should gather up those tears into one dark, deep, briny ocean, and doom you to drink from the bitter fountain? — forever drinking and forever dry — thirsty and drinking, but never satisfied. He is able, and it would be just. And you know that you would call in vain for a drop of water from the pure, cool fountain that flows on and on, forever, near the throne. None ever pass the gulf. 'Nor thieves, nor covetous, nor drunkards, nor revilers, nor extortioners, shall inherit the kingdom of God.' And such are ye. Dear child," said Hester, " I pity you, and God pities you. That is what I used to tell Winnie. Darling, God pities you. He can help you to bear this life-long burden. Do you ever ask him, dear ?"

"Yes, auntie, and something tells me that if I should go and stay with father, I could get him to sign the pledge. Can I go?" She looked up timidly into her face.

"Fossie, you don't know what you are asking, dear. Your grandmother Lentell is very cross and selfish, and aunt Abigail is much like her. You could not stay there; my little girl would die." Hester told her all the circumstances of her birth, how her mother had been neglected, how very low she found her, and nursed her back to life again. "And ever since," she said, "I have watched over you in sickness and in health. And now I am growing old; I am beginning to feel infirm."

"You, auntie?" said the child. "Why, I thought you were young. How old are you?"

"O, I have passed the allotted time of man's life. I am more than threescore years and ten. I thank God for so large a measure of health and strength.; but it cannot last always. Some time I shall want the little one I rescued from death, cherished so tenderly, and loved so well, to lean upon. I, in my turn, shall need to be cherished. Will Fossie do it? or does she want to go and live with those who have never done her a single act of kindness, and blamed me for bringing you to life?" The child wound her frail arms around Hester's neck impulsively, saying, —

"Darling auntie-mamma shall have her baby to take care of her when she is old and sick. I will come back long before that. I will, auntie; I know I shall. And I will bring my father with me, and he shall plant the garden, and cut the wood, and sleep in grandpa's room. O, won't it be nice! And then you will forgive your little Fossie all her naughtiness — won't you, auntie?" Hester looked down earnestly into the sweet, pale face which was now radiant with hope, and sighed, for she saw no chance to hope. "You will forgive your little Fossie?" she again inquired. "Say that you will, and that I may bring him here when he is all cured. May I?" Her eagerness aroused Hester from a fit of abstracted thinking. She clasped the child in her arms, saying, —

"Why, yes, my darling; of course I shall forgive my Fossie. She has been a good little girl so far, and I hope she always will be. I don't expect she will be faultless."

"Well," said the child, "may poor father come here when he gets well of drinking?"

"Why, yes, indeed, he may, my dear, and welcome." Again the child clung to Hester's neck, this time in silence. Hester and Martha were puzzled at the strangeness of her conduct.

"I don't know," said Martha, when they were alone, — "I don't know but we shall have to let her go up there, and see for herself. It is strange what has possessed her."

"Good by, little pet," said Hester, a few days after this conversation. "Take good care of aunt Martha till Winnie gets home, and then Howard will bring you over to uncle Giles'. And we will go from there to grandpa's — won't that be nice?" Fossie clung to Hester's neck, and seemed loath to part from her. She crept to her room, and wept long and bitterly. She then took a scrap of paper she had been sacredly keeping for the occasion, and commenced writing word after word till it was covered. She folded it with a sigh, saying, —

"Well, she will forgive me; she has promised it, and she never lies. I am glad she won't know it for a week, and I shall almost get him to sign by that time. No one has ever told him how wicked it was; and he don't know he has got a little Fossie to love him." She tied up some of her dearest treasures in a little bundle, and, stealing out at the back door, took the road which she had been told led to grandma Lentell's.

"It is only seven miles up there. Let's see; auntie told me once, when I asked her, that it was a straight road from the tavern. I know where that is; and I must turn off at the right hand. I can find it. And the house is built like my uncle Mason's. I guess they will be glad to see me. I will tell them what I came for. Why, I thought I should come to the tavern by this time." And the little feet went faster and faster, the little heart beat quicker, and the breath came harder. "It is a great ways farther walking than it is riding," sighed the tired traveller. "I shall have to rest. I wish I could find such a beautiful arbor as Christian did to rest in. I haven't any roll to lose, only my bundle, and I could hang that on my arm. O, here is a nice, cool place under this tree. I can lean my head against the tree, for it aches. I am glad aunt Hester promised to forgive me, and glad I learned to write. Now she will know where I am, and won't think I'm lost. I will say my prayers first." She knelt on the green grass, and prayed that prayer which she had so often and so sincerely uttered, closing with, —

"O Lord, save my father, and help me to reform him, for Jesus' sake." That was the last she remembered. Two hours passed, and she still slept. She was aroused by the rattling of wheels, and sprang up bewildered from her long, deep sleep, just as Mr. Trueman reined up his horse.

"Why, little Fossie, is that you? I thought you would be farther along. Come, get into my carriage. Aunt Martha is distressed about you, dear."

"O, Mr. Trueman," said the child, distressed in her turn, as she saw her bright dream of happiness vanishing, — "O, Mr. Trueman, please let me go. O, let me. God wants me to. I have asked him a thousand times, I should think, to save him, and he hasn't done it. I know he is waiting for me to go to father, and lead him back. O, let me go — let me go. I *must!*" She knelt there on the grass again, folded her hands, and prayed this time that she might be allowed to go on her pilgrimage. "It is only seven miles," she said. "I will come back long before aunt Hester gets old and lame. I will, Mr. Trueman; I will bring father, and we will kill the fatted calf, and you shall come and eat some it. Dear, good, kind Mr. Trueman, don't take me prisoner," she said, as he alighted from his carriage, much affected by what he saw and heard. "O, don't take me prisoner and put me in jail, for I am not a deserter. I wrote it all on a piece of white paper; and I want to go back myself and confess, when I have found my mission. I heard aunt Martha tell aunt Hester she believed I was saved for some kind of a 'mission.' Aunt Hester nodded, and whispered, 'Perhaps it will be to save her father.' I heard it; but they wouldn't let me go; and so I went. O, don't carry me away from my 'opportunity!' Winnie lost hers."

"Be calm, little Fossie; I shan't take you prisoner, and you are not a deserter; you are a good little girl. But I want you to go home with me now. See, the sun is almost down; it will be dark soon. You have had no dinner, and will have no supper. You will have to sleep out in the damp, dark night, and get cold, and die, perhaps; and then you will lose your 'opportunity.' But," he continued, "if you will go home with me, they will let you go. They must; and I will carry you with your clothes, and come up in a week, and see if you want to go home."

"I shan't, Mr. Trueman; I shan't go home till father goes with me, and then I shall want to come. I shall want a new hat from your store, and some clothes that are nice and clean; and aunt Hester must come out to meet us, and kiss him, and put a ring on his finger; for grandpa is dead, you know, and she will do just as well." Mr. Trueman smiled sadly as he handed the young enthusiast into the carriage. "I am glad they don't call me a deserter. I was afraid they would. That is awful

— isn't it? They shoot them in the army; and I didn't know but you would take me prisoner — that means to take people where they don't want to go. I hope they will let me use my 'opportunity,' and go to my 'mission.' Winnie said father loved children; and I am growing so fast, I was afraid I shouldn't get him to sign if I waited." Hester and Martha stood anxiously watching at the gate when Mr. Trueman rode up with the little truant. Fossie seemed embarrassed when she met them, and commenced crying. "Mr. Trueman says I am not a deserter; and I was coming right back, just as soon as I had done God's errand: that is what he saved me for. I knew you would be so glad. What made you come home so soon, auntie?"

"Why, darling, aunt Martha sent for me. You have frightened us."

"*I*, auntie? Why, I wrote it all in a letter. I thought you would know where I was."

"O, birdie bird, didn't you know it was a long, long way for a little girl like you to go alone? — didn't you, dear? You might get lost, and have to sleep out doors, and take cold. O, darling, don't ever do such a thing again;" and Hester kissed the little pale, sweet face, from which the joys of childhood had been driven by that accursed love of gain which pampers the drunkard's love of drink. Martha left her work, and knelt by the child-heroine, who was bound to their hearts by such a mysterious cord.

"Little Mary," she murmured, — "my Mary, grandpa's Mary, — welcome home for a night. To-morrow, if you wish it, we will send you. But, precious, you will see hard, rough times. It won't be like this home. They don't love each other there."

"Won't they love me?" said the child. "I guess they will. God will make them; he is going with me." Hester was weeping; it was a strange sight for little Fossie. Martha often wept; she was used to that.

"Don't, auntie — don't cry," she said; "Fossie will stay."

"No, darling. I am willing you should go. I was thinking of the past, dear — of the past; thoughts which you could not understand came crowding into my mind — thoughts and feelings buried long ago; for I have lived a great while in this world of changes. I was thinking how many, many years I longed, with an indescribable longing, to learn something of my father, who perished on the ocean; it was supposed shipwrecked at sea in a gale. They knew the ship was lost, and the crew were never heard from more. My mother clung to the vain hope that he was saved. It was before I was born, Fossie, just before; and they said my mother watched and waited, with a pale, calm face, month after month. She watched and waited silently, wasting day by day. They hoped her helpless baby would arouse her from this waiting, listening posture; but no. She talked to me of papa, my dear papa, saying, —

"Hush, hush!" with her finger to her pale lips — "hush! the captain is coming — hush!" and thus she sat, straining every nerve; but he came not. They carried her far and near; they did all they could to save her; but she died, listening and waiting. They tell me that when dying she started up, and reached out her arms, saying, with a smile of angelic sweetness, "At last! at last!" and expired, leaving me a helpless infant. Fossie, I was older than you, I think, when I gave up the idea that I should see my father. I listened eagerly to stories of wanderers returning. I imagined him a captive on some lonely island. I thought of him as a prisoner, and wished that I was a man, so that I could go and find him. I dreamed of him as returning poor, old, and sick, and sometimes as rich, and with a princely bearing. Child, I can't blame you. Your father was manly, and had noble qualities; go and save him. I will give you his last letter to your dear mother when she was dying. I will read it over and over with you, until you can read it to him. It may do him good. Tell him you are sent to claim the fulfilment of that sacred promise. · Tell him his Harmony is waiting and watching for him in heaven, and Jesus is waiting to forgive and save." Fossie had listened attentively to Hester's narration.

"And so you didn't find your papa? He was hidden in the sea. What made you feel better about him?"

"It was my mother's dying expression. When I was thinking it over one day, and weeping, it came into my mind with great power, that as the golden cord was breaking, and the tried spirit released from its sufferings, my father came to meet her. And from that day he was dead to me."

"Did you tell any one of your feelings?" said Martha. "I never heard of it."

"No," was the reply; "they never knew anything about it; and I heard more than they thought, or I never should have known that I was not in my own father's house. It was chiefly visitors that spoke of these things; Mr. Lovering's family never. So, now, dear, you shall not have to run away to find your father.

Since you wish it so much, we will consider that it is from above, and bid you God-speed; for I know you have sought counsel of him in your childish way. Who knows but you may save him?"

"O, I shall, auntie — I shall. And when I come leading him home, I want you to come out with mother's wedding ring, — Winnie will let you have it, — and put it on his little finger, and kiss him and me. And aunt Martha must attend to the fatted calf, because she is the youngest; and Mr. Trueman is going to put clean new clothes on him out of his store. He said he would when we were riding home; and he said he might work in the store, too. O, won't the girls be glad, and Wallace, and all?"

"Yes, we shall all be glad, and methinks there will be joy in heaven when that day comes," said Martha, reverently. "But you will have to give me notice," she continued, sportively, "or I can't get a good fat calf for the joyful occasion."

"O, that won't be any matter, auntie. It means that we should be happy, and have something good, as we do Thanksgiving Day — doesn't it? Will you both promise?"

"Yes; we will do all we can, dear. So pleasant dreams; for to-morrow your work, as a reformer, begins in earnest."

CHAPTER XXXVIII.

Love's Golden Key, or A New Era in the Lentell Family.

"Are you my grandmother?" said little Fossie, as Abigail Lentell opened the door. Abigail laughed a coarse, derisive laugh. It was so strange, so new, to the child, that she started back, and looked up earnestly into the sympathizing face of Mr. Trueman, and then back into the unsympathizing face of Abigail.

"What do ye want?" said Abigail, sharply.

"I want my father, and he lives with my grandmother."

"Well, I ain't yer granny, nor yer father, ye see. Whose young one are ye?"

"I am aunt Hester's little girl, I am, and Morgan Lentell is my father, and my grandmother's name is Mehitable Hum," said the child, innocently. She had heard Elida call her that name till she really thought it was so.

"O," said Abigail, sneeringly, "ye come by one of yer aunts — did ye? What do ye want of yer father? The sot can't do nothin' for ye. They needn't pack ye off up here; we've got 'nuff to do to maintain him in his laziness. So ye may tramp back."

"But I want to see my father," was the reply, as the child folded her soft, delicate hands, and looked pleadingly into the hard, sharp face. "I want to see him —I must. I have come to cure him of drinking rum, and then he shall go to my home, and not trouble you any more."

"Pretty tall doin's for a little scrimp like you." Abigail was softened a little by the tearful earnestness. "Come in, an' see what yer granny says. 'Twon't do to put on no Loverin' airs 'fore her. C-a-l-l?" This was said reluctantly, with a nod towards the carriage.

"No, I thank you," said Mr. Trueman. "I will sit here until you see whether the little Fostina will be permitted to stay and get acquainted with her father's family. She has longed to come, but her friends feared she would not be welcome, and I perceive she is not. But yesterday she actually started on foot, and alone, and walked until, overcome by fatigue, she sat by the roadside and slept. It was nearly dark when I found her there, and she begged so hard to be allowed to come, that I promised to bring her to-day. You see she is a brave little thing, and thinks a good deal of the Lentell connections."

"What! run away from the Loverin's' to come here? Sho! she didn't, though!"

"Yes, she did," was the reply; "she is determined to form your acquaintance. She is a frail child; be tender of her if she stays. But I hope she will be willing to return with me. They will miss her sadly at home."

"They will, hey? Well, come, Fussy; that's yer name—ain't it? let's go to granny. She's lame as a horse. She'll like ye to bring her things, and take up her stitches. An' I'll bake ye a turnover and twist ye a doughnut, I guess, if ye wanted to come an' see us.

Don't be scairt; the old woman is cross, but she never bites, an' it's easy 'nuff to git out of the reach of the crutches. Ye wanted to come an' see how yer granny lived — did ye? I like yer grit."

Fossie looked pained and puzzled.

"They talked badly to my Jesus," she thought, "and I am his disciple; so I must bear it. I wonder what a granny is. I will wait and see."

"Marm, here's Morgan's youngest young one, an' she's the right sort, too. Why, she run away from Hester an' the rest on um to come an' live with us. She'll be handy to pick up yer stitches."

The little wiry, witchy woman had grown more wizened and withered-looking than ever. The wrinkled face, with the sharp gray eyes sunken beneath a rim of black, looked hideous; the long chin hung loosely; the blue lips missed the sharp grinders, and the long nose seemed peering in at the open door of the mouth. Fossie looked, and shrank away — not so much at the ugly features, the long, wrinkled hands, with the light cords and the dark ones stretched lengthwise through them, the dark nails at the tips; but the look of cold scrutiny, the entire absence of any kind of loveliness in expression, voice, or feature, shocked her. She remembered what Hester and Martha had told her.

The old lady finished her scrutiny.

"Whose young one did ye say it was?"

"Morgan's," screamed Abigail. "You never saw her after she was a week old or so."

"What did ye say she was here for? an' where did she come from?"

Again Abigail screamed the information, saying, —

"Yer granny's as deaf as an adder. Ye'll have to pipe up. Ha, ha, ha!" was the conclusion of Abigail's second version of the story.

"She'll cure him! I guess so. The evil one couldn't do it."

"I can't," said Fossie; "but God is more powerful than the evil one, and he can cure him. Satan don't want to."

"Bravo, little Fussy! you'll do," said Abigail.

"W'at is she a-sayin', Nabby?" with a curious look.

"O, she says the Lord can beat the devil any day — that's all."

"Ha, ha!" said Mehitable; "she's none of yer Loverin's; she'll do, Nabby; let her stay. She's wuth 'bout as much as a taller candle for help; but we've got 'nuff to eat. Good for Hester; I'm glad on't. They want 'er. Well, I guess we can buy 'er as pooty things as them Loverin's. O, hum, hum! Well, take off yer things, an' Nabby 'll give ye a doughnut. Got any twisted ones, Nabby?"

"What do ye say, Fussy?" said Abigail, in her pleasantest tones. "Will ye stay an' eat red apples, an' butternuts, an' 'elp Nabby make the links? Ye can punch um with the new puncher. Ever seen one? Got a new one. An' we make cider sarse. Did ye ever eat any?"

"Yes," said the child. "What are links? Those long things that we fry and eat?"

"Yes; an' ye shall have plenty of punkin pie, too; so run an' tell the man that yer goin' to stay."

"O, yes, I mean to stay if you will let me. And I can punch the links, I guess. I stick a fork in them sometimes to let the water out. Will that do?"

"O, you'll do, I guess."

Fossie climbed up into the carriage, saying, —

"O, Mr. Trueman, I didn't know; but I shall stay — I must. My Jesus bore the cross for me, and I can stay here for him."

Mr. Trueman saw the turn things were taking. He knew the state of Mrs. Lentell's heart towards Hester and the Loverings. He saw that the child would not only be tolerated, but petted in their way, if they could torment Hester and the Loverings by so doing. A low, base motive, to be sure, but it would make the child-missionary more comfortable, her life tolerable.

"Fossie dear," he whispered, "don't speak of Hester or the Loverings; your grandmother and aunt dislike them, and they won't like you if you do. Think of them often, dear child, and love them. They have been good and kind to you, and love you as they do themselves. If they say unkind things about them, just you keep those little lips closed. Don't get angry, but ask God to help you bear it. It won't hurt auntie, or any of them, and it will help you to save your father."

"May I speak to father about them, if he will let me, when we are alone."

"Yes, dear; tell him how good they are. I shall call to see you in a week, and then perhaps you will go home with me."

"O, if I could! but the prodigal won't come to so soon; aunt Hester thinks so. I shall have to wait."

"Perhaps," was the reply, "you can sow some good seed, and leave it for the Lord to water; we will see. Good by! I shall come and see how you like your little girl in a week," said he, as Abigail came out to see where "Fussy" was, as she persisted in calling her.

"O, we'll do nicely. Tell them Loverings we can dress her and send her to meetin' as well as they. She's a bright one, and knows which side her bread is buttered on. Win is a stuck-up school-marm, they say, an' Wall 's gone a-sogerin', an' Lide's gone to the mill. *She* allers knew a thing or two. I hate yer stuck-up folks."

"She is at home learning dress-making now," was the reply.

"Sho! she ain't, though — is she? Well, they're all 'bout alike. We'll try to get some of the stuck-up-ness out of this one. - She's the first of um that's been near us since Hester stole um."

"Well, good afternoon," said Mr. Trueman. "I must go. Good by, Fossie."

"I am going to ride just down to the corner, aunt Abigail," she said. "I will run right back in a moment, and punch the links, or do anything you want me to."

"That's a good one," said Abigail, who supposed it was said in jest, and not that the child was in utter ignorance of what punching the links could mean.

"Mr. Trueman," she whispered, holding her hand before her mouth, "you don't think that my grandmother is a witch — do you?"

Mr. Trueman smiled.

"Why, Mr. Trueman, there are some witches. There was one in the Bible that raised up Samuel, you know; and I have seen a picture of one on a broomstick," she said, confidentially. "Did you ever see it?"

Mr. Trueman tried to look grave as he replied, —

"There were some, I know, in King Saul's day; but I think he caused them all to be destroyed, except that one; and she died soon after that, and there have been none since." He spoke very decidedly, and with a great deal of assurance.

"Well, I am so glad," said Fossie. "My grandmother does look like the picture I saw. Perhaps that was one of the old ones that Saul killed."

"I presume so," said Mr. Trueman; "but you may be sure she is not a witch, or she would not be suffered to live. She has worked very hard, and is old, and hasn't practised the Christian graces. That is what makes her look so forbidding, for in a measure we come to look like our lives. If we are habitually cross and selfish, we look ugly; if kind and loving, we look pleasant and peaceful even in old age. Good by."

Fostina returned to attend to her opportunity, as she called it, and overcome difficulties an older and wiser head than hers would shrink from encountering. She said God was going with her, and he did go. Everything she said and did was "brave," and "smart," and "bright." Verily the Lord turneth the hearts of men at his will. Suffer she must from their coarseness; it was new and irreverent to the pure-minded child. How often she remembered what aunt Martha said — "They don't love each other there"! How she missed the love! She was puzzled to understand their language; it was a new dialect. But she was a zealous little missionary, and God taught her, and shielded her from their bitter hate.

Mr. Trueman went home thinking more meanly of intemperance, wherever it might be found. In the palace, or in the hut, in the parlor or the bar-room, in high places, or low places, at home or abroad, all the same — the meanest, the weakest, and the most damning vice men or devils ever indulged in. He groaned as he thought how little the Maine Law had accomplished. "And yet," he thought, "I must admit it, that it has accomplished much here, where it has been in force."

He sighed that in places of trust and honor the evil was increasing. Those set to guard the interest and virtue of the nation were turning traitors to the nation's good, and drowning their God-given faculties in the intoxicating cup. "Shame, shame on such meanness! Set up to govern the people, by the people, and cannot govern a little clamoring appetite! To govern the people, and *such* a people, and cannot govern self! Shame, I say, shame!" He spoke aloud; his horse stopped, put back his ears, and listened. "I don't mean you, old Charlie; you are more of a man than they who sip wine at the card-table, or in the gilded saloon, though they pass in the 'best society,'" he said, sarcastically, "and drink from a golden goblet, or a silver cup. Go on, old Charlie; you will never die a drunkard, nor make another so; and in God's sight, I think you are more noble and worthy than they who do such things. I can't see the point of difference; getting drunk is getting drunk, whether the deed is accomplished by the best of imported wines and brandies, or on rum and cider. O that men would see this, and act up to their high prerogatives! If I were the voice of the people, none but men who were temperate in all things should govern this people — men who could rule their appetites and passions, and rule the people in justice and equity. Then, and not till then, shall we be truly prosperous and happy."

"Where is my father, aunt Abigail?" said Fossie. "I want to see him, and begin my mission."

"That is a good joke, Fussy. How come they to give you such a homely name?"

"O, my name is Mary Fostina; but they call me Fossie."

"Sho! Is that it? Well, Fussy will do, for you are a strange little thing; not a mite like the young ones in the other room."

"Aunt Hester said I was a good girl," said Fossie, as she raised those large, dark, mournful eyes to her aunt's face.

"O, you'll do," said Abigail, laughing, "you'll do. I'll buy ye a china mug, with a flower on it, to drink milk out of, if ye won't git homesick."

She was touched by the child's expression, which was a strange commingling of smiles and tears, of sadness struggling with mirth. Her very artless truthfulness was mistaken for wit, and they called it droll.

"I should like a china mug very much," said Fossie. "Did you say there were children in there?"

"Yes, a grist of um; but they won't beat you, Fussy."

"Well, I am glad; I shouldn't like to be beaten. Who are they?"

This was said in the child's own peculiar ingenuous, demure way, which was her greatest charm. Abigail was delighted with it; she laughed again, and her voice was a shade softer, as she said, —

"O, they are uncle Simeon's children. He's gone a-sogerin'. They've got a proper pooty little one in there. You shall play with that one."

"I should like to, but I shan't have much time to play. I must help you all the time I can get."

"What are you larfin' at, Nabby?" growled Mehitable. "You act like a fool. You'll scare that young one's senses out."

"Sho! I guess not," laughed Nabby. "But I believe she'll kill me a-larfin'. Marm, she thinks she's goin' to be chief cook an' bottle-washer, an' shan't have time to play. That ain't much like Sim's young ones — is it?"

"Ha, ha! no; that's true for ye, Nabby. Well, she's a real Sharp, that one is; she looks like our kind of folks. There ain't a bit of Loverin' in her, or Lentell either. Nabby, you are a sight like my folks. Your father was a nice clever man; but he hadn't gumption enough — that's all. I never'd orter married him. O, hum!" And the old lady swayed her body back and forth in bed, where she sat most of the time, with the Bible wrong side up, mumbling over the bits of texts she had heard now and then, or spelling out with great difficulty a few verses.

"Where is my father? I want to see him."

"Well, you won't want to more'n once, I reckon. He's in there, drunk. He works in the forenoon, and gits drunk by dinner time. Ye'd better not meddle with him to-day, but wait till mornin' when he's sober. Wait, and see if he'll know ye."

It seemed a great while to wait; but the obedient child cheerfully submitted.

When Mr. Trueman informed Hester and Martha how he had left their darling, they were truly grateful.

"It is the Lord's doings," said Hester. "Dear child! I hope and pray that the time may be short, for her sake as well as ours. How we love her!"

"What a comfort she was to us all!" said Martha.

"She is a strange child, so thoughtful and wise beyond her years, and yet a very child in artless simplicity. How I miss her! I shan't sleep a wink to-night, I do believe. Don't you suppose she will lie awake and cry all night?"

"O, no, I think not," said Hester; "she is a young philosopher, that child is. She will cry as if her heart would break, say her prayers, and go to sleep."

Hester's well-poised voice trembled as she commended their darling to God that night.

"Martha, I am growing old," she said, sadly; "I feel it. But that dear child's faith has prevailed. It was her Christian love that cast out fear; don't you see it? She said they would love her. God would make them; and he has. How wonderfully he fulfils all his promises to those who trust in him. 'According to your faith be it unto you.'"

CHAPTER XXXIX.

UNCLE LEVI. — SAD SCENE AT THE SUPPER TABLE. — THE NOBLE WRECK.

"Marm, supper's ready," screamed Abigail. "Come, pick up yer crutches and begin to hobble."

Fossie's eyes filled with tears as the poor old lady wended her way slowly and painfully to the table, with Abigail's help.

"O, how lame!" she thought; "poor grandmother! I will pick up her stitches, and read to her." She looked at the distorted features, the dark veins, and the large cords on the hands, and fairly shuddered. "What if she should be a witch? How did Mr. Trueman know they were all dead? But then, if she was a witch, she would ride to the table on a broomstick, when she was so lame." She took a deep breath, and began to watch for her father. She longed, and yet she feared to see him. A tall, lean man entered the room, and without word or sign to any one, commenced eating voraciously. Was that father? No, he was younger than aunt Abigail. No, that wasn't the ragged man she used to see.

"Levi," said Abigail, "this is Morgan's child. She that was born when he's in jail. Why don't ye look at her?"

He raised his sharp gray eyes suddenly, and looked at the child. Their eyes met. Levi started.

"Why," said he, "is that the baby? She looks like Harmony, some."

"What is he sayin', Nabby?" said grandmother, impatiently.

"Why, he says *she*," pointing with her knife, "looks like Harmony."

"Levi, you talk like a fool," was the reply. "She's a Sharp, has got the Sharp eyes, an' forrad, an' nose. I tell ye she's a Sharp, and she shall have my red cloak made into a little red ridin'-hood, like Sim's gal, and go to meetin' with um. Nabby, can't ye fix it to-night? I wan't her to look smarter 'n any on um."

"O, I'll do it before she wants it," said Abigail, who agreed with mother in her ambition about the child's looks. "We'll make um stare — won't we, marm? I'll git her the best hat I can find."

"Ha, ha!" and the old lady opened her mouth very wide. She looked more like a witch than ever, when she brought her crutches down angrily, and said, —

"Levi, don't you let me hear you say she looks like Harmony, or I'll beat ye over the head."

"I should like to see you doing it," was the curt reply. "I just want you to remember that I was twenty-one long ago. I don't stand crutches now, or tongues, and I shouldn't mind going into the army. Five or six hundred dollars don't grow in the country. I could sell the stock, you know."

"O, they don't love each other one bit," mused the little missionary. "I wish I could teach them to love."

"There, there," said Abigail, "don't mind what the old woman says; she's a child. If you go, I'll go. Ten such cows as we've got, and four such oxen, and two such horses, can't be found every day. What a shame to sell um! Sim's gone and left his grist of young ones for us to look arter. What's the use to talk? Jule is slack."

"Julia is good enough," said Levi, "and so was Harmony; and that child looks like her. I am glad she's come, — a little ray of light you see, — for home has been a Tophet; that's all. Abigail, you know it. It is work and scold, and eat and sleep: that's been the programme. I hate it. I had as lief go to war, and shoot somebody, as to be shot at all the time, and can't shoot back. I wish she would strike me once; I'd go." He raised his voice to a high pitch. "Marm, I tell you this child looks like Harmony, and she is pretty. Now cane me if you dare!"

Fossie covered her face and cringed, expecting to hear the blow, the crashing of dishes, &c. The poor strained hand clinched the crutch, and the gray eyes, sunken behind the dark rims, glared at Levi, — nothing more, — as the blue lips muttered, —

"O, hum! I'd orter expect it; this is what comes of marryin' third cousins. O, hum!"

"Don't be scairt, Fussy." ("What a name!" said Levi.) "There won't be any bones broken; and uncle Levi likes ye, and he'll take ye to see the 'grand craven animals,' as marm read it the other day."

"What is it, aunt Abigail?"

"O, the caravan. There is monkeys in it. Ever see one?"

"No, but I have read about them. I brought my books, and I'll read you about it when I have time."

They were interrupted by a heavy, shuffling step. The

poor inebriate's troubled sleep was disturbed by the loud talk. He caught the name of Harmony now and then. How it startled him! He had not used it, nor allowed others to, for years.. He raised his head, brushed back the tangled locks of rich dark hair, and listened.

"She is pretty, and she looks like Harmony," he heard Levi say, defiantly. "Now cane me if you dare."

He started up, and crawled off the bed nervously.

"Who've they got there?" he muttered, with an oath. "Who looks like her — like her?" he groaned. "O, God, she wouldn't know me. Why, I meant to forget her. Curse them! they've brought it all back — all back."

He stopped in the doorway which opened opposite Fostina. He leaned weakly against the door, with pale, parted lips, red, wild eyes, tattered garments, and matted locks. How haggard he looked! What a wreck! How like a noble castle in ruins, with hingeless gates, tumbling walls, and broken battlements!

O, what a noble wreck! The tall, manly form was there; the pale, white forehead was there; but it seemed as if the honest, loving, manly soul had been banished from the noble mansion of God's own making, and a demon, half defiant and half afraid, stood fearfully looking out of the windows of the soul, abashed at those strange, beautiful, mournful eyes, which rested with an unutterable yearning look upon him. He reached out his arms with a quick, frantic gesture, then drew them back fiercely, and, smiting them on his broad chest, exclaimed vehemently, —

"O God! O God! it is the same look. *Her* eyes, how they followed me to the road — out of sight — yes, she stood in the door and looked." Again he smote the broad chest, madly. "O God, what a look that was! How it haunted me! How it stood between me and the jug, till she died! And then it followed me — followed me day and night, till I cursed it, and I never saw it more."

This was said with a shudder, and in a hoarse whisper.

"Never any more; and I drank and drank till I drowned my misery, and got revenge; and it was sweet." He raised his voice. "You told me to drink, old woman. Have you got enough of it?"

"Yes, yes; God knows I have," was the low, muttered reply.

"That is what comes of your ugly, domineering, selfish disposition," muttered Levi, as he left the room.

Poor, frightened, trembling little missionary, Did her heart fail and her faith waver for a moment, as she bent lower and lower in her seat, saying, —

"Dear Jesus, what shall I do? what shall I do?"

"Do ye think ye can cure him, Fossie? do ye?" whispered Abigail.

She, too, was pale and trembling. There was something awful in the language, tone, and manner of the fallen man. It was like a wail of despair, or a prayer half uttered, or a muttered curse. She could not read it. She had not seen the tears nor heard the prayers which had been put up for that man; knew not that the Spirit of God was striving in the dark, dark soul.

"I can't cure him. O, no! I can't, but God can. The prodigal son was poorer and worse than he. He ate with the swine; but my poor, poor father has good nice food, and a little girl to love him."

SAD SCENE AT THE SUPPER TABLE.

Morgan Lentell took a step nearer.

"Who be you?" he gasped. "Who be you? Her ghost?"

"I am Mary Fostina, your little girl. I love you, and Jesus loves you. I have come to tell you something beautiful when you are sober."

"Sober?" he muttered. "Who told you I drank?" he said with an oath, which shocked Fostina. "Who is Jesus?" he mused; "I used to hear about him. She used to tell the children about him. But, child, he's done loving me; don't speak of him."

"There, Morgan, eat yer supper," said Abigail, with a degree of pity in her heart she had not felt for a long time. "Eat; here is some cold victuals: you like it."

"Yes, father, sit by me and eat; for I am your little girl — your baby that you never saw. I have come to live with you a long time. Aunt Abigail and grandmother say that I may. Ain't they good? I want you to love them."

He looked at her in great perplexity.

"Those are *her* eyes," he said, with an oath. "Abigail, who is it?"

"Why, it is your own child — she that was a baby when Harmony died."

Abigail used to listen in a kind of bewilderment, as little Fossie talked of her hopes and plans. "What a droll little thing you be, Fussy!" was her only answer. Fossie soon learned that aunt Abigail did not mean disapprobation by that term, and so it ceased to pain her. The dear child had trials. She could not speak of those who occupied her thoughts so often. How she desired to see them, to hear their loving words, to tell them all her thoughts, to lay her head on their bosoms, and look into their dear, sweet faces. In vain Abigail made twisted doughnuts and turnovers, with the curious crinkle round the edge, with the light crisp crust, or bought her sugar hearts. She missed the love which had seasoned everything in her other home. So she waited, and labored, and thought of the fatted calf, the ring, the new hat, and, above all, a father to know and love. She smiled, and played with the children, and waited hopefully on till the end. There were days at Mehitable Sharp Lentell's which were real holidays to the child-missionary; days when the married daughters of the family, with little boys and girls, came home — children who had been taught to love one another, and respect each other's rights. Little Mary, as their mothers taught them to call their cousin, was a favorite among them. She was too modest and unassuming to excite envy in hearts fortified as theirs were by love. And then her good will was a sure passport to aunt Abigail's and grandmother's hearts. It amused them very much to hear grandmother call her a " Sharp young one " — her, the demure, quiet, thoughtful maiden, so affectionate and kind. " She means that she is like *her* family; her name was Sharp," their mothers explained to them. Uncle Simeon's wife was quite literary; she found books and papers in her part of the house. But the child-missionary denied herself the privilege of reading, and almost of eating or sleeping; at least, she felt willing to, when she could in any way promote the work for which she was a cheerful exile from the home and friends she loved. There were dark days, cloudy days, stormy days for her — days when her father would not permit her to approach him; and then she hovered around him, watching for her "opportunity," as she called it. Uncle Levi plucked the nicest fruit for Fossie, listened, with his eyes closed and his head leaning on the back of his chair, to her artless conversation about God and heaven, about Christ and salvation, about things she had seen and heard at school — sad things and amusing ones, for the little, wise, old-fashioned child had a fund of anecdotes. She always heard everything, and never forgot. Sometimes, when she went to the village with him, or about his work, he inquired concerning Hester and the Loverings, and was much interested in her account of their way of living and doing.

"What! have prayers night and morning? I thought such things were for ministers, or men, at least."

"Why, I guess not," was the reply. "Grandpa is dead, you know, and the altar must be kept up. Why don't you have an altar, uncle Levi? It would make us all better and happier." She waited; he seemed uneasy.

"O, I suppose you had rather pray to God alone in your room; that is just as well, I guess. That is the way I do."

"You pray?" said Levi, looking up under his heavy, shaggy eyebrows; "you pray, little May-day?" He called her that often when they were alone.

"Tell me what you mean, uncle Levi, by calling me May-day. Is it a good day?"

"O, I mean that you are pleasant and lovely." Levi felt half ashamed that he had spoken words which his mother always called "weak as dish-water," until the human nature in his soul was paralyzed and put fast asleep.

The child had aroused his slumbering faculties, and he

was hungering for something to feed upon — something he had not found in his home. Yes, he was hungering for sympathy — for something human to love, something to live for besides his cows, and oxen, and horses. They were the only living things he had ever loved: they were like old friends, but now they did not satisfy him. His brother's children he might love, but he feared his mother's derisive laugh — Abigail's sarcasm.

"Abigail is different," he mused, as they rode along. "Little May-day, what shall I buy you at the store?"

"Let me think," said the child; "some maple sugar, please. No, no, uncle, don't buy me anything. I love you well enough now. Buy aunt Abigail and poor, lame old grandmother something. Aunt Hester says little deeds of kindness, little words of love, coax out the better feelings, and kindle the flame of affection. I guess grandmother's never were kindled."

"No," said Levi, bitterly, "she never had any affections. She fed and clothed us, as I take care of my cows and horses, only not so kindly. May-day, you would have been a north-easter, if you had been brought up here."

"Should I?" was the innocent reply. "Don't you love your mother, uncle Levi?"

He looked at the child silently, almost sternly, a moment, and then said, "Do you love her, or your father?"

"Yes, I love her, but not as I love them at home. I want to make her better, but I don't want to go and put my arms about her neck, and love her hard. O, I can't love them enough! I wish you would go and see them some day."

"Well, I will," was the prompt reply. "I will; and you shall go and see them, little one. It is too bad!"

"Will you, uncle Levi? How happy I am! For when I stand and look out of the window towards there, I wish I had wings like a bird, so that I could go ever so often, and right back to my mission."

"Let's see; what is your mission? — to eat turnovers and sweetmeats?" he said, smiling into her face.

"You are very pretty when you smile, uncle Levi. Aunt Hester will like you," said the child. "But don't you remember what my mission is? Why, it is to reform my poor father. I feel so, without any, you know. The children tease me about it. That is what I stay here for; and I like you and aunt Abigail too. I am going to help her punch the links, when you kill the hogs; she says I may. Kill them as easy as you can — won't you, uncle Levi?"

He laughed, placed his broad, brown hand on her head, and said, in a voice so low and tender, —

"Little one, you are not like us. I don't understand it. What makes the difference?"

"I don't know, I am sure. Grandmother says I am like her Sharp folks." He frowned.

"She — well, it isn't true. You are like your mother, child. She was a Christian — the only one that I ever knew. I didn't always treat her well. The old cock crows, and the young ones learn. But I remember her. She was very lovely and good." There were tears in those sharp, deep-set eyes, and a little tremor in his voice, as he said, "Mary, we were not brought up right: that is what ails us. It isn't a good place for a child like you to live. I like you, but I want you to go home. Abigail likes you. I never thought she could like anything before. But your father is a real sot;

there isn't any help for him; so I want to carry you home before the sweetness is turned sour." She folded her little hands, and raised those large, beautiful eyes to his, mournfully, as she said, —

"I promised aunt Hester and Martha that I would certainly bring him, and I must. Please let me stay; only let me go with you to see them."

"Well, have it your own way; you are a strange little thing." Those were happy days for the child, when she went to see the loved ones.

"Marm musn't know a thing about it," Abigail told Levi and Fossie. "It is lucky she's deaf." Abigail indulged her youngest brother more than ever since the war. The querulous old lady muttered and mumbled her disapprobation, and read, "C-h-i-l-d-r-e-n, o-b-e-y y-o-u-r p-a-r-e-n-t-s i-n t-h-e L-o-r-d! O, hum! I never'd orter married yer father, Nabby. He was a nice, clever man, but he hadn't gumption, and he was my third cousin. Children never prosper when there's blood relation. There's a cuss on 'em."

"Fiddlesticks!" said Abigail, aside; "it's your tongue that has cussed us, and allers will, fur's I see. I wish yer loom and yer wheel had been sunk, and yer tongue tied. So there! I'm tired on't." Fossie looked up, with a frightened, grieved look.

"Aunt Abigail, did my grandmother use to scold so when" — she was about to say "when my mother lived here?" She stopped, confused.

"When what?" said Abigail.

"When she was young and well."

"Yes, and worse. She was always at it — work and fret, work and scold. Father never had a minute's peace in his life."

"Didn't he, aunt Abigail? Well, I am sorry, for she can't ask him to forgive her, now he is in heaven; and she can't get in there, for I guess she don't love God."

"Sho!" said Abigail; "yes, she will. Christ died for sinners. We shall all get in there somehow. I wish I was there now; for if Levi goes to the war, I can't live — that's all." Fossie was thinking what to say to Abigail: she saw her mistake.

"Will my father go to heaven as he is? Will he, aunt Abigail?"

"How do I know, child?"

"Well, would he be happy there without rum?"

"No, no, child. Run and get yer turnover: it's mince, with raisins in it."

"Yes, aunt, I will in a minute. It is nice. You are so kind to me, and I love you ever so much! But you can't go to heaven unless you are a Christian — no one can. We must repent and believe, — the Bible says so, — or we can't go to heaven. Won't you read it, aunt Abigail? — won't you? I want you to go to heaven."

"I'll think on't. There, run and see what yer granny wants. What a fool I am to humor that young one so!" mused Abigail. "I can't fret at her — I can't; and it may be true — it may. Marm's doctrine don't make any on us perfect. Pshaw! I won't be led round by a young one — and that Harmony's, too — I won't!" she said, spitefully.

But she was led, nevertheless. Yes, "a little child shall lead them." Mary Fostina's "opportunity" came at last. God sent a sickness upon the father; it was severe while it lasted, and left him very weak. The little girl hovered near him, watched over him, combed out the dark, rich locks, and petted them as Harmony used to. They were yet beautiful. She washed the soiled face and hands when he was stronger, and caressed his hollow cheek, which yet bore traces of manly beauty. She kissed the pale, high forehead, and said, softly, —

"Mother loves you, father. She is waiting for you in heaven. Jesus loves you. You thought he didn't; but he does. O, he loved you, and died to save you. Aunt Hester loves you, and Winnie, and Wallace, and Sunshine love you. That is what we call Elida. And papa, I mean to call you papa, now that you haven't drank any rum this week. Yes, your little Mary loves you, papa. I feel so badly when they call you sot and drunkard! O, I feel so badly, when you were such a beautiful man! Aunt Hester says so. They all say so. O, papa! papa! you promised mamma — my darling mamma! — when she was dying, that you wouldn't drink rum any more; and she will be disappointed if you don't leave off. Papa, won't you promise your little girl that you will never, never drink it any more?"

She fell upon her knees, and, with clasped hands, prayed, without waiting for a reply, —

"O God, help him to promise! O Jesus, save him! save him! and let me have my father to love." Abigail, hearing the child's pleading voice, stepped to the door and peeped in. The sight affected her. It was as if the child had been inspired by the Holy Spirit. It was a solemn, sacred sight. "Will you promise, papa?" she said, looking with a half doubtful, half hopeful look; "will you? Here is the very letter you sent her; and aunt Hester says she believed you. Say, papa, will you promise? Don't speak till you can." Then she told him, more calmly, her little plan, — how she was to lead him to her home, when he was all well and cured of drinking. "And we shall all be so happy!" she said. Morgan Lentell was weeping; it was long since he had wept: but he was very calm.

"Mary, I dare not promise. I have a demon in here, which clamors day and night for 'rum! rum!' 'Tis hell on earth. I can't escape it." Abigail withdrew to weep alone; she was ashamed of tears.

"O, but, papa, you have promised in this letter. Hear me read it — hear me." She read, pointing with her finger. He listened and groaned.

"O, I dare not promise. God knows I would like to reform, but I can't, I can't; it is too late."

"Dear papa, if God knows you want to reform, you can; for if you want to, he will help you. Winnie has wept for you; I heard her say she had wet her pillow weeping for you, and prayed for you; we all have. Won't you promise to try? O, you *must*." He gazed long, and almost tenderly, into the pale, tearful face.

"Harmony's face," he thought. "It *must be*. The eyes are hers; yes, it is the same look, tender, yearning, and mournful. I promise!" he whispered, hoarsely; "I promise, Harmy — I promise; God help me." In a moment the child fell upon her knees, and poured out her heart in praise to God. The sobs of the sick man startled her. She said, "Amen," abruptly, and arose to quiet him.

"It is done," she said; "it is done. Now go to sleep, papa — dear papa. My mother loved you. God loves you. Jesus loves you. You will repent, and believe, and be saved. There, go to sleep; it is done; I haven't lost my opportunity, as Winnie did; I went to find it."

Dear child! She was a little heroine at home, doing God's work bravely and well. How those two hearts grew together, as she hung with a mother's tender fondness around the returning prodigal! Reader, you would have wondered had you seen them walking to the small house near the swamp, day by day, and entering the dark, damp, dismal room, hand in hand, and coming forth with calm, peaceful faces, only that you know this was the child's chosen place for an altar. Yes, there they went to pray. Little Mary's altar it was. She prayed, and it was there she produced the pledge Hester had written for her to sign, and said, —

"Papa, it was in this corner I was born. Here mother died; the bed stood here, you say. Sign it right here, dear papa; perhaps God will let her see you sign it." He took the pencil, and wrote, with a trembling hand, —

"I will leave it off, God helping me."

CHAPTER XL.

Elida's Visit. — The Soldier's Funeral, or the Laurel Wreath.

Levi brought a letter one day, directed to Mary F. Lentell. It read thus: —

"My darling Sister: What you have told me about aunt Abigail, and the rest of them, makes me want to come and see them. Uncle Levi I know, and like already. Please ask aunt if I may come and stay a week or two. I won't make her a bit of trouble; and if she has dresses to fix or make, I will do my best; for Mrs. P. trusts me to do the best of work. They will tell me I have what grandmother calls 'gumption.' I think she will take me to be a Sharp. So, little sister, coax them to let me come. Your affectionate sister,

"Elida Lentell."

"I can't have none of yer stuck-up folks here," said Abigail. "Dress-maker! Miss Dress-maker! You don't want her — do you, Fussy? Aunt Abigail can git yer dresses cut in the village, and make um herself." Levi looked eagerly at the child. Would she dare be truthful? He saw the color go and come; tears glistened in the mournful eyes, the lip trembled for a moment, and then, with a brave effort, she spoke quite calmly: —

"Aunt Abigail, I love my sister very much, and she isn't stuck up, I guess; she isn't as big as you are; and she makes nice dresses. And she is so funny, she makes us all laugh! So I wish you would let her come — please, do. I should like it better than ever so many turnovers and things." She threw her arms around Abigail's neck, and kissed her again and again. "Aunt Abigail, say yes."

"There, there," said Abigail, as she shrank away, half ashamed of being caressed, it was so new — "there, Fussy, don't eat me up." She smiled. "You're a queer little thing. Ask uncle Levi if he'll go after her. May be it'll make him more contented. Granny'll fret, unless I can make her think she's a Sharp, from the crown of her head to the sole of her foot."

"You are the *darlingest* aunt Abigail I ever had," said Fostina, patting her on the cheek. "Uncle Levi will go, I know. I see it in his eyes." She went and leaned confidingly against her uncle's shoulder, and looked up into his face. "Won't you, uncle Levi?"

"I guess not," he said," smiling. "Dress-makers are bad things to have round; but aunt Abigail can *employ* one, though," he said, archly.

"Why, no, uncle Levi; dress-makers are not bad, I know. My sister isn't. You have seen her — isn't she funny? She made you laugh. But she is real good, though. Won't you go for her, and let me go with you? I will give you my new book that Winnie gave me, that has the elephant and the monkeys in it."

"O, that will be fine!" said Levi. "I'll go. When shall we start?"

"Better go now," said Abigail; "it's pleasant, and

the pears 'll be gone afore long." Levi took the letter, and read it.

"It is a neat thing," said he. "Abigail, if you and I had more learning, it wouldn't come amiss."

"Sho!" said Abigail; "if I'd been to school as much as you have, I'd be satisfied."

"Nabby, who's that letter from? Simeon? I'm afeared the rebs 'll kill him. O, hum! I'd orter knowed better 'n to let him gone. Jule 'll have the pinshin, I s'pose. I allers had yer father's. He fit at Concord an' Lexin'ton, an' helped take Burgwine. It allers made him shudder, an' laugh, too, when he told how they went in one *solid flanax*, right at the pint o' the bagonet, an' took him with flyin' colors. Ha, ha, ha! Didn't they bring him down a peg? I allers like to see yer stuck-up folks brought down. They hild him prisoner o' war — didn't they, Nabby?"

"I don't know nothin' about it," said Abigail. "You burnt up the hist'ry of it, that father bought, 'cause the boys wanted to read it."

"Get your information out of the ashes," muttered Levi, starting up, and striding out to the barn.

"Nabby, who did ye say that letter's from?"

"I didn't say," said Abigail, impatiently. "It is from one of Morgan's young ones. She wants to come and see if you think she's got the Sharp gumption. She is goin' to do our dress-makin'. Levi says she's a smart one," screamed Abigail.

"Looks like the Sharps, did you say, Nabby? Ha, ha! How mad the Loverin's ill be. Good for um. Let her come, Nabby. Likely 's not she can learn to spin an' weave."

"Not in this house," muttered Abigail. "I wish yer loom was burnt."

"I'll be ready in just forty minutes," said Elida, gleefully, when Levi and Fossie arrived; "for I am a Sharp, you see, and can do things quickly."

"Dress as plainly as possible, darling. Grandmother Lentell has a perfect horror of what she calls 'stuck-up' folks," said Hester, who could do little but look at and hold her baby. Martha was busy getting supper. Hester was learning to lean upon her a little now; for she could no longer deny that she felt the growing infirmities of old age.

"You will think me childish, Mr. Lentell," she said, "and I am. You see I have had a pretty large family for a maiden lady, and I love them all, foolishly, I suppose. You can have no idea how I miss this little pet," she said, folding her in a loving embrace; "she is the youngest. I miss the boys, too. Wallace is first lieutenant, and he so young! They call him very brave. He has never had so much as a scratch. Albert Gray, Elida's intended, has been wounded slightly; his sister's husband has been sick: we have felt anxious about him. George is in a fair way to get an epaulet, as he promised to. He is rising, and very popular. Perhaps you don't know my boys, though. I was speaking of George Lovering, Fossie's cousin. I wish the war was over; it is destroying thousands of lives, and souls, too, I fear; for it is, and must be, demoralizing." When Fossie and Hester were alone, she said, "When think I shall see my darling leading home the prodigal? I have got the ring all ready."

"Well," said the child-missionary, rising up from her

nestling-place, "I think I will come in the spring. You see, I have promised to help aunt Abigail chop the meat and punch the links with the new puncher; and after that it will be too cold to walk home, and they won't like it if I don't stay. And now that I can come and see you, and Elida is going to stay a little while, and father has signed, it won't be so hard." She breathed a deep breath, and waited for a reply.

"Why, my precious darling, auntie wants you very much; and if your poor papa could come and live with us, we could nurse him up, and he would be less likely to take to drinking again. Here there would be less temptation. Mr. Trueman would find some employment for him. Perhaps uncle Levi will bring you; it would be a long walk."

"O, he can't drink again, auntie, now he's signed. And then you wouldn't see us coming, and meet us with the ring."

"O, yes, I should. You could wait in the road till I came. Wallace and Winnie are going to buy him an entire new suit of clothes — boots and all. But, darling, you must say, stuff the 'sausages;' 'links' isn't proper; and 'sausage-filler,' instead of 'puncher.' That is the old-fashioned way."

"Well, I will tell aunt Abigail; she don't know it."

"No, dear, you had better not; she wouldn't like to have you." Hester had a long talk with Levi, who very willingly acceded to her wishes, and promised to bring them in a few weeks.

"We shall miss her," he said, with a grim smile; "but she is better here. I shan't speak of this till the time comes. They would be willing to lose Morgan;

for since he stopped drinking, he can't do a chore of work."

"O, well, he will when he has rested and recruited a while; and then he can find employment here, or go back, just as you and he can agree," said Hester. Elida was the same fun-loving child as ever, only a shade more thoughtful. She met aunt Abigail as if she had known her for years.

"Now tell me how to look like the Sharps, so that grandmother and I can hitch our horses together, as the old saying is," she said, in her queer way. Abigail laughed.

"You'd better look out for the crutches, if she thinks you look like Hester or the Loverin's."

"O, but I will look like the Sharps. Haven't you got a picture of one of them?"

"No; that's the only one," said Abigail, pointing at the bed; "and she don't look as she did, I can tell you. Between workin' and frettin', she's ready to blow away. Better take yer knittin' when she's lookin', and knit like a horse."

"Do your horses knit?" was the jocose reply. "Then I'll buy one when I earn enough, for I certainly wear out stockings very fast."

"What is she sayin', Nabby? I wish ye wouldn't mince so. I want to hear once in a while. O, hum! that's what comes of marryin' third cousins."

"She wants some knittin'," screamed Abigail. "She's goin' to arn enough to buy a horse, she says. She's got the right kind of grit — ain't she, marm? and looks as you did when you's a gal — don't she?"

"Where's my best specks, Nabby? I want to look

at her. I've forgot how I looked. You say she looks like me. Ha, ha! Horace said I was handsomer 'n Hester once." Elida drew down her face, and, seating herself in the range of the specs, commenced knitting. She dared not raise her eyes; she was full of suppressed mirth, which she had to restrain with all her might.

"She's a Sharp," said the old lady, with great satisfaction. "She looks like me, you say. Well, I guess she does. I wish my leg was well. I'd larn her to spin an' weave. She could have my loom an' arn a horse mighty quick. Ha, ha! Good! she ain't none o' yer stuck-ups. Nabby, git her some of yer doughnuts, and let her stay. There's victuals enough. She's got the Sharp nose," she muttered, feeling of her own. This was too much. Elida commenced coughing and choking; she rushed out of the house, out of sight, and laughed till the tears ran. "Git her some of my 'oarhound, Nabby. I used to cough when I was her age; it cured me."

"There, uncle Levi, you've found me," said Elida, laughing so that she could hardly speak. "Don't tell them; I couldn't help laughing, it is so funny! My poor nose — O, my poor nose! Grandmother says it's the real Sharp, and I look like her. You see I can't help laughing; I never could. I've got the bump, I guess. Don't tell them." The laugh was contagious. Levi laughed. Abigail came out with the candy, which the old lady always kept on hand as an infallible remedy for coughs.

"Here, take it," said Abigail, "and tell her you're better. She'd cane ye if she knew what set ye to coughin'. Don't your nose ache?"

27

"I am foolish to laugh so," was the reply. "Poor old lady! I am glad she liked my pug nose; but it struck me as decidedly droll to hear her call it the Sharp nose." Morgan Lentell did not take to the merry-hearted girl as he did to her more quiet, thoughtful sister. He had an indistinct recollection of a pouting little maiden, who stamped her tiny foot, and said, —

"Go away, naughty man. I won't be your little girl. I b'long here, and my name is Sunshine, it is." But she made herself useful in many ways; worked button-holes for Levi, and starched and crimped grandmother's caps very nicely, who, true to her early habits, was scrupulously neat. Abigail finally permitted her to fix over her black silk dress, "so as to have it ready to wear if Simeon should be killed."

"Lide's got the real Sharp gene," said grandmother, as she turned the clean crimped cap over and over, with childish satisfaction. "None of the Loverin' blood in her, I tell ye, Nabby; she's a Sharp."

"She takes arter her aunt Nabby — don't she, marm?" said Abigail, with a sly wink at Elida.

"You, Nabby?" she said, evasively — "yes, I s'pose so. You took arter me, when you 's a young one, under foot all the time. Ha, ha!" Grandmother's laughs seemed not to come from the heart. They were hollow, joyless, soulless, and made one feel like weeping.

"I will come every year and crimp your caps, if you want me to," said Elida, "for I like to stay here."

"She's goin' to be married when the war is over," said Abigail, "and then she won't think of granny's caps or Nabby's doughnuts."

"Yes, I shall think of crimped caps and aunt Abigail's doughnuts, and cheese, too, for they are the best I ever ate."

"Pshaw!" said Abigail, well pleased with the compliment. "Pshaw! I can't cook much. I wonder where Fussy and Morgan are. That child makes me think of an old hen scratching for a dozen chickens. She follows her father, and watches him every minute. He don't seem easy if she is out of sight a moment. I caught her mending his pants the other day. Her little white fingers warn't much bigger 'n the darn-needle she was usin'. She thinks he never can drink again, because he's *signed*. Poor thing! she hain't lived as long as I have." Elida felt reproved by her little sister's devotion to their father.

"I will go and find them," she said. "Where do you think they are?"

"Down to the small house, as likely as anywhere." She had shrunk from going there; but she went, thinking,—

"I live for self, Winnie and Fossie for others. Wallace is fighting for home and country. I wish I had a mission." She listened at the door, and heard a child's voice pleading at the throne of grace. She opened it softly, crept to the side of the two kneeling figures, and knelt; and when the low "amen" was uttered, she wound her arm around Fossie's neck, and wept, saying,—

"Little sister, your work is not yet done. Teach me to be a Christian."

"O, I am not a Christian," said the child. "I am Christ's little one, father says. Aunt Hester and they at home can teach you. The Holy Spirit will teach you. Don't cry, Elida."

"O, I must. I am a sinful girl. I laugh and sing, and leave the hard work for you, little sister."

"Well, it is my work, Elida. God will give you some pretty soon, it may be, and then you will do it, I know." Little prophet. O, how little she knew the significance of those prophetic words! They three sat there in the dark, damp, dismal room, and talked of the dear sainted mother in heaven, of aunt Hester's home, of grandpa's bedroom, where the prodigal was to sleep, of the ring, the clothes, and the fatted calf.

"Dear father," said Elida, "I know you will love me the least of all your children, I am so unlike the rest. But I am going to be good to you. I wish I was different. What makes me so 'chipper,' as grandmother calls it? and it is the right name. I want you to love me a little — won't you?"

"Yes," was the quick reply, "I will; and I will tell you some time what makes you so different. There is Abigail's horn: it can't be tea-time."

"Fussy Sharp, where've ye been to?" said the querulous old lady. "Nabby can't light my pipe worth a cent."

"Marm is uncommonly pious to-day," said Abigail. "She has read the Bible ever since you went out. There, she is at it again. Listen. She boasts of not goin' to school, and I used to think it was smart; but I've done with that. I wish I knew something."

"In S-a-l-e-m, Salum, a-l-s-o, also, is his t-a-b-e-r-n-a-c-l-e, ta-barn'a-cle. Nabby, who is he a talkin' about there? I've been to Salum; I've never seen any ta-*barn*-a-cle — have you?" Abigail laughed; Levi laughed. "That will do to go with your 'flanax' (that's what she calls *phalanx*), and the other day she read about the 'bell-e-ge'rents'—belligerents she meant."

"Nabby, what's he sayin'? Why don't ye tell me whose"—here she spelled it again, and pronounced it—"ta-*barn*'a-cle it is?"

"Marm," said Abigail, "we're laughin' at your larnin', that ye got in six weeks. Better read to yerself."

"Ye be—are ye?" said the old lady in a rage. "I never brung ye up to treat yer betters in that way. Didn't I spin and weave, and buy and sell? and warn't my family as well off as if I'd spent my life in a book-cover, like a worm? O, hum! I never 'd orter married him: he was my third cousin," she muttered.

"There are uncle Edward and aunt Hester," said Elida, turning pale; for she saw the deep grief in their faces, in spite of all their efforts to be strong, that the stricken heart might lean on them. "Aunt Abigail," she said, clutching her nervously by the arm, "I know some one is dead."

"O, may be not," was the reply. "Don't tell marm who 'tis, or we shall have a scene." Elida stood trembling, with her cold hands pressed firmly over the white, white face. Abigail opened the door. Hester and the doctor saw at a glance that their errand was comprehended, perhaps exaggerated.

"Come in, for God's sake," said Abigail, "if ye can help her. She's dying, I do believe."

"O, no," said the doctor; "she will be relieved when I tell her that Albert is only wounded, and wants her to come and nurse him."

"Nurse him!" she said, the hands unclasping.

"Where is he? How? or when? O God, I thank thee that he is not killed, and I may see him again."

"Be calm, darling, be calm," said Hester. "Lucy has a mightier grief than yours is yet. Albert, we think, will certainly recover, with you to nurse and uncle Edward to look after him. He will go with you." They did not tell her then that he was crippled for life; they felt that she could not bear it. "But alas! we cannot raise the dead. Poor Frank! poor Emma! and poor, dear, stricken Lucy!"

"Then George is dead," said Elida, as she commenced to weep. "O Lucy! Lucy! What if — O, I could not bear it! I have been so hopeful and giddy, when they have been facing such perils, enduring such hardships for me. When can we go, uncle Edward? O, I wish I could fly! Where is Wallace?"

"On his way home with dear George's remains," was the reply, "and very well."

"Nabby, who be they?" said grandmother, impatiently; "and what's to pay? Is Simeon dead — hey? Do tell me."

"Elida's beau has got shot in the leg, and her cousin is dead, and these are her friends come for her to go home."

"O, hum!" was the reply; "I'm glad 'taint Simeon. I wouldn't take on so, if I's Lida; why, I didn't even cry when your father died. She can't go — can she? She hain't got your dress done."

"Pshaw!" said Abigail; "here, come in this way," opening the parlor door. "Let me get ye a cup of tea afore ye start."

Hester gratefully accepted the offer. This had been a hard, trying day. Yes, she would be glad of a cup of tea. She felt weak and weary. She must find Fossie and her father. She must see Levi if possible. Wallace would remain at home on furlough. If they could come home before he returned, what a comfort! Hester prepared Elida very gently for the worst, and yet she almost fainted when she knew that the poor limb was gone forever, and that henceforth the tall, manly form would be shorn of its graceful beauty and strength.

"If I could bear it for him!" she said; "if it could be me! O, Albert! Albert! your sacrifice has been great — greater to you, perhaps, than the loss of life, but to me infinitely less. Auntie, I am glad I learned dress-making," she said, with a half smile. "God is giving me something to do. I have lived for self so far."

"Yes," said Hester, "God is indeed giving you a work to do; and I feel confident you will do it faithfully. Dear child, I want you to trust in Jesus. Give your heart to him, and all will be well."

"Auntie, I want to be a Christian. I see the beauty of true religion more and more. There is an entire lack of Christian principle in grandmother Lentell's family. It pained me to see the poor, decrepit old lady treated so disrespectfully. She is their mother, and so aged! They laugh at her ignorance, when, it may be, she had no one to insist on her going to school. I verily believe I should have been as ignorant as she, had I lived in her day, and followed my own inclinations. You had hard work to get me started up the hill of science — didn't you, auntie? I thank you for taking the trouble, though I thought it hard at the time. Auntie, I see it now. I wanted to live for fun — that was all."

"I pity your grandmother," said Hester. She did not tell the young girl how much she had to blame her for. "I pity her; she had no one to cultivate her affections or educate her. On the contrary, her parents before her gloried in their ignorance, and hired her to stay from school. For her want of mental culture she is not responsible; but, Elida, she is responsible for her want of Christian culture. If she were an earnest, trusting Christian, she would challenge respect from all reputable persons."

"O, how long the time seems!" said Elida, walking up and down the room. "How can I wait? He may be worse — dying even. I may never see him alive."

"I feel that he will live," said Hester, calmly; "I think he will. Only think how slowly the hours must be dragging along at uncle Frank's! No hope for them — nothing to do but to wait and weep. Think of them in their desolation, dear! it will help you. Think of poor Lucy! *nothing* left for her but the cold, cold clay. No word, or look, or sound — nothing but the mournful privilege of burying the loved one, and weeping over the honored dead. He was brave, noble, and generous, and has left a name; was lovely, and they loved him; and when the sorely-smitten hearts have sobbed out the mighty anguish, and gained relief in that way, then the love and the noble needs of daring will come to comfort and cheer them in their darkened way. Pleasant memories, bequeathed to us by the dying, are better far than wealth. You, dear child, have a sad, sweet meeting to look forward to; so hope on to the end."

The village bells tolled long and mournfully on the day when Wallace arrived with the dust of his friend and brother in a common cause. There was a laurel wreath on the bosom of the dead, and epaulets on the shoulders, and glory such as a king might covet enshrouding the soldier's clay. The aged pastor, who had officiated very acceptably in the absence of the young man who had taken his place at the altar, followed the little procession, with bowed head, to the stricken father's house. It was he that dedicated him to God at the baptismal font; it was fit and proper that *he* should say, "Ashes to ashes, and dust to dust," when they buried him.

Reader, you understand it all. O, you know how the pulses stop, how the soul seems to shrink and shiver when the lid is closed, and how the cold earth, as it rattles on the coffin, grates upon every nerve. Instinctively you wish to shield the dear one. In your anguish, you forget that the casket is empty. The soul is gone, but yet the dust is precious.

"I thank my God," murmured the weeping mother, "that we could bury him, and keep his hallowed dust from sacrilege. Isn't it a comfort to you, dear Lucy?"

"It ought to be," she said; "but I can't, O, I can't feel it yet. Dear Mrs. Lovering, let me go to mother. O, let me go. I shall distress you. I never thought he would die. I'll come when I feel stronger. O, shall I ever?"

"Yes, dear, you will grow calm and peaceful some time. This is your first great sorrow, and it is hard to bear; I know it. If you could have been married, it would not seem so sad. We love you as a daughter, and for dear George's sake, love us — won't you?"

"I love you all, and George could not have been

dearer than he was. But in the selfishness of my great grief, I wish we could have been joined in the holy bonds of marriage. I could speak of him so much more freely, and feel that I had a right to speak his praises, and talk about his love." Reader, these scenes have been so familiar in the last few years, that I need not dwell upon them. And then they followed each other so rapidly!

There came a sorrow — you remember it — so much deeper and broader than any which had preceded it, that we, for the moment, forgot all other griefs. It was not the family circle alone that had been broken; nay, verily, a nation's chief had fallen; at such a time, too, and in such a way! And then the mourning came so very near to the rejoicing! It was as if death had entered the banquet-hall at the hour of feasting, and smitten, with cruel hate and malice never matched before, the honored master, and left the happy guests dumb with grief. O, who can picture the scene!

One day there came news — "Richmond has fallen!" How we had looked, and longed, and waited for that news! It meant to us peace, instead of war — dear ones at home again; it meant everything desirable. It was a day which would emancipate our noble, self-denying, imprisoned soldiers from a doom than which there never was anything more terrible; and God grant there never may be a place inhabited by men so full of woe and terror! Famine and death, in its most hideous form, went hand in hand; literally, it was a place of skeletons. O God of justice, is there a place for such men as those who gloated and gloried in the hunger and thirst, in the blood and tears, of helpless men, mocking even the agony of *such* a death — is there a place for such men and such women to repent?

Thou, God, knowest. Well, we thought our calamities were over; freedom had triumphed over oppression — right over wrong. Was it strange that we were almost intoxicated with joy? Was it strange that the very church bells danced and made music to the nation's heart, as it beat exultant, and said, "Hurrah"? Even the deadly weapons of war, the cruel instruments of death, were forced to cease their work of destruction, and make melody! The nation's heart was full: it could not be expressed; and so the cannon roared, the drums beat, the bells rang, and men said, "Hurrah!" children shouted, "Hurrah!"

Even the mourning ones — they whose beloved lay mouldering on the enemy's soil — smiled brightly, and forgot their sorrows; and, amid the joy and exultation, devout thanks went up to God, the Giver of it all.

It was only a little while, you know, almost before the noise of sudden mirth had been hushed into quiet thankfulness, that the stunning blow fell upon us, and the great, honest, loving heart, upon which we had come to lean with a child's confiding love, lay motionless in death. Yes, God had raised up for us, in the hour of our extremity, an honest man. He had been like "the shadow of a great rock in a weary land." We rested in his shadow; it was a pleasant shade, and we loved it; not blindly, for we had tried it, and it had not been found wanting. And they buried *him*, too — our Lincoln, the nation's hero, an able, honest, truthful, temperate man. It was a nation's funeral, and the tears were honest tears of sorrow and regret. But, after all, we did not fully realize the magnitude of our loss. Our grief would have been despair, perchance, if we could have seen the future, as it came surging on, freighted with the most tremendous interests to us and the world.

Yes, we should have been paralyzed with fear and consternation, could we have seen the future, and realized how unskilful, unsteady, and utterly unreliable, was the hand which held our nation's destiny.

CHAPTER XLI.

Our last Call on the different Families in Our World. — Harmony's dying Wish accomplished, her Faith rewarded, or the Conclusion of the whole Matter.

The war is over, of course you know; or at least the noise of battle and the call to arms have ceased. We hear no more about drafted men, and high bounties, or victories and defeats. Mr. Trueman has not been idle. He has discharged the duties of collector faithfully at home, and acted as paymaster in the army of the West with great acceptability, with the rank of major. Honest, self-denying worth has been rewarded. His business at home has not suffered. Walter has learned to talk straight way about, long ago, and, with mother's and sister's help, he has attended to home trade successfully. Could you look in upon the family circle, now that they have been reunited, you would thank God, with us, that there is such a thing as a united, happy family, who "love God and keep his commandments," "in honor preferring one another." And you would see, also, that second marriages, if sensibly formed, are pleasant and profitable to all concerned. An own mother, be she who she may, could not comfort and console Lucy in her deep affliction better than the step-mother; and Lucy clings to and leans upon her as a daughter should. Mr. Frank Lovering's family have been chastened by their affliction;

drawn nearer together, if possible, since they laid their first-born away in the silence of death. A new cord is drawing their thoughts upward, and uniting them to God, "who doeth all things well." The Loverings, generally, are enjoying as much happiness and prosperity as is common to the lot of man. They are reaping the benefits of an early Christian training, and cultivated minds and hearts. Dr. Edward has an extensive practice, and is doing much good. Mr. Giles is Mr. Giles no longer, only in name. He has been with Him "who is meek and lowly of heart," and learned of him. Old habits stick to him, he says; but he is fighting the good fight, and will finally triumph. Ann is a revised edition of her former self; happier than we supposed she ever could be. Christian love works wonders, imperfect as it is in the human heart. It was the children's mission to teach Ann to love, first themselves, and through that human love she may yet learn to forgive, and ask forgiveness and wisdom of "Him who giveth liberally, and upbraideth not." Elevia seems not a day older than she was when she went home to die, as she and we supposed. Her early dream of returned affection and a happy home is realized. The Wileys are Wileys yet; God pity them! They too, are reaping the reward of their doings. Their daughter, whom they loved, it is true, with a sordid love, which is born of earth, has disappointed them sorely. They taught her to be selfish and self-seeking; and so, when, in the progress of the war (after she had recovered from her mortification and chagrin at failing to win Howard Trueman.), the fair maidens of the loyal North wrote patriotic letters to the soldier boys, Envena cast in her lot also. She was deceived by an empty title, a gay exterior, and caught at a hook which *appeared* to be golden, but it was only sounding brass. The fast young man came to see her. The father said he was too fast, altogether too fast. "But he looks well; he makes a show." He was a captain, and might be general.

"As likely as not he will be general," said the doting mother. "Hold on to him, Venie, and see."

"I shall be likely to,"· said the daughter. "Mrs. General Cowell; it sounds well. Won't they envy me? Mamma, I shall be married in rose-colored silk, with white lace looped up over it with orange blossoms and geraniums, and nothing but a japonica in my hair. Aunt Ann may go; I shall be rich enough without her paltry fortune. I wonder which of the children will get it."

"My daughter, you mustn't look ahead too far," said the proud, happy mother; " hold on,· and wait."

Had they known Captain Cowell, they would have been certain he would not wait. There was property enough to tempt a man with an empty purse, an empty heart, and an empty title which did not pay; for he assumed it without Uncle Sam's consent. He came often. "Officers could get leave of absence," he said; and then he loved her so. He might die in battle, — he might, — brave captains were often shot in battle, — and then she could inherit none of his property, or glory, or pension, not even his name. And so one day, without the consent of parents, the rose-colored silk, the white lace, or even the japonica, they were married privately; and then, in spite of parental frowns, the bride and bridegroom had such a honeymoon as is seldom seen. It was more than bright, it was brilliant; it was more than joyous, it was jubilant. They rode, they walked, they feasted. In the church they smiled, and looked into each other's faces and smiled, and crept closer and closer to each other; and the people smiled — a half mournful, pitying smile. But the end came, the bubble burst. The counterfeit was discovered when too late. Self-seeking ended in abasement.

I intended to tell you, at some length, that Howard graduated from the Theological Seminary with honor; paid a visit to the soldier boys, and labored for them three months; came home, obtained a very desirable settlement in a pleasant, thriving village, and married our favorite, Winnie Lentell, the successful teacher, who, in spite of many obstacles, was greatly beloved by her scholars, as well as numerous personal friends. But my book is getting too large, they tell me; and then the wedding was a calm, thoughtful, grave wedding; they realized what they were doing, but were happy, nevertheless, calmly, sensibly happy. And now they have been married some years, but their tones are not less tender, nor their smiles less sweet. Envena is not envied by any one to-day; they pity her, and none more than the gentle, loving Winnie, as she folds her birdie boy to her mother bosom, and caresses the sweet head nestling there, or goes quietly into Howard's study, to see if the minister is grappling with some mighty thought, or whether he has mastered his theme, and waits for her to listen to the result, with the satisfaction of a loving heart in the success of the beloved one. They are happy, very: why should they not be? They live for others, and not for self alone; for eternity, and not for time only. God bless them and their baby boy. Its name is Georgie. Winnie's heart has been disciplined and tried, until, Howard says, there is nothing left but the pure gold; and she is the most contented and happy little wife and mother in the land.

"Howard," she says, "is so generous, noble, and strong, that I am satisfied. God has cleared up the clouds that hung over my childhood, and I ought to love him, and I will praise him while I live."

Poor Envena! she is sadder and paler now. The little innocent one at her bosom calls up no pleasant emotions, no happy smiles; nothing but vain regret. She is not a general's wife; O, no; she knows not that she is a wife at all. Her husband has not been heard from, though she has sought for him with the energy of despair. No such name appeared among the captains of the regiment in which he served; but a man answering to his description was counted among the deserters of our army. Only this they knew: that bill after bill came in to Mr. Wiley on his daughter's account — the price of her few weeks of joyous revelry during the honeymoon. They paid them, in silent amazement, and thought to hush the matter up. And now, as the months roll on, and the disappointment takes deeper root in their hearts, they speak of their daughter's bereavement, and say that her husband "the captain," died for his country in a Southern prison. But they can get no clew to him; and there is no state aid for her, or the fatherless little girl in her arms. O God! help and bless the little one, and bring it into a better life!

Mr. Stillman is moving along at a slow pace — nothing better, but rather worse. Mrs. Stillman is going on in the right way, keeping boarders for a livelihood. Jack, poor, misguided, ruined Jack, died on the battle-field, honorably, she thinks. Well, let her think so; give her this little comfort. It would do no good to enlighten her; but his comrades know that he was shot in a drunken fray. Poor Jack! you might have been a great, good, noble man, with a different training.

Clara, once the belle of the village, is sitting quietly in a comfortable easy-chair, reading a little, working a little, or resting a little, as the case may be. She is beautiful yet, though the roses and the healthful roundness have departed from her cheek. She is an invalid, and always will be, until the mortal shall have put on immortality in the better life. The beauty which she now wears is the beauty of holiness; the light in her eye is the light of eternal love; the peace of God is resting upon her; and she, too, is satisfied, or will be when she shall awake in his likeness, and behold him as he is.

"I thank God," she says daily, "that I am what I am — a feeble, suffering invalid; and not a child of sorrow sold unto sin, steeped in pollution, as my companion and playmate, the beautiful, the queenly, but fallen Regena Steele has become. O Regena, Regena! would that I could snatch you like a brand from the burning, and save you from the wrath of an offended God!" she said often; until one day an enormous trunk came to the village depot, containing the cast off finery of poor, misguided, lost Regena Steele, and also a written account of her journey from the boarding-house to her "elegant city home" *prison,* her desertion and despair.

"My pride triumphed," she wrote, "and I, in my turn, became the destroyer, the betrayer, of innocence. But my reign is over. Ere this reaches you I shall have gone to sleep, never more to wake. There is no hereafter — none. I am glad. I could not meet the just and holy God the Bible speaks of — I couldn't. But it is well enough to believe in him while we live. I wish I had. Mother, had you sent me to meeting, and taught me the religion of the Bible, I should have been happier in this life, and useful to my fellow-men, instead of what I am and have been. But it is no matter now; my wrongs are all avenged. The wretch who made me what I am died, no matter how. I am weary and sick of life — of self; and, now that I can endure it no longer, I, too, go to rest in the bosom of mother earth. Farewell. O, I am longing for rest. I hold that in my hand that will give it to me. Farewell forevermore."

Mrs. Stillman and Clara enjoy much in spite of adverse circumstances. Our Father in heaven pity and comfort them. Let us cross the street and enter the house where the first Mrs. Gray fell a charred and blackened victim to Mr. Stillman and the rum he sold for gain, which was cursed of Heaven, and proved a curse to him. The house is changed since that terrible tragedy. How changed it is, and for the better! There is a stepmother in it, too. So you see, reader, that the happiness of a family depends on whether it is composed of true men and women, and obedient children, rather than upon anything else — don't you see it? Step-mothers are blessings, inestimable blessings, when the own mother is gone, to return no more, if love, purity, and fidelity prevail in the family circle; and there can be no happiness where they do not, be it own mother or stepmother that sits at the head of the table, presiding over all.

Mrs. Gray, the second, was a rare jewel; and the children " arose and called her blessed; her husband also praised her." She was a good, judicious, own mother to Henry Herbert, who is now settled on his father's homestead at the West. Hattie is very happy, only that she misses home friends. They think of coming East, now that Elida and Albert cannot go to them, as they at first intended. Their purposes are broken off. And she was a good mother to her husband's children, too, and a tender, loving mother to little Ella Gray, the youngest pet. There was no room for envy in her motherly heart. All honor to the mother of them all. The lame boy, who had lost his good right leg in his country's service, and his happy little Sunshine, call her blessed. Theirs was a peculiar wedding. There was much sad tenderness mixed and mingled in the heart-felt congratulations of friends, it was so different from what they expected before the war! On account of Albert's feeble, almost helpless state, the return of the prodigal was delayed until spring. The little missionary was content; she was teaching them to love. Her work there was not done.

Lottie and her husband, the young pastor of the village church, call Mrs. Gray blessed, as well as Hattie and Henry Herbert. Little pet will lisp it soon; and Mr. Gray, the elder, is the most blessed of them all in the possession of such a wife. She is the planner of all their happy schemes, the sharer of all their joys, and the bearer of all their sorrows. And Hester, the strong, the noble, the generous, the loving Hester, seemed to be the grandmother of them all. How they loved and venerated her! And aunt Martha — the gentle, care-taking, loving Martha — was the household aunt, you see; Mr. and Mrs. Gray's aunt, Henry's and Hattie's, Albert's and Elida's, Lottie's and the minister's, Howard's and Winnie's aunt, I mean. But to Fossie and Fossie's father she was more, a great deal more, than aunt. Hers was a mother's love for them. O, let me tell you that the fatted calf was killed and eaten some time since, but not until Wallace and Elida came with their precious hero soldier, crowned a martyr to freedom. The little missionary spoke a prophecy when she said, —

"God will give you something to do, sister, and you will do it; I know you will." Hester spoke truly when she said, "God is preparing a life work for you, and I feel sure you will do it faithfully." Hers was just the disposition to cheer the wounded hero, and make him forget his loss. It was Hester that gave them a deed of half the old Manlie mansion, which was kept in good repair, and seemed not to grow old any faster than its mistress.

It was Martha, the aunt of all of them, and Mrs. Gray, the mother of them all, that fitted it up, with a little store in one end, and everything nice and cosy, so that the children could be happy. "Albert must have something to do," they said, "or he will miss the strength and freedom of other days."

And so the noise and smoke of war rolled away, and the sun shone in the Manlie house clearer and brighter than ever before. For the little willing exile, the child-missionary, had kept her promise, and come home at last, leading the prodigal in his right mind. They fed and clothed him, bound up his bruises, and poured the oil of consolation into his weak and wounded spirit. For he had been among thieves, you know.

Little Mary, — grandpa's Mary, auntie's Mary, and

now papa's Mary,— you shall wear him as a crown of joy and great rejoicing in that day when the Judge of all the earth shall count his jewels. Little Fossie, thy faith hath saved thy father; go on hoping, and trusting, and working, and waiting.

"Wallace Lentell, Groceries, Grain, &c."— that is the new sign over the old one where Mr. Trueman's name had stood the test of many a storm. "Trueman and Son, Dealers in Dry and Fancy Goods," is the sign overhead. A fine establishment it is now, refitted and refilled. There is a new house over the way, almost finished. Whom do you think it is for? It is no secret. Wallace and Susie Trueman, they say, will live there, and Morgan Lentell, the reformed inebriate. What wonder if he is proud of his children! Only he has no reason to be *proud: pleased* — that would sound better. He has done nothing to form their characters; other hands and other hearts did that.

Well, he is grateful; they are all grateful, and as happy as love and gratitude can make them in this fallen world. Such a time as they had when the prodigal returned! The Loverings were there, — all of them, — little and big; the Truemans, ditto; only one baby in the family, you know; that is Howard's: Mason Giles and family, too.

Aunt Ann "s'posed she must go to take care of the pickanins," she said, with one of her grim smiles, which was half a tear, I ween. Aunt Abigail was there, with her black silk dress on, and a pale, sad face, softer than it had been, for Simeon was dead — *starved* in the Southern prison-house of death. That was the hardest of it all, she said — he to *starve*, when the house was full of food. The hand of the little missionary had unlocked the door of her heart, and let the light of a holy, purifying love into her soul. A little leaven will leaven the whole lump, perchance. Levi was there, too. He and Abigail smiled at each other when the child-missionary touched his arm, and whispered,—

"Stop here, uncle, please. It must be a good way off, you know. Aunt Hester will see us." And she did—came to meet them; placed the ring on his little finger, the same ring which he had placed upon Harmony's many, many years before.

"God bless you, Morgan; in the name of your sainted wife I bless you! And, now that you are freed from your terrible bondage to drink, I welcome you to our home and our loving hearts. God bless and keep you, and at last unite you to her who loved you to the last. Come and receive the blessing of your children — *her* children and *our* children."

Mr. Lentell stood with his head uncovered, and bowed very low. He was too much affected to answer only by a firm clasping of the hand, which had so often ministered to the necessities of his wife and children. Little Fossie did not dance for joy. O, no! Her emotions were too deep to be expressed in that way. She watched the proceedings with a calm, deep interest, with her small hands folded tightly, her head bent forward, drinking in every word with an intensity of emotion painful to behold. If I am not mistaken, a tear glistened in Abigail's eye. Levi was much affected. He opened his strong arms, saying,—

"Little Fossie, come to uncle: you have done it all. God bless you, little Fossie; you have shamed me out of my sullenness and selfishness; and now I mean to live for something better than self." Fossie crept into the open arms, and nestled there, saying,—

"It is God that has done it, uncle Levi; I couldn't. I am only a little girl; but they said God had given me a mission; so I went to find it. I am glad I did — O, so glad!" and then the strong emotion of the child found vent in tears. Levi patted the head of the weeping child, and brushed a tear from his own eye, impatiently. Abigail was distressed to see her weeping so.

"Don't, Fossie;" she called her that now — "don't cry; you have more reason to laugh, child. You've done us good. Aunt Abigail shan't forget ye; and ye've promised to come twice a year, and help her and uncle Levi to crawl out of their crusts, you know. I was a crabbed old thing when you came, child, and should have died so, only for you. Come and shake hands with me now, and say good by; for I shall miss ye as much as Hester and the rest on um did." Fossie threw her arms around Abigail's neck, and kissed her with real affection.

"Yes," she said, "I will come, auntie" (she dared to say "auntie" now) — "I will come and help you and uncle Levi about your mission."

"What do you mean by that, Fossie?" said Abigail.

"O, I mean taking care of poor grandmother, and not minding if she does fret; she is so old and sick, you see."

"Yes, I see," was the reply; "I'll try to bear it better: good by."

"I shan't hear a word of your going home till you have tasted of the fatted calf," said Hester; "it would be too bad. Come, get right out of the carriage; put your horse into the barn; I will send a boy to help you." They were not very loath to stop when sufficiently urged by Hester and Martha, joined by their nephews and nieces; that was how they came to be there.

"We must be careful not to embarrass them with attentions, or slight them," said Hester to the company before they entered. Winnie and Howard met them cordially, and held up the baby boy for a little notice. Elida received them as old friends, and led them to her hero husband with fond, tender affection; and they looked upon him with reverent pity. They knew how brave he had been.

"If Simeon could have come home in that way, I should have been satisfied," said Abigail.

"Yes," said Hester, "it was the hardest of all to have him starve; it was a cruel, cruel thing. God reward them."

"He will," said Abigail. "I believe in future punishment now; it must be true." Wallace introduced Susie Trueman, the future Mrs. Lentell.

"And here is my husband's sister," said Elida; "Lottie Gray that was, Lottie Elwood that is. O, there comes Mr. Elwood, her husband and our minister. He married us, — Albert and me, — and I presume he will do the same kind deed for Wallace and Susie soon," she said, archly. "Now I think somebody ought to make a speech. This is a great occasion. Come, uncle Levi."

"I am not clever at that business," said Levi. "I can hold a plough and drive a team; that is about all. Make one yourself, Elida; you are a Sharp, you know," he whispered. Elida laughed.

"I, too, think some one ought to make a speech," said Morgan Lentell, turning to Hester, who was standing by his side. "I want to thank you now, and here, for making my children what they are — for doing what I ought to have helped you do. I never could have done for them what you have done, and I thank all the friends for their kindness to them. May God reward you all. I feel unworthy to call myself their father. But," he said, "if God will help me, and you can bear with me, they shall yet love and respect me before I die. Some time," he said, with great emotion, "I may tell the world how this child" — he placed his hand upon the head of little Fossie — "sought and saved me; but not now." After a moment's profound silence, Hester said, in a cheerful voice, —

"I am more than repaid for all I have done — I may say *we*; for I have had many and cheerful helpers. Yes, I feel amply rewarded for all the anxiety of the past; for I have seen the dying wish of our darling Harmony accomplished, her faith rewarded, and I am satisfied. Henceforth I have little to do but lean on those loving hearts, and rest; for I am old, now, and weary. Little Fossie promised me she would come back with her father before I needed her; and she has come just in time. But," she added, in a still more cheerful strain, "I only brought home four, and now I give you back as good as seven; and seven as good and intelligent children as you will find, I don't care where you look. Haven't I been successful? Now let me go and see about the fatted calf, or Martha will have cause for complaint, like Martha of old, and there will be no gentle Master to rebuke her."

CONCLUSION.   443

"She won't complain, aunt Hester," said Wallace, "so long as she has grandmother, and Mrs. Trueman, and Mrs. Gray, with others of like stamp, to assist her. Stay; you have done enough for one human being, and done it well enough to satisfy yourself, I hope. Let us minister to you, our guardian and friend from childhood until now." Grandpa Lovering appeared, announcing that supper was ready, his face radiant with happiness. Mr. Lovejoy asked a blessing upon the sumptous meal, and the united family, and all present, in his usual happy manner; and Mr. Elwood, the young minister of the parish, returned thanks for all God's goodness to them! from a full heart, fervently; and then the company were entertained by a few patriotic songs. These children were all singers, and Lottie Elwood was leader of the village choir, as well as wife of the minister.

Fossie listened to the fine tones of a beautiful, new piano with delight. She had not seen it before. Grandpa's room had been newly painted, papered, and furnished with great care and taste by Winnie. Elida, with her lesser means, but no less loving heart, had placed a beautiful book-case in one corner, with a few choice children's books upon it, and a picture of "After the Nap"—three lovely little girls—over it. And then other friends brought offerings to the child-missionary. After the singing, Wallace and Susie led Fossie to the instrument, where Lottie still played, and inquired,—

"How do you like it?"

"O, it is very nice," said the child, in her sweet, quiet way; "it sounds almost like heaven. Did you buy it, Wallace?"

"Yes, little sister; Susie and I bought it for you, darling." He stooped and kissed her.

"Mine!" said Fossie; "why, I can't play, brother Wallace. I think it is beautiful, though!" And the little white hands clasped instinctively.

"Well, you can learn," was the reply. "A little girl with your patience and perseverance can learn to make sweet music, I know; and you have a pretty voice, too."

"You are to be my scholar," said Susie, kissing her tenderly; "and by-and-by, when I can teach you no more, Lottie will make a finished player of you."

"That will be nice!" said the little girl. "I hope I shall learn. And grandpa's room is very pretty — isn't it?"

"This is to be your room, darling," said Hester; "yours, dear, while you wish to stay in it; and may it be long. Your father shall have grandpa's bedroom for his own. You have brought that to your brother and sisters — to us all — which money could not buy; and it was fitting that we should do something for you. This is one of the reasons why we consented to let her spend the winter with you," she said to Abigail. "We wished to surprise her; and then our time has been so occupied with fixing Elida's part of the house."

"Likely 's not you won't want to come to see us, Fossie," she said, "now you've got such nice things."

"Yes, I shall, auntie. I like nice things, but I like folks better: I shall come. And you and uncle Levi must come and hear me play 'Yankee Doodle,' when I learn it, and 'Star-spangled Banner' — won't you?"

"Why, yes, I guess we must. Good by, little chick."

"I want to send something good to grandmother," whispered Fossie.

"You shall, dear," said Hester; "and I will put up some sweetmeats for uncle Simeon's children — poor dears! Abigail, I wish you would bring your brother's widow and her children down here some day. You must all be lonely."

"Like enough I may," muttered Abigail. She had not opened her heart enough yet to take Julia in, although the children were gaining ground every day. They were storming the castle bravely, encouraged by Fossie and uncle Levi. Did ever the children fail? No, not when they had fair play. Reader, if you have a powerful imagination, you can get a better idea of the happiness of the family whose father was lost and is found, dead and is alive again, than I can give you. Grandpa Lovering rejoices with a great joy over the prodigal in his right mind, as well as over the reformation of Mr. Giles.

"Elevia is as happy as the rest of my daughters," he says, with a quiet smile, saddened by the thought that Charles still sticks to his eleven and four o'clock drams, in spite of their entreaties. His second marriage proves a pleasant one. The little widow Payson spoke truly when she said, —

"I shall never be sorry, and I hope you won't." No, he was not sorry. She was a treasure to him and his family. They didn't mind the bustle: the real goodness was there. They too were satisfied; and she used to say, "My cup runneth over."

Patient reader, a little more, and I have done. It is autumn again. The new house is finished. Wallace is married. His father, much improved in health and spirits, is busy in the store about such things as he can do. He is calmly happy. Mr. Trueman's family receive him as a sacred trust from their daughter Winnie, who lives in a distant village.

"We will do all for his happiness that you could, Winnie," they said, when she lamented leaving him, now that he was found.

"I thank you," was the grateful reply.

"It ought to be happiness enough for me, I suppose, to have him as he is; but we mortals are hard to please." Let me tell you that Ann Thropee is still further revised, so that you would hardly recognize her as the hard-faced woman she was. Well, she has been several times to spend a few weeks with Winnie. "I s'pose I must go and see that young pickanin," she said, the first time she went after Georgie's birth. "I wonder w'at I must buy for 'im."

"A wheelbarrow," suggested Master Mason Eddie; "buy him a wheelbarrow." Ann laughed.

"Well, ducky, I s'pose I must. He'll be old 'nuff to w'eel it some time. I wonder w'at them carts, sich as rich folks cart their young ones in, cost?" she continued to Elevia: "I mean the black, shiny ones, with the silver things on um. Winn's good as the best on um. I want 'er to 'ave one."

"They are quite expensive," said Elevia, "but very pretty and useful. One would last a great while with Winnie's care. I will give something towards it."

"You won't, then," said Ann; "if I can't pay for't, she shan't 'ave it; that's all. 'Ow much be they? Can ye tell?"

"O, from ten to fifteen dollars."

"Pooh!" said Ann; "that's cheap. I'll buy 'er one, an' put the w'eelbarrer inter it."

Mason Giles, with his juster views of life, had compelled his father to do Ann partial justice, and she had all the money she wished to spend now, with her habits of personal economy. Elevia smiled complacently, as she contrasted Ann with her former self, and thought how successfully they had covered the skeleton in their house with the mantle of charity, until it had become something to love.

Ann was not faultless yet; but she was being moulded, slowly and surely, into the image of Him who is love itself. She, and Mason, and Winnie, and Hester, and all the Loverings, had helped in the glorious work; but the little children in the house had done more than they all. God bless the children, and finish their work in his own good time.

One more call, and my work is done. Mehitable Sharp Lentell still sits upon the soft, clean bed, with her Bible in her palsied hand, straining the poor sunken eyes to find something to atone for her one great sin, as she says.

"Nabby, I'll go to heaven. I never wronged nobody, I didn't. I've worked hard and been honest. Say, Nabby, shan't I go to heaven?"

"I hope so, marm. Fossie says Christ came to save all who will repent. Can't ye repent, marm?" screamed Abigail.

"What is that you say, Nabby? Repent! I'd like to know what for. O, hum! I'd never orter a married him: he was my third cousin."

"O, dear!" sighed Abigail. "Marm!" she screamed,

"don't harp upon that: they marry own cousins sometimes; that's nothin'. Think of things you've done worse' n that — sins against God and yer feller-men."

"You lie, Nabby!" said the old lady, fiercely; "you lie! I never sinned worse 'n that. What if I did put in a teaspunful o' laudanum, instead o' ten drops. I wanted him to sleep till the will was writ. That never killed him." She paused, with a frightened look. "It didn't kill him — did it, Nabby? O, hum! hum!" rocking the witchy-looking body back and forth. Abigail turned pale. Was she a murderer, then? A feeling of horror and disgust crept over her. She remembered her kind, patient father — his sudden, mysterious death. She felt faint and dizzy, as she thought how her young heart had been steeled against that father by her mother, and she felt like shaking her by the arm in anger; but she thought of Fossie's injunction, of Jesus, and of God.

"Marm," she said, "there will be no rest for ye, here nor hereafter, if ye don't repent."

"I tell ye," said the old lady, "I know I never 'd orter married him; but I can't help it now. Don't bother; I'll do well enough." With a pain at our heart, we leave her muttering and mumbling over the Bible, spelling out the words, as if her salvation depended upon that. "O, hum!" we hear her say, as we departed, "I'd never orter a married him, Nabby. But I'll go to heaven for all that. It was only a spunful o' laudanum I gin him; that didn't kill him, Nabby — did it? Say, Nabby." Abigail told Levi of this talk, and they both shuddered, and looked steadfastly into the fire tha' burned, and flickered, and flashed, and died; and s' they looked and thought. Levi broke the silence saying, —

"She has been a terrible woman, Abigail, if she is our mother; and we were following in her steps till Fossie came, dear child." Another pause.

"Ye might as well out with it, Levi. I've seen how it's been goin' between you an' Jule this long time," said Abigail, with a forced laugh. "I shan't stand in yer way this time."

"Shan't you, Abigail?" said Levi, taking her hand as he had never done in his life before. "Well, I am glad; Julia is good enough for me. Simeon loved her, and she loved him as she will never love me. I can't expect it. I had determined to marry her if I had to sell my half of the place, and leave the state. Simeon's children shall be my children. But if you will treat Julia kindly, we can be happy here together. And, Abigail, Julia would like to help take care of mother, if you will let her."

"She needn't," said Abigail, tearfully; "it's my business to do that. Julie is good enough; she'll do, Levi. But half o' the property ought to go to Morgan. I didn't think marm was so bad."

"It shall," said Levi; "I promise you it shall. Come, go and tell Julia that she will do; she will know you mean a good deal by that. She always said that you had a kind heart underneath."

"There is sin enough in it," said Abigail, "if that's all."

She did go; and now the children climb upon her knees, and talk of their dead papa, and cousin Fossie, and the kitten, and the new kite that uncle Levi has promised them. And aunt Abigail makes twisted doughnuts, and round ones, and turnovers. And they pick up the apples, and help her peel them, and pick the chips, and put on a stick of wood, and do a thousand little things for her. And if she cannot bring her tongue to say "dear" and "darling," she calls them pet names, nevertheless, such as "ducky," and "kitty," and "bossy," and she loves them well. And they, with childhood's generosity, return the love with interest. Julia is happier than she ever thought it possible she could be when the sad news came that Simeon had starved in prison. O, that was hard to bear! Theirs is a happy family now, only there is a living skeleton in it.

They talked the matter all over together,—Levi, and Julia, and Abigail,—and finally the Noyes and Atwood places were sold, and half of the stock, excepting one horse, and old Rosy, Fossie's pet cow. They went one clear, bright day, a happy company of them, as many as could be stowed away in the covered wagon; Abigail, and Julia, and pet on the front seat, three children on the back seat, and Levi on horseback, leading old Rosy, the cow. Fossie clapped her tiny hands gleefully this time, and Levi said she actually danced for joy. She is looking rosier now that the great hope of her life is realized. Hester, and Martha, and Elida were pleased with Fossie's present from aunt Abigail; for it was Fossie's cow "to keep always," she told Albert. "And you shall have nice new milk to make you strong again."

"I'll drive you a load of hay, Fossie," said Levi, "to feed her with this winter. And you will have to milk—won't you?" he said, quizzically.

"Why, I don't believe I can," said the child, sadly.

"O, you needn't," said Elida; "sister will milk. I can learn, you know."

"And I can learn," said Martha. "I will see to the cow till we can find a boy to adopt. We need one — don't we, Hester?"

"Yes, Martha, I think we do. It will be nice to have plenty of milk; we are much obliged to you, I am sure." And they all went out to the barn, so long unoccupied, to admire old Rosy, which was only three years old, after all, and a beautiful creature.

"It seems like old times," said Martha. "If there is any creature I love, it is a cow." Morgan Lentell wept when they handed him the purse, saying, —

"Take it; it is yours. We never realized how much you had been wronged till recently. And this horse is yours. You and Wallace will need it in your business. I want to see your name on the sign, too. There is money enough to enlarge your business. I am going to trade here in the future; don't cheat me — will you?" said Levi, trying to laugh away the tears. Susie came out to admire old Charlie — a fine beast, fleet, strong, and gentle, and only seven years old. She petted the horse, and felt that she could gladly kiss her new uncle. It was just what they wanted, she said, to complete their happiness, which she thought was full before.

"I do believe we are the happiest people in the world," she said, putting her arm through Wallace's.

"No, you are not," said Elida; "we are; Albert and I are the happiest." Abigail, Julia, and Hester, Elida, and Fossie, had come over to congratulate them and witness the surprise.

"We have got the prettiest cow in the world," said Fossie, "and shall make lots of butter; for uncle Levi is going to bring some hay. And if she ever has a bossy, like the one she had last winter, I shall give it to you and Susie, Wallace, to pay for my piano; and papa shall have some milk."

"Bravo, little Fossie!" said Abigail; "you'll do, yet."

"And my little girl shall ride with father often," said Mr. Lentell, with emotion. He was looking back; he was thinking of Harmony and the past. "O that she were here to enjoy our property!" he said, softly, to Hester.

"She is far happier than we; let that comfort you," said Hester.

"O that she were here, so that I could ask her to forgive me!" said Abigail, mournfully. "I believe an evil spirit possessed me to treat her so. We have been blind."

"I rejoice that you now see," said Hester. They returned, and found Martha's tea waiting. Fossie played "Yankee Doodle," and several other tunes. Levi said it sounded pleasanter than mother's loom used to. He would like to have one of the girls learn to play.

"Buy her something to play on," said Abigail, "and I'll risk her learning." Levi and Abigail felt relieved, now that their duty was performed. "We have never felt right about things at home," they said to Hester, "but had no idea Morgan had been so foully wronged. Mother talks about her getting the writings made out often now; father had no hand in it, she says. I am glad justice is done him at last, so far as we are concerned."

"So am I," said Hester. "I respect you for the steps you have taken; you will be far happier. Let us be friends in the future; and may our Father in heaven

CONCLUSION. 453

bless you, and lead you to a higher life and a better hope."

Wallace hastened to connect his father in business with himself. "It will strengthen and encourage him," they all said. The Lovering farm has been somewhat encroached upon by the steady march of New England enterprise, and the quietness and romance of the beautiful Merrimack, disturbed by the busy hum, and stir, and commotion of a manufacturing city. But the old farm-house has bravely stood the test. True, its exterior has changed very much; the poplar trees have given place to shrubs and flowers of a more modern date. "Old Tom," the family horse, has long since gone to rest; the cider-mill ceased its grinding. The "river road" still abides in beauty; but it is less cosy and secluded than when Harmony and Morgan plighted their troth beneath the willows. And now, as a pale, sad man walks back and forth under the shadowing trees at twilight, his eyes rest on the many lights which gleam from the factory windows. But he is thinking of the beautiful light which flashed upon his pathway in that very spot, and beamed so brightly upon him for a few short years, and then went out in such loneliness and neglect. "O God," he murmurs, "forgive me! I can never forgive myself."

www.ingramcontent.com/pod-product-compliance
Lightning Source LLC
Chambersburg PA
CBHW022137300426